✷ The American Film Institute

....

Getting Started

in

Film

✸ The American Film Institute

·······························

Getting Started

in

Film

Emily Laskin
Editor

Anna Lisa Korobkin, Assistant Editor

James Hindman, Deputy Director, AFI

Jean Firstenberg, Director, AFI

PRENTICE HALL

New York   London   Toronto   Sydney   Tokyo   Singapore

Prentice Hall General Reference
15 Columbus Circle
New York, NY 10023

Prentice Hall and colophons are
registered trademarks of Simon & Schuster, Inc.

Manufactured in the United States of America

1 2 3 4 5 6 7 8 9 10

Library of Congress Cataloging-in-Publication Division

LC: 92-7853

Contents

■■■■■■■■■■

Foreword *by Emily Laskin* ■ ix

Acknowledgments ■ x

The American Film Institute ■ xi

History of the American Film
Institute ■ xiii

Introduction *by Jean Firstenberg* ■ xvii

1. THE SCREENWRITER ■ 1

Frank Pierson

Nora Ephron

Tom Schulman

2. THE PRODUCER ■ 29

George Lucas

Peggy Rajski

Gale Anne Hurd

3. THE DIRECTOR ■ 55

Lawrence Kasdan

David Lynch

Martha Coolidge

Robert Wise

4. THE CINEMATOGRAPHER ▪ 91
   Haskell Wexler
   Caleb Deschanel
   Allen Daviau

5. THE PRODUCTION DESIGNER ▪ 120
   Jim Bissell
   Richard Sylbert
   Patrizia Von Brandenstein

6. THE COSTUME DESIGNER ▪ 141
   Jeffrey Kurland
   James Acheson
   Robert Fletcher

7. THE CASTING DIRECTOR ▪ 161
   Juliet Taylor
   Johanna Ray
   Marion Dougherty

8. THE ACTOR ▪ 179
   Barbara Hershey
   Clyde Kusatsu
   Danny Glover

9. THE AGENT ▪ 205
   John Ptak
   Ronda Gómez-Quiñones
   Rick Nicita

10. THE ATTORNEY ▪ 228
    Stephen Barnes
    Melanie Cook
    Don Tringali

11. THE FILM EDITOR ▪ 249
    Carol Littleton
    Dede Allen
    Thelma Schoonmaker

12. THE SOUND EDITOR ▪ 271
    Tom Holman
    Walter Murch
    Richard Anderson

13. THE COMPOSER ▪ 300
    Elmer Bernstein
    Maurice Jarre
    Herbie Hancock

14. SPECIAL EFFECTS ▪ 327
  Robert Greenberg
  Michael Backes
  Scott Ross

15. THE CRITIC ▪ 350
  Leonard Maltin
  Sheila Benson
  Richard Schickel

16. THE PUBLICIST ▪ 378
  Mickey Freeman/Joe Sutton
  Michael Levine

Foreword
■ ■ ■ ■ ■ ■ ■ ■ ■

It is often said that film is a collaborative art form. That collaboration is guided by the director. Although the director leads the creative team, that assemblage of people—the cast and crew—involves the intellectual, spiritual, and physical coordination of many talents. The distinctions and subtleties of the process shift from film project to film project. The absence of absolute definitions becomes clearly apparent when one tries to break down those components for the purpose of a career guide. The simple ordering of chapters becomes fodder for debate.

The interviews that appear in this text are intended to give the reader an overview of the kinds of creative career opportunities available in film—what kind of preparation may be appropriate, what the profession entails, typical time commitments, the rigors of each craft, the inherent stresses and frustrations, the joys and potential success. Interviewees were identified and selected based on the excellence of their work. With that as a given, we have attempted to profile people with varied backgrounds, educational preparation, and film experience in order to best serve the reader's needs and interests. We also have tried to offer interviews with filmmakers who work outside of Hollywood.

Interviews with the initials "JF" were performed by Jean Firstenberg, Director of The American Film Institute; those with the initials "EL" were performed by Emily Laskin.

Every film is a new creation, and every film team has its own balance and dynamic. There are no definitive answers, there are only guide posts. We hope some are provided within.

Emily Laskin

Acting Director
Development and Public Affairs

Acknowledgments
·················

Many people contributed long, hard hours to the creation of this book. The American Film Institute (AFI) is deeply grateful to all the creative professionals who contributed their time to be interviewed. Many of the individuals included herein participate in and support the work of the AFI in other varied and significant ways. It is their commitment of time, energy, and thought that made this book possible.

Thanks must go to Jean Firstenberg, Director of the AFI, for her support and participation in several interviews; James Hindman, Deputy Director, for his editorial guidance, encouragement, and enthusiastic support; the Education and Publications Advisory Committee of the AFI; the staff of the Louis B. Mayer Library at AFI; Greg Beal; David Chadderdon; Bill Horrigan; Ilana Kern; Odette Salvaggio; Eraine Schmit; John Schmit; Stephanie Toia-Lytle; Devon Wall; and Michael, Nicholas, and Joseph Laskin.

Special thanks to Deborah McRae, who masterfully transcribed the bulk of the interviews and to Anna Lisa Korobkin, who persistently scheduled interviews, transcribed, corresponded with interviewees and photographers, prepared the final manuscript, and generally kept the project on track and on schedule.

Many thanks to Barbara Gilson at Simon and Schuster, whose assistance, expertise, and patience were invaluable.

The American Film Institute

■■■■■■■■■■■■■■■■■■■■■■■■■

The American Film Institute was created in 1967 as an independent, national, nonprofit organization by the National Endowment for the Arts to "preserve the heritage and advance the art of film and television in the United States." Through a series of interrelated programs emanating from its offices in Washington, D.C., New York City, and Los Angeles, the institute conducts activities around the country that work toward the achievement of its primary goals:

- to increase recognition and understanding of the moving image as an art form
- to assure preservation of the art form
- to identify, develop, and encourage new talent

The American Film Institute

∎∎∎∎∎∎∎∎∎∎∎∎∎∎∎∎∎∎∎∎∎∎∎∎∎

History of the American Film Institute

"We will create an American Film Institute, bringing together leading artists of the film industry, outstanding educators, and young men and women who wish to pursue this 20th century art form as their life's work."

With these words, President Lyndon Johnson signed the National Arts and Humanities Act of 1965. The legislation created the National Endowment for the Arts (NEA) and, in turn, the American Film Institute was established as an independent, nonprofit organization dedicated to promoting the art of the moving image: to preserve the film classics of the past, advocate an appreciation of film and television in the present, and help to train the filmmaker of the future.

The institute's first chairman was Gregory Peck, and George Stevens, Jr., was named the founding director. Initial funding came from three sources (each at the $1.3 million level): the National Endowment for the Arts; the Ford Foundation; and the member companies of the Motion Picture Association of the Board of Trustees from private, foundation, and corporate sources.

Setting an immediate pattern for the AFI's activities, one of the first projects undertaken by the AFI was a "rescue" operation to locate and preserve 250 rare and historically valuable films. Since then the AFI film collection at the Library of Congress has totaled close to 25,000 motion pictures, spanning the spectrum from Laurel & Hardy films to *Lost Horizon.*

In 1969 the AFI established its conservatory, the Center for Advanced Film Studies, at Greystone, the Doheny mansion in Beverly Hills. Among the crop of young filmmakers who studied at the Conservatory during its first year were Jeremy Paul Kagan (*The Chosen, The Adventures of Natty Gann*); Caleb Deschanel (*The Black Stallion, The Right Stuff, The Natural*); Matthew Robbins (*The Sugarland Express, Batteries Not Included*); and Paul Schrader (*Taxi Driver, Mishima*).

In Washington the AFI opened its exhibition program at the National Gallery in 1970, moving in 1973 to its own theater at the John F. Kennedy Center for the Performing Arts. By 1970 the AFI's publications program was underway with the *AFI Guide to College Courses in Film and Television,* the *AFI Catalog Project,* and a series of oral histories of filmmaking: *American Film,* debuted in October, 1975. The AFI's first feature-length Film-on-Film was *Directed by John Ford,* made in 1968 by Peter Bogdanovich, three years before he became internationally known for *The Last Picture Show.*

John Cassavetes became the first Filmmaker-in-Residence at the Center in 1972; in 1973, the AFI began what has become perhaps its best-known activity with the presentation of the first Life Achievement Award to John Ford. The Life Achievement Award has become the highest honor a filmmaker or actor can receive, and the annual ceremony is telecast worldwide. Subsequent recipients have included Fred Astaire, James Cagney, Frank Capra, Bette Davis, Henry Fonda, Lillian Gish, Alfred Hitchcock, John Huston, Gene Kelly, Jack Lemmon, Gregory Peck, Barbara Stanwyck, James Stewart, Orson Welles, Billy Wilder, William Wyler, Sir David Lean, and, in 1991, Kirk Douglas.

One of the most notable programs run under the AFI auspices is the Directing Workshop for Women, which, beginning in 1974, has given dozens of professional women the chance to direct motion pictures. Lee Grant, Randa Haines, Nancy Malone, Neema Barnett, and Jan Eliasberg are just a few of those who have honed their directorial abilities under this program.

George Stevens, Jr., resigned as director of the AFI in 1979. His successor was Jean Firstenberg, who has served for the past twelve years, overseeing the AFI's continued expansion, which has included a major improvement of facilities. In 1981 the AFI acquired the former campus of Immaculate Heart College on Western Avenue in Los Angeles. Occupying four buildings spread over eight acres, the campus provides a spacious home for the institute. More than 1,500 men and women have received training at the conservatory, now called The Center for Advanced Film and Television Studies, including Bob Mandell, Michael Dinner, David Lynch, John McTiernan, Jon Avnet, Marshall Herskovitz, Ed Zwick, and Amy Heckerling. In 1985, the Center became the first film school to be accredited by the National Association of Schools of Art and Design. That same year the AFI became the first art institute to be included in the California Education Facilities Authority Pooled Bond Program, which infused the institute with $6.7 million from the tax-free bond issue to refinance the acquisition and renovation of the campus.

The AFI has continued to encourage new filmmakers with grants and programs that have steadily extended into new areas, and television is now firmly within the AFI's purview. Since 1981 the institute has sponsored the National Video Festival and its touring program of new and innovative works, and operates a Television Writers' Workshop and the state-of-the-art Sony Video Center on the Los Angeles campus. AFI graduates have produced numerous telefeatures, including *LBJ: The Early Years,* by Peter Werner; *The Burning Bed,* by Jon Avnet; and *Special Bulletin,* by Marshall Herskovitz and Ed Zwick, all of which have won numerous awards.

The AFI continually strives to showcase new works by emerging filmmakers, most visibly through the annual AFI/Los Angeles International Film Festival, which is rapidly becoming one of America's most respected film festivals. The AFI Independent Award—the Maya Deren—was created in 1986 to recognize the contributions of independent film and video artists and to raise public awareness of their work.

In September 1989 the institute celebrated the approaching twenty-fifth anniversary of the establishment of the NEA with a "Back to the Rose Garden" event in Washington, D.C., at which President George

Bush said: "For almost a quarter of a century, the American Film Institute has nurtured and celebrated the art of the moving image. In doing so, it has had an immense impact on the mind and soul of America."

Preserving, training, and celebrating; for more than twenty years the American Film Institute has sought to fulfill its mandate to support this greatest of American art forms, the art of the moving image.

Introduction

■ ■ ■ ■ ■ ■ ■ ■ ■ ■

As we celebrate 100 years of cinema, we look back and reflect on the changes, evolutions, and technological developments—from the sophistication with which films are made today to the multiple modes by which we view them. One critical element has remained the same: the talent, dedication, and passion required to be a filmmaker.

Film has matured as an art form. It is acknowledged, recognized and respected as such. It has taken its place next to the more traditional art forms of the preceding centuries. It holds a very special place in our minds, hearts, and souls. Film inspires, educates, changes our opinions and attitudes, and even motivates us to action. We mark the passage of time with references to when we first saw a particular film and what it meant to us. Sitting with several hundred other filmgoers in a dark theater still has the ability to spark a sense of wonder, awe, and pleasure as only this remarkable American art form can. Whether we are watching these magical flickering shadows in a theater or at home, the sheer power of these images, with all their immediacy, familiarity, artistry, and even silliness, causes us to marvel at our global telecommunications network that has created a world so close and so connected.

Filmmakers are a special breed. They are at once inspired individualists who nevertheless are entirely reliant upon numerous colleagues to bring their artistic visions to the screen. This volume offers a profile, a small sampling of the kinds of people who shape the films we enjoy;

individuals whose collective creative talents conceive and execute imaginative and compelling stories that become part of our cultural heritage. It is their collaborative efforts that have built our remarkable American film heritage and have established and sustained our love for film.

Jean Firstenberg   James Hindman
Director   Deputy Director

ONE

······

⭐ The Screenwriter

The screenwriter is, initially, the most critical component of the tapestry of a film. The potential success of any film lies in the strength and uniqueness of its story—the sole responsibility and inspiration of the screenwriter. Screenwriters work in many genres: fantasy, science fiction, drama, tragedy, comedy, action/adventure, etc. Screenplays can be original or can be the result of adaptations from other media (plays, novels, short stories, etc.) Writers can work alone or in collaboration with the director, producer, or a writing partner.

The salary range for a screenwriter varies widely and depends on whether or not screenplays include treatments or are first drafts with options for final drafts, or whether the writer is only handling a rewrite or polish. For the various categories compensation ranges from $5,000 to $53,000. A screenplay in great demand by the production companies may sell for over $1,000,000. Writers are eligible to join the Writers Guild of America (WGA) (213-550-1000) once they have accrued twelve units of credits as described by the WGA's "Schedule of Units of Credit," based upon work completed under contract of employment or upon the sale or licensing of previously unpublished and unproduced literary or dramatic material. Employment must be with a company signatory to the WGA.

Frank Pierson

. . . .

Frank Pierson was born in Chappaqua, New York, and graduated from Harvard University in 1950. He spent the next eight years as a journalist for *Time/Life* magazine. Since 1960 he has been a television writer/director/producer for such productions as "Have Gun—Will Travel," "Naked City," and "Route 66." He received Academy Award nominations for co-writing the screenplays *Cat Ballou* and *Cool Hand Luke,* and garnered the Oscar for his screenplay *Dog Day Afternoon.* He co-authored the 1976 version of *A Star Is Born,* and wrote and directed the television movie *The Neon Ceiling,* and the feature film *King of the Gypsies.* His recent credits include the screenplay adaptation of *Presumed Innocent.*

EL: When were you drawn to screenwriting or to film?

FP: Like everybody in the age of film, I spent a lot of my childhood watching films. My family, particularly when we lived in New York and in places where films were available to us, used to attend rather sophisticated European films that were not much in vogue in the late thirties and early forties. I didn't think of making a career of screenwriting until my mother became a screenwriter. She wrote an autobiography that was made into a film in the early part of the war. All the male screenwriters were off fighting in the war, so she was offered the opportunity to write the screenplay, which she did, and that led to a career. When I returned from the war, I stopped in Hollywood, and she got me onto the lot at Warner Brothers. I watched the shooting of a scene from *Humoresque*. It was magical, this world being created before your eyes (in those days everything was being created artificially on the soundstage). I'd been away three years, and I went back to finish college in the East, but that vision of the soundstage was always lurking in

2

some dark alley of my subconscious. I had big problems dealing with the Oedipal competition with my mother, I guess. I didn't attack it directly for a couple of years after I left college. My first job was as a reporter working for *Time-Life* magazine.

EL: How did the journalistic experience fit into your screenwriting?

FP: Again, it was a matter of being exposed to so many different kinds of situations, doing a story where you spent weeks or months traveling around with cops through the ghetto, or spending time with a dying cancer patient while the photographer was taking pictures for *Life* magazine. At the same time I went to glitzy Hollywood parties covering the stars and all that gossipy stuff. And then I covered military affairs and science and watched the people who govern our nation at rather close quarters. One got much closer to them then than the press can now. It was a wonderful job at that time because in those days *Time* and *Life* opened doors that are no longer open to the media.

EL: When did you put your feet firmly into screenwriting?

FP: I was working out here in the *Time-Life* Bureau, and the low salaries and the disillusion with *Time-Life*'s political distortions of the news began to bother me. Journalism is a young person's career; nobody should stay with it for a lifetime unless one gets a personal forum, or becomes an editor who can control the policies of a magazine or a newspaper. There comes a moment when you have to make up your mind to do something different. I'd spent a lot of time with movie people on movie sets and began to believe that I could do film. I decided that I would write on weekends in whatever spare time I had. I tried to do that, but it just didn't work. So finally I just quit my job. I decided to use my savings to buy whatever time I could—to see if I could break into the industry. It took me two years.

EL: Describe the evolution of your writing process. Do you write now in the same way as you did then?

FP: Not at all. In the beginning you don't know whether you can do it at all. The first few years are spent simply learning the craft, learning how actors work, learning how directors stage and mount scenes, what's possible with a camera and what's not. This technical and craft stuff dominates your thinking—or it did mine. After a bit I was able to set that aside and address the substance of the story. That's when it gets scary. You know that this scene has to be a certain type; you know what it's supposed to do in the structure of the piece, but you haven't the faintest idea of what the scene is going to be like. That induces sheer terror because you begin to think, "Where are the ideas going to come from?" You set aside the clichéd ways of doing that scene; you set aside the ways everybody else from Shakespeare to Ibsen to Paddy Chayefsky did that scene. You know, the same scenes keep coming up again and again in story after story; how a man tells a woman that he loves her, how a woman leaves a man, how someone tells another person a loved one is dead. We've seen all these situations again and again, and yet your task is to make them new, surprising, true, specific to this story. That's the point at which some kind of original thinking begins, and the creative solutions arise. It's absolutely petrifying to have to confront that in the early years of your career. What I've achieved, I guess, is a fair confidence that if I sit there long enough the answer will come—and most of the time it does.

EL: Do you write every day?

FP: I write on the computer every day for at least two hours, but my unconscious is working all the rest of the day. After years and years of writing every single day, holidays included, I've become addicted to it. If I don't write, I get very difficult to live with, so that everybody around me says, "For God's sakes, get to your computer, and do some work so we can bear you for the rest of the day!"

EL: Do you work on more than one project at a time?

FP: Yes, but it's really on again, off again. In other words, I work on one thing for a week or until I finish a draft, and then I go on to something else. It's very difficult to do one thing in the morning and then something else in the afternoon. I've done it at times, but I'm not very successful working that way.

EL: In the thick of the process, do you share the material with any select person or persons?

FP: Oh, sure, with a number of people, other writers. There are a number of us who trade things around. I'll send a script to Sydney Pollack for his opinion, and he sometimes sends his to me. Alvin Sargent and I trade sometimes. There's a lot of that. I think it's a practice left over from the time most of us in the older generation of screenwriters and directors broke into the trade. I remember fondly the days when we still went to the studio and there was a collegial atmosphere. You knew a lot of other writers, what they were going through and what they were doing. That's long since vanished; everybody works at home now. We have a breakfast club at the Brentwood Mart where a lot of us meet every morning—a table full of writers and directors. It's an echo of the old "writers' table" that used to be a fixture in the studio commissaries back when people were still punching time clocks.

EL: We hear so much about film as a collaborative art form, but it seems to me that the writer must spend much time in solitary endeavor.

FP: The writer wasn't always as separated from the actual creative process. It's become much less a collaborative medium in recent years. Usually one director, a star, or, in rare instances, a producer so dominates what's going on that everybody else is really just feeding that person material. There's very little feeling of the teamwork that used to exist.

EL: Do you gather your ideas from newspapers, from out of the blue, or from personal experiences?

FP: All of those places. Sometimes driving on the freeway you'll just have a notion about something. For example, what would happen to somebody who, sitting in a jam in the middle of a freeway says, "Oh, fuck it, I don't want to do this anymore," and takes an action that leads to another action. You find yourself daydreaming, and sometimes those ideas turn into stories.

EL: What skills do you think a good screenwriter needs other than being a good writer?

FP: Command of the English language is a wonderful thing that has very largely vanished. I'm astonished at the number of screenplays, even in this age of computer spellers, that are difficult to understand because the language is so poor. A screenplay is a very tight document and closer to a poem than to a novel because of its compressed nature. I'm talking about good screenplays, not the 99 percent of commercial dog-food out there. You compress a great deal of information and feeling into the fewest possible words, and trying to create in that way requires a precision most writers lack. A good screenplay is written to be performed, which is a totally different idea.

EL: Do you recommend that a young person interested in developing such skills read specific, dramatically successful screenplays?

FP: Sure, I've done that all my life; that's how I first began, by reading my mother's screenplays and any others that I could scrounge from her friends. They were tremendously helpful. More than anything else, I would recommend some acting classes. You're writing these things to be acted, not to be read. One of the difficulties I have with executives reading screenplays (and even directors) is that they'll look at a scene, and from the way they talk about it, I realize that they have read it wrong. What I have done for a long time is actually insist on reading a great deal of the screenplay aloud to them. Bob Towne does that, too. In fact, Bob and I once lobbied the Writer's Guild to make that a negotiating position in our contract: that the form of delivery of a screenplay would require the person at the studio who makes the ultimate decisions, the CEO, to close the door and turn off the telephones for three hours while the screenwriter reads the screenplay aloud.

EL: It's dramaturgy in cinema, and it's interesting that every theater has a dramaturge but there is no such position in film.

FP: There used to be a story department at the studios that was usually headed by a writer/producer who served somewhat the function of a theater dramaturge, but it's a position that has been done away with. We now have development persons, and most of them have never made a motion picture and don't know how. They are scouts looking for deals; they don't have lunch with writers and directors, but rather eat with agents.

EL: How does one become adept at different genres?

FP: I don't know the answer to that. I think that some people have a natural dance rhythm that leads them to do a particular dance style very well, and that's what they tend to stick to. No doubt that stems from a natural ability and feeling. I've never been aware of genre as such. I need to find the particular form in which a given story can express itself, and then I write it that way. *Presumed Innocent* was the first thing I've done that I thought of as genre film, a courtroom drama. Frankly, I found that aspect a huge pain in the ass.

EL: Is it frustrating to be saddled with adaptation? Does it present its own set of challenges to be met on different ground?

FP: No, actually you're ahead of the game if it's a book that readily lends itself to adaptation. I think of an adaptation in this way: I've read the book or seen the play that I am adapting. I begin to imagine the movie it could become by asking myself what in me responded to it. What does it mean to me? When I've figured out the answer to that, which I suppose is finding the theme, I take that and think, OK, using this theme, this mood and feeling, this musical tempo, how would I write this as a movie? One then begins to create the movie from there which is ground zero. The book or play is a bank of spare parts, and you use whatever you need to create a new entity, which is the movie, and throw away the rest. I make myself very unpopular with novelists this way.

EL: Do you think in words or do you think in images?

FP: I know exactly how I would stage every scene and where the actors are in relation to each other, the furniture, their entrances and exits, etc. On a current project I've designed a set, so I can show the director how the scene is going to play. I think the writer owes the director and the actors very specific imagery of what exactly is happening, whose point of view we're viewing. Once I've communicated that to the director, he may have an entirely different idea about how to do that. I'm not trying to tell him how to direct his picture, but if I can show him how I see it then he is in a better position to start from that and create his vision any way he chooses.

EL: At this point how much of what you do is cerebral and how much is intuitive/instinctive?

FP: Leading an audience through a story is a very cerebral enterprise, especially if you're doing something such as a courtroom drama. At the same time, the emotions are the factor that draw an audience into the theater, and they come from other regions of the mind and heart. Consider the word "actor"; we don't call them "speechmakers" or "vocalists" or "orators"; we call them *actors* because they *act*. What they *do* on stage or on camera tells us what they are feeling. Often what the actor says is clearly a lie, because what he's doing at the same time is telling us something completely different. Those are the complexities that you have to deal with. You have to allow your unconscious and your conscious to do battle with each other without refereeing. Very often you look at the computer screen with utter amazement and say, "My God, where did that come from?" It comes from the unconscious, and you need to get in touch with that in order to write well.

EL: Has the computer changed the way you write?

FP: Yes, no question about it. I've been working on a computer now for almost ten years, and I think it's added three years to my creative life. We never knew in the old days how long our script was at the end of a day. You'd have these tatters of paper all pasted together. Now you can print it out every day, and you know exactly how long the thing is. You can try things that you never would have tried before because it was too exhausting to do it manually.

EL: Do you think that today film school is essential, helpful, or unimportant to a young person considering a career as a screenwriter?

FP: I think it's important because the competition is so intense, and you need any help that you can get. There are film schools where a talented student can learn much of value. On the whole, however, I'm against them, certainly at an undergraduate level. If I were running a film school, I would do it strictly at a graduate level, open to anybody over the age of thirty. I would look for people who have led a troubled and disastrous kind of life. Many kids from USC, UCLA, or Columbia never had anything bad happen to them. They're twenty-seven years old, and all they know is what they've seen on "Cheers" and in George Lucas films. They produce imitations of imitations of imitations of life that are not interesting to me. Even the Coen brothers, who are terrifically entertaining, are all style. Give me a person who's worked in an emergency ward for ten years bursting with rage or joy or thirst for revenge and is full of stories that pulse with the blood of real life. But what we're getting is trendy idiots who are already rich making TV ads for underwear and perfume.

EL: What are the biggest changes you've seen during your career?

FP: The fragmentation of the business. Now we work at home until we suddenly get together on a production, work very intensely together for a few weeks, and then it's over. The result is that there is less and less feeling of sharing artistic and business experiences. One of the first offices I had was off a long hall with a row of doorways. Bob Rafelson, Bob Altman, Paul Mazursky, Carl Reiner, Howard Fast, John Cassavetes, Henry Jaglom, and Jack Nicholson were around. When you got stuck on a scene, or you had a problem with your life, somebody had a door open. Everyone was delighted to talk instead of having to write. It was a wonderful way to cross-fertilize our instincts and our feelings about the business and the art. That kind of thing has pretty much gone by the board, though it still does exist. Another big change has been the deaths of the old studio czars, the Harry Cohns, and the generation of studio heads who came right after them, most of whom were writers. They thought in terms of a story they cared about and hoped that the audiences would identify with. The succeeding generations have sold out to the conglomerates. There is an infestation of the business department with lawyers who have completely changed the way contracts are written and the way business is done. This has materially changed the atmosphere in which we work and not for the better.

EL: Is there any advice you would give to a young person considering screenwriting or working in film?

FP: I remember during one of the summers when I was trying to break into the business, I wrote seventeen half-hour shows in seventeen weeks. I couldn't sell any because they were bad. It took a long time for me to find out why they were bad. I got very discouraged, and at one point I said to a friend of mine who had read some of my things, "Tell me, am I wasting my time? Should I just give up? I don't want to embarrass my friends, and I don't want to embarrass myself." He replied, "Listen, I don't really know, because I don't know what you can become. All I know is that the only ones who are doing it now (being writers, directors, etc.) are the ones who never stopped!"

Nora Ephron
■ ■ ■ ■ ■ ■ ■ ■ ■ ■ ■ ■ ■

Nora Ephron was born in New York to Henry and Phoebe Ephron, the screenwriters of such films as *Carousel* and *The Desk Set*. She attended Wellesley College, graduated in 1962, and soon joined the staff of the *New York Post*. In 1968 she began doing freelance work, and during the next few years she served as contributing editor for *New York* magazine and became senior editor and writer of a column on the media for *Esquire*. Three collections of her articles have been published, including *Wallflower at the Orgy, Crazy Salad: Some Things About Women,* and *Scribble, Scribble.* In the late seventies she began her screenwriting career with a television movie entitled *Perfect Gentleman.* She was then partnered with Alice Arlen to write the screenplay for *Silkwood,* which earned them an Academy Award nomination. In 1986 Ms. Ephron adapted her novel, *Heartburn,* for the screen, which was directed by Mike Nichols. Her current credits include the screenplays of the critically acclaimed *When Harry Met Sally,* directed by Rob Reiner, *Cookie,* directed by Susan Seidelman, and *My Blue Heaven.* Her first directing project is the feature film *This Is My Life,* for which she also wrote the screenplay.

EL: How did you prepare yourself to be a writer?

NE: I knew that I wanted to be a journalist in high school, partly as a result of reading a lot of things such as "Brenda Starr" and "Superman" comics, and partly because there was a spectacular journalism teacher at Beverly Hills High School. That was what I wanted to be from the time that I was thirteen or fourteen. I later went to Wellesley College, and it didn't have journalism courses. When I moved to New York, I became a reporter at the *New York Post* where I worked for five years as a journalist. Later I became a freelance writer. I worked as a freelance writer for ten years writing columns and essays in *Esquire* and various places, and books that were collections of my essays were published. I didn't think very much about screenwriting at all. I can't remember if I was already married to Carl Bernstein or not, I probably was, when the movie of *All The President's Men* was going to be made. Carl and Bob (Woodward) were not happy with the first draft of the script, and they asked me if I would help do something that would indicate to the people who were making the movie what they had in mind. Carl and I rewrote the first draft, which was something that I now realize we should never have done. It was a horrible thing to do in terms of courtesy to another writer. However, it was an extraordinary lesson for me in screenwriting: We didn't change a huge amount of the script (we changed a scene here and a scene there), and I essentially ended up retyping quite a lot of Bill Goldman's script. It was like going to film school, because he's a very economical and gifted writer, and you really learn just how good a writer is when you have to retype his words. He didn't speak to me for many years because of this and I don't blame him.

As a result, however, a couple of people read that script and asked me if I wanted to do a women's caper movie. So I wrote a script about a group of women who rob a hotel and called it *Perfect Gentleman*, and it was made into a TV movie. It was not very good. In fact, it was one of the worst things I've ever seen. I saw it when I was pregnant with my first child, and I'm amazed he survived the experience! But because I had a script that had been circulating, I got another job.

I did an unproduced musical for Paramount, and then I did at least three drafts of *Compromising Positions* for Warners which was never made with my script. Then I did *Murder At Elaine's* for Warner Brothers, one of my favorites of my many unproduced scripts. Then I finally got lucky. Meryl Streep wanted to do the Karen Silkwood story, and Arlene Donovan at ICM had read one of my many unproduced scripts and suggested that I would be a good person to do it.

EL: Could you describe your writing process and whether it's different with a partner?

NE: It's very hard to describe my writing process because I do think it varies from project to project. It depends on whether you're doing original material or whether you're adapting something. When I do a completely original movie like *When Harry Met Sally*, I spend days just taking notes, writing little scenes, little snatches of dialogues, little ideas, observations about people I know, stories I've heard. That's the kind of movie that comes straight out of your head. I based a lot of the character of Harry on Rob Reiner, so to help myself I had some interviews with him and with the producer, Andy Scheinman. Basically, you just sit and sort of noodle for a long time, and then you outline it. I don't outline so violently when I'm working alone. I have a general idea of where I'm going. Sometimes I may get to a section where I need to do a rough outline of it, but usually I just know when I start in what the beginning, middle, and end are supposed to be. A certain amount of it is logical; you have certain logical things you have to do when you start a movie, and you know what they are.

When I work with a partner, either with Alice Arlen or with my sister Delia who really are the only two people I've written screenplays with, I do very extensive outlining. You sit in the room together and spitball back and forth, and the outline is almost but not quite the scene. There's a lot of dialogue and a lot of jokes in it, if it's meant to be funny. There are things that may not be used, but the idea is to get as much down in the outline as you possibly can even though you may not use it. You can free-associate a lot, and you can put in a lot of asides to one another going back and forth in an outline. Sometimes we do everything together; sometimes we go off and do each section separately.

EL: Each writing dialogue for different characters?

NE: No, the same because we've got the outline there. It's very hard to give any kind of rule about what I do because every movie is a little bit different.

EL: Do you find your characters from people you know, do you invent some, or is it a combination of both?

NE: It depends. For most of what you write, you have some idea of who the character is but you may not know that person. You can do movies like *When Harry Met Sally* where Sally is 90 percent me and Harry is

90 percent Rob. Then you can do movies like *Silkwood* where I'm not anybody in that movie. I do not think I could work with a partner on an original script. However, the advantage of working with a partner in the movies is that, first of all, movies are collaborative anyway, so you might as well start collaborating from the very beginning. Second, there is so much dialogue, and it's very easy to do dialogue with another person. Third, you come at something from a different aspect from someone else, and that's always good for the material, as long as you are in agreement on what the material is. When you start with something fact-based, you have a given. Your given is that your character is Karen Silkwood who worked at Kerr McGhee and she died on this-and-such a date. She had a boyfriend she lived with and a roommate who became a lesbian. That's given; you can't disagree about that. You can disagree about a million details; you can negotiate and argue and come at it from a million different points of view. But it's important to agree on what your basic story is. The only time Alice and I tried to do an original together, we had a very nice idea, but we couldn't agree on anything because nothing was a given.

EL: When you do a story such as *Silkwood*, a true story that had had a lot of public profile and awareness, how do you find the balance between the actual events and the things that you need to change for dramatic purposes?

NE: I think we were unbelievably careful in *Silkwood* to ensure that the things we made up were not the main part of the story. We created Cher's girlfriend, for example, who was a beautician in a funeral parlor, but it didn't seem to us to violate what the story was.

EL: When you're writing a script, do you have other people read it as you go?

NE: If I'm the writer on the script, I don't really show it to many people—maybe my agent and a couple of other people—then the studio reads it. I'm directing a movie now, and I'm showing the script to almost anyone who can help because what's in the script is basically my decision.

EL: Since you are moving into directing, will you abandon screenwriting or do both?

NE: No, I love the idea that I might be able to do both. One of the reasons that I wanted to do this movie with my sister or with a partner was that I think you need somebody to be the writer if you're going to be the director. I don't mean that all directors do, but I need somebody to keep reminding me, "You can't do this." and "This isn't working"—all those things it seems to me that writers are good at nudging directors about.

EL: So the move to directing may be to have more power over the story?

NE: It isn't so much to have more power as that there are things that I want to make movies about; one of these is women. The number of women directors is so small, and the number of men who are interested in directing movies about women is so small that it seems to make perfect sense for me to do this.

EL: In what way did your experience on the set as the writer prepare you to be a director?

NE: I was on the set almost the entire time on two Mike Nichols movies and on one Rob Reiner movie. These were not the worst people to go to school with.

EL: As you hire your crew as a director, and considering your interest in women's stories, will you give more attention to providing more opportunities for women?

NE: I haven't been conscious of making more effort to hire women, partly because it would never occur to me not to hire women.

EL: As a writer on a film, what has been your relationship with the director and the producer?

NE: I've had movies where the relationship with the director was as close as you could have. Mike Nichols and Rob Reiner are unbelievably generous about letting you be on the set and letting you say whatever is on your mind, far more generous than I can imagine my being, now that I look back on it. They were just wonderful to me. Nonetheless, all the movies that I worked on with them were their movies. In the end the director goes into the cutting room and you're not there. I've also worked on movies where a distant relationship with the director existed, and I worked on one movie where I couldn't stand the director. All of those things are possible.

EL: What's the most frustrating thing about being a screenwriter?

NE: When you start out as a screenwriter, you can't imagine how different the movie is going to be from what you started with. Sometimes you like it, sometimes you don't, but you are continually amazed at how your idea of it differs from what's actually happening. Have you ever had that experience where you anticipate going to a party, or a job interview, or a meeting, you're anxious about it, and you have a very clear idea of what the room will look like, who will be there, what it will be like, and what might happen? Then you go, and it's not at all like that, and in that moment your initial visual idea is completely erased from your brain. You can't remember what you had in mind; all you know is this is not it. That happens continually on movies you write—both on the movies you like and the movies you don't like. Eventually you stop being frustrated about it, and you face the decision about it, which is that either you accept it, this is how it is, this is the way it's going to be, or you decide to direct. I wouldn't say that I started directing out of frustration, but there's no question that when you write a script it's yours and by the time it becomes a movie, it's his. I use the masculine pronoun for obvious reasons because most of the time it's a he. The movie that Rob made out of *When Harry Met Sally* was a better movie than the one we started with, and I loved the experience of working with him on it. That's a movie I look at with complete and total happiness because I think we made the best possible movie we could have from the script—which is rarely true from the screenwriter's point of view. Then you can make a movie that doesn't work out at all, and you say, "I could have screwed up this screenplay (as a director) just as much as the person who directed it did and at least I wouldn't be so frustrated about it." You can either choose to accept what you do as a screenwriter, accept the limits of it, and understand that it's fundamentally only a blueprint for the movie. Or you can try to get a little bit more control by directing, and I'm sure that has its frustrations. I'll let you know what they are when I've discovered them.

EL: Can you identify anything in your training and experience as a journalist that has served you well as a screenwriter?

NE: I believe that the best training anyone can have for writing is journalism because it's the cleanest, simplest writing. I think my movies are well-written movies; I'm not referring to the dialogue, but to things such as set descriptions and things like that. Most screenwriters do a very good job at that, so it doesn't make me unique in any way but it is certainly a thing that has helped me. The continual question of journalism—"What's the point of this?"—is a question that you constantly have to ask yourself in a movie: what's the point of this scene? what are we trying to get to? where is the truth here? I wouldn't say that journalism taught me to write a screenplay; the truth is I'm not sure *what* taught me. *When Harry Met Sally* falls into absolutely no known structure that is in any of those books on how to write a screenplay. Whether you think it's bad or good, there's no possible way that a computer wrote it, which is not true of a lot of the movies you see. If the question behind your question is what helps one to become a screenwriter, I don't know. From my background, it seems to me that I learned a lot just doing it. The people you work with teach you a lot about writing.

EL: What advice would you give to a young person who wants to pursue screenwriting, either in terms of formal preparation or experience?

NE: My advice would be not to do it until they're older. One of the best things about journalism is that I spent almost twenty years seeing and doing things, not just going to the movies but covering political conventions, trials, and even a war. This may not be evident in my work, but the point is, it is. It's very much a part of who I am as a person. I don't know what happens to people who start writing screenplays in their twenties because it seems to me that they're not going to see enough to write movies about. But on the other hand, they may have better imaginations than I have. Still, I think being a journalist is the best writing training there is.

Tom Schulman

■ ■ ■ ■ ■ ■ ■ ■ ■ ■ ■ ■ ■ ■

After attending Montgomery Bell Academy in Nashville, Tom Schulman majored in philosophy at Vanderbilt University. He began writing with the hope that it would lead to a career in directing. After spending a semester at USC Graduate School of Cinema studying film production, he joined the Jack Garfein's Actors and Directors Lab in Los Angeles, where he spent three years acting, writing, and directing short films and plays. In 1985 he wrote *Dead Poets Society,* which was produced by Disney's Touchstone Pictures. Touchstone then signed him to work on the script *Honey, I Shrunk The Kids.* He has since written the comedy *What About Bob?* which starred Richard Dreyfuss and Bill Murray, and his screenplay *The Medicine Man,* starring Sean Connery, was filmed in the Amazon.

EL: When you were starting out, to what extent did you share your writing with other friends or other writers? How did you get feedback?

TS: I had three or four close friends who were kind enough and honest enough to read my scripts and tell me the brutal truth. I learned that when you start probing you find that half the things you think you are communicating aren't really coming across. I'd ask, "What did you feel was going on in this scene?" and I'd learn that the reader was getting something completely different from what I had intended. I found that if I could force myself past the pain and disappointment of my friends' "bad reviews" and stay open to what they were saying, I could really improve my scripts. My friends were incredibly helpful over the years, like yardsticks against which I could measure whether I was getting any better.

© Touchstone Pictures/Francis Duhamel

EL: Can you describe your working process? Where do you get your ideas? How long must they germinate?

TS: When I get an idea I write it down or put it into a computer file. As the ideas pile up in my subconscious and start worming around, a few will start pushing their way into my train of thought. I'll think— That idea—it's bugging me.

Something about it is interesting, but I don't know what. It could be a character, an interesting twist in the story, a line of dialogue, anything. I keep lists, and I'm always playing with the lists on my computer screen—moving the better ideas to the top and the dogs down. If an idea becomes insistent enough, I put it into its own file and start making more extensive notes about it. Soon I might have 15–20 pages of notes, many just stray ideas based on the original idea. Then I print all the pages, slice each paragraph up, lay them out on top of the desk, and see if there's a story. If there is a story I try to evaluate it. I ask myself, Were you lucky today, punk? Could this story actually be worth a damn? Is there anything of value here trying to get out? I really have to force myself to trust my own subconscious; force myself to stay in a place where logic is not necessarily hard and fast; force myself to free-associate. If anything starts to stick in my gut at that point, I know I'm onto something. The process I just described works particularly well if one feels in a state of—dare I speak its name?—writer's block.

Occasionally, I get what I know is a great idea and simply sit down and write it from beginning to end. Other times the idea percolates for a long time, coming a lot like a dream. Why do certain things bubble up? I have no idea. All I know is that you have to trust your unconscious, allow yourself to relax, and let thoughts speak to you. Writing also produces a lot of anxiety, and I have tried to learn to let that anxiety spur me into action—push me into making my stories better. In whatever you write, it's important to constantly demand more from yourself to avoid clichés and develop something you've never seen before—something fresh. Any idea that is less than fresh should be left in the computer memory.

For me, the most important part of the writing process is writing the story. Once I have a story I'm satisfied with, I feel great, and I like to crank out the first draft in a few days. Most screenplays are not that long—20,000 to 25,000 words. I've found that it's better for me to write for twelve or fourteen hours a day and finish the first draft in three or four days than it is to do it at a more leisurely pace. Unfortunately, I have a habit of procrastinating. Some masochistic part of me simply refuses to calmly sit down and write five pages a day for a month. Instead I'll organize paper clips, read the sports page, or brush the dog until suddenly I've got five days to write the entire script. I don't recommend it, but it seems to work for me so far.

EL: Writing is a very solitary activity. Do you share your materials with other people during that process?

TS: Most of the time I discuss the idea quite a bit, particularly in the story stage. I think you can approach a first draft in two ways: You can either discuss the story extensively, work up a detailed outline, and then write the first draft. Or you can write the whole script without discussing it or working the story out at all, and hope that by the end of the first draft you'll have figured it out. I have occasionally resorted to doing it the second way, but I believe it always pays to think a story through completely *before* writing it. When I first started writing I said to myself, God, this idea is so good it is going to write itself. I discussed it with no one, blasted through the first draft, and then after 120 pages discovered that I didn't have a clue as to what I was writing about. I had to rewrite the whole thing and it was particularly messy because I found myself clinging to bits that I liked that didn't belong on the planet, much less in that script. It was an ugly process during which I became an extremely unpleasant human being. The wisest course for me is to tell the story over and over to my wife or friends and to see what their response is, where they're interested, where their attention is wandering, etc. Then, when the story is really working (or when my wife looks like she'll kill me if I ever mention it again), I sit down and write the script.

EL: Where do you find your characters, and how do you develop their voices?

TS: I start by basing my characters on people that I know or have met. In the first few pages of the first draft, I conjure up images of the people I know, but then the fictional circumstances take over and the characters develop fictional lives and personalities of their own. I play the characters myself. I think that's why having acting experience is important for writing. At the Actors and Directors Lab, Jack Garfein made the directing students act on stage for a year. It terrified me—but it was wonderful training. In writing, you create the circumstances and the needs of each character, and from there it's like an acting improvisation with you— the writer—playing all the parts. Each time you play a scene you learn a little bit more about each character—what he or she is going through and wanting from the other characters—and you play each part again and again until the scene feels right from every character's point of view. If you're writing fiction, the characters could turn out "larger than life" because they're doing things that average people don't do. The characters are driven to extreme behavior by extreme circumstances.

EL: Let's say you've written a script and it's going into production as a feature film. Can you describe your relationship with the producer and director? How do you ideally like to work?

TS: *Dead Poets Society* was an almost perfect experience. The producer, Steven Haft, optioned the script and said to me, "This is a movie I want to make. I don't want you to do any rewrites yet; I think I can get a studio interested in it just the way it is." He delivered on that. Peter Weir ran the show, but making the film was a happy and collaborative process because we all shared the same vision of the movie. Often that's not the case; a producer or studio will buy a script for the basic idea and then either ask you to completely revise it or they'll hire someone else to do it. Or they might spend years with you writing a movie about which everyone is in agreement, then hire a director with a totally different vision and suddenly you're off the project and someone else is rewriting it. In the best of situations, the process of rewriting is one where the original writer and the director work together to make the story as tight and strong as possible, while at the same time incorporating the director's ideas that help to make the story "his"—personalizing or tailoring it to the director's vision. The director should be completely connected to the material emotionally and believe in it as much as the writer. That's the feeling I got from Peter Weir, and he even went me one better. He knew I wanted to direct, so he let me sit by his side and observe and say or ask whatever I wanted. He talked about why he was making certain choices, about the how and why of the performances, etc. He was incredibly confident and open, and that attitude pervaded the entire production. There was no pretense or ego from anybody.

EL: Do you still want to direct?

TS: Yes, I'm going to direct the next script I write.

EL: Are you interested in directing what you've written or what other people have written?

TS: Both.

EL: How much do you write on assignment and how much do you write original projects?

TS: *Dead Poets Society* was a spec script; *Honey, I Shrunk The Kids* was an assignment. *What About Bob?*, which is shooting now, was an assignment. *The Stand (The Medicine Man)*, due to shoot in January, was a spec script. So, it's been 50/50 over the last few years. One of the advantages of writing on assignment is that the idea has already been bought by a studio or a producer. It's ready to go. To write on spec is to take the risk that no one will like your script, and you will have wasted a lot of energy and personal investment.

EL: Are your spec scripts given greater attention now?

TS: Yes. If movies get made and are successful, you get more attention. It's the nature of the business.

EL: Could you briefly describe your relationship with your agent, what that relationship should be, how you chose an agent, and what services the agent provides?

TS: My relationship with my agent is ideal. I think he understands me both personally and professionally, and he works hard for me. A good agent strives to place the client with the producers and studios who appreciate the client's work and will treat him or her with respect. A good agent doesn't typecast the client. A good agent doesn't necessarily have the same personal taste as the client, yet he or she is *genuinely* supportive of and enthusiastic about the client's work. The agent/client relationship can be very close. It is often compared to a marriage, and there's some truth in the comparison.

When you're first starting out, getting an agent is difficult. Get your material to as many agents as possible and remember that it's hard to get good agents to read your scripts. You'll have to do everything you can—lie, cheat, beg—just to get agents on the phone. Sometimes an agent will say, "I want to be the only agent reading your script, and I want two weeks to read it," and you will have to respect that. But generally speaking, I think it's best to blanket the town with your material if you can, because agents pick you—you don't pick agents.

Look for someone who is excited about your writing, believes they can sell you, and has recommendations for people you should meet—and pray that list doesn't include other agents!

If an agent decides to represent you, it's a good idea to find out how much time the agent is going to spend working for you, particularly when the agent has other clients who are his or her breadwinners. How often does your agent want you to call him? Does he want to advise you as to what to write? Do you want that kind of advice? Something you won't learn until later is how much rejection of your work the agent can handle before he stops working for you. The relationship usually starts out with good feelings and high expectations, and, if your work sells right away, those feelings last. If you don't sell, the agent might eventually lose interest, but rarely will you get a call saying, "I don't have time for you; it's not working out." Some agents will never drop "cold" clients. They see no reason to encourage any client to leave when even the most unlikely client could suddenly turn around and write the next megahit. If an agent is particularly callous, you could endure months of unreturned phone calls. I have been through that, and it was torture. So I suggest discussing the possibility of "divorce" at the very beginning and coming to an agreement as to how separation will be handled if it becomes necessary. No one wants to be dropped by their agent, but a quick rejection is far better than a slow one. Time is precious.

EL: What's the most frustrating thing about being a screenwriter?

TS: The struggle to get my material to the screen in some form approximating the way I wrote it. Once you've sold your screenplay, you've lost control over it. No matter how much you might believe in a line of dialogue, a character, a scene, or even the entire story line, if a star or a director (and you know who you are) thinks that something is not working, it's gone. Changes can be forced upon you at any stage of the process—from the first rewrite right through the final preview of the finished film. There's a lot of frustration. Writers are the above-the-line doormats.

EL: What are the joys?

TS: The day-to-day joys are the surprises: the unexpected lines of dialogue that suddenly come from your characters' mouths, the new twists that suddenly make a story exciting. The greatest joy is the audience response. Seeing that people have gotten something positive out of your movie—hearing from people who are so moved that they call you up, or write to tell you how much your movie meant to them. There's no substitute for that because that's ultimately what it's all about—moving people. *Dead Poets Society* was an overwhelming experience—a dream come true. It took four long years to get it made, but the response made the years of struggle worthwhile.

EL: I think many people were moved, though I'm sure that it was originally not considered commercially viable.

TS: I was called on the carpet by several producers who said things like, "Why in the world did you write something like this? Certainly you know that no one's going to *make* it or go see it. My God, poetry . . . *Dead Poets Society* . . . listen to that title, where's your ear?" I knew that was going to happen. I wasn't so naive as to think that it would just suddenly provoke a reaction of, "Oh, this is interesting; let's make it." Getting it made took finding people who were willing to take risks. Once they took the risk, others couldn't understand how it ever was considered a risk in the first place. But believe me, to most people this was not a commercial-sounding property.

EL: Can you suggest other personal skills or characteristics, other than creativity, good writing skills, and understanding dramatic structure, that a good writer will need?

TS: Openness and interpersonal skills are important. Writing is communication, so learning to talk with other people, to listen, to be open to change is important. I think many writers are afraid that if they are open to critical input they will lose their individual voices, but the greater danger is closing off; it never hurts to listen. There are quite a few people out there—people who might not be considered "creative"— who can have extraordinarily helpful ideas about your script. If you're willing to listen, you will make major breakthroughs. Learning how to listen to criticism is so important. A lot of people whom I knew in the early days—incredibly bright and talented people—would tenaciously defend their first drafts, in spite of criticism or suggestions, and refuse to change anything. That led to rejection. One in a million first drafts is that good. The trick is learning to ask questions, and probing, and figuring out what's really behind all the criticism. Often, readers can't say exactly why a screenplay is or isn't working, but buried in their criticisms is a gem of an idea. Finding those gems is the key to rewriting, and rewriting is the key to successful writing.

EL: Is film school valuable, or can someone succeed as a screenwriter without it?

TS: I don't think it's essential. The most important part of the writing process is not attending classes or studying how to write, but *writing*. So, whether you're in film school or not, you're going to get better if you keep writing and working at it. If you keep writing— which is essentially a process of staying open to your idea long enough to make the most of it—if you're willing to work hard and take input from good people, you'll get better, and you won't need film school. Which is not to say that film school is not valuable; it is. It can expose you to a wide variety of films and ideas, it can teach you how movies are made. Film school also provides you with a daily exchange of ideas with a peer group. But if you're not in film school, don't despair. You can find help in night school classes, acting workshops, the back seat of your Ford Mustang, all sorts of places. Of the people whom I trust to counsel me about my writing, only one went to film school.

EL: Any other advice you'd give to young people?

TS: First, start writing. I'd like to offer a quote by Goethe that I keep near my computer: "Until one is committed, there is hesitance, the chance to draw back, always ineffectiveness. Concerning all acts of initiative (and creation) there is one elementary truth, the ignorance of which kills countless ideas and splendid plans: that the moment one definitely commits oneself, then Providence moves, too. All sorts of things occur to help one that would never have otherwise occurred. A whole stream of events issues from the decision, raising in one's favor all manner of unforeseen incidents, meetings, and material assistance, which no man would have dreamed could have come his way. Whatever you can do or dream you can, begin it. Boldness has genius, power, and magic in it. Begin it now."

Know that the process of getting scripts sold obscures the real work. The real work for the writer is writing. In the beginning, when you don't have an agent, maintaining your focus is difficult. Even when you have an agent, it's hard not to get enveloped by the business side of things. However I firmly believe—and the early part of my career bears this out—that the more energy you spend focused on selling or thinking about what will sell, the less likely you are to write a good script and the less likely you are to sell. A friend of mine used to say, "A good script will get made even if it is left on the floor of a public bathroom," and deep down I believe that. So maintain your enthusiasm about your work, write about themes you are passionate about, believe in the power and magic of movies, demand the best of yourself, work hard—and all the rest will come.

Just be sure you choose the public bathroom at CAA.

TWO

■■■■■■

★ The Producer

The producer often develops the material for a film, usually beginning with a script or story that he/she chooses. The producer hires the director and the crew (with the exception of the key creatives hired in conjunction with the director). He/she arranges for financing, meets with the studios, negotiates deals for marketing and distribution, and works hand-in-hand with the director throughout the shooting. The producer is responsible for the film's budget and schedule from pre- through post-production. He/she is the first one to come onto a film and the last one to leave.

There is no set minimum wage for a producer. The salary he or she receives is dependent upon the budget of the film, the time the project consumes, the status of the producer, and whether he or she owns the production company or is just a hired producer. Payment may range from $2\frac{1}{2}$ to 5 percent of the film's earnings. Producers may belong to the Producer's Guild of America (213-557-0807), which has a membership of 450. Membership is permitted if one is currently employed as an executive producer, producer, or associate producer with a contract guaranteeing credit as such. Membership is also permitted if one has executive producer, producer, or associate producer credit on any of the following: a) one feature film, b) three television movies, c) six 1-hour television shows, or d) thirteen half-hour television shows.

George Lucas
■ ■ ■ ■ ■ ■ ■ ■ ■ ■ ■ ■ ■

Born in 1944, George Lucas grew up in Modesto, California. He attended Modesto Junior College, where he met cinematographer Haskell Wexler, who encouraged him to pursue filmmaking and helped him gain admittance to the University of Southern California film school. While serving as a teaching assistant, he made "THX 1138:4EB," a science fiction short that he later adapted to the big screen as his first feature film. He gained recognition for his screenplay and direction of the film *American Graffitti,* which was nominated for five Academy Awards including Best Picture, Best Director, and Best Screenplay. Following the success of *Star Wars,* which he also wrote and directed, Mr. Lucas executive-produced and co-scripted the two sequels, *The Empire Strikes Back* and *Return of the Jedi.* He then served as co-executive producer on *Raiders of the Lost Ark* and the sequels, *Indiana Jones and the Temple of Doom* and *Indiana Jones and the Last Crusade,* all of which he also co-scripted. Other producing credits include *More American Graffiti, Willow,* and *Tucker.* In 1978 Mr. Lucas founded his own production company, Lucasfilm, Ltd., located in Marin County at Skywalker Ranch, his multi-million dollar production center. The facility encompasses film research and special effects facilities, screening rooms, editing areas, film libraries, a guest house, and a recreation area.

JF: Please discuss what you think filmmaking is or should be.

GL: There are always certain realities at work. Film productions operate somewhat like an army because you're trying to coordinate a lot of people to bring about one particular plan and focus a lot of energy into one moment. It has to work like a well-trained unit so that all the pieces come together for a brief period of time. Sometimes it's right for a moment, then it falls apart again and comes together again for another hour in a different way and falls apart again. All the pieces have to be tuned together because the moment in time is frozen forever on a piece of film, and you're stuck with it. It's also like a football game. Sports and battle have this same criterion—there's no second chance. You have to deal with the play at the moment, so it's a challenge. I've been involved with some film schools, and film schools have a tendency—in my experience—to protect. It's a jungle out there, and students sometimes are completely confounded by the standard they must reach. It's like brain surgery too; one can't fool around. Filmmaking is a very difficult occupation. A lot of students I've known over the years whine, moan, feel put upon, feel they've got this giant wall to scale. Well, school is the easiest wall, and getting through film school is a piece of cake for some students. Getting to direct the first movie is a little bit harder. But the second movie is really difficult unless you make a hit movie your first time out. It just keeps getting more difficult, the older you get.

JF: What is the best kind of environment a film school can offer?

GL: There's nothing wrong with failure; you don't need to protect people from the experience of failure. Sometimes people make films that don't work; instead of admitting those things teachers say, "Well, that was a very interesting *effort.*" But the world isn't like that. The secret is to succeed at something extremely experimental or know you failed and why. That's what I did in film school. I never did anything safe or conventional. I did things that were so far out I was in trouble all the time. But eventually I pulled it off. I did fail at times—it was embarrassing, and I certainly heard about it, but the secret was that ultimately I succeeded in doing things that were out of the ordinary. That called attention to my films, and that's how I got to be successful. Film schools have a tendency to protect mediocre people who really don't have "it." The film school should operate more like law and medical schools. It's a matter of proper admissions. I believe they should operate with a professional school form of admission in which one has to apply six months in advance and go through an interview. Even if you haven't made a movie and have average grades, if there's something about you

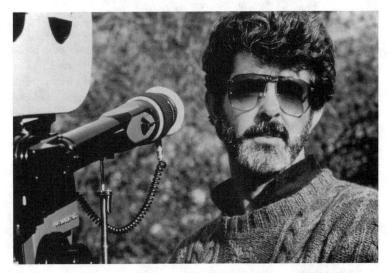

© 1987 LucasFilm Ltd/Keith Hanshere

that causes somebody at that school to say, "This guy's got something," you might have a chance. I also feel that for the first year schools should admit twice as many students as they do now, and state very clearly at the beginning, "Half of you are going to be out of here because you're going to flunk. If you can't prove yourself the first year, you aren't going to stay." At least the teachers would get a chance to work with students and select those who show promise.

JF: What do you think is the best way for young people to train?

GL: I believe in film schools because they're the fastest way to learn. There are a million roads to Mecca, and you've got to take the one that suits you best. For me, film school was a great concentrated way of learning a lot about film. I got in by a fluke. I didn't know anything about film, but I had an interest in photography and in becoming an illustrator. I went to the movies and I watched television, but I didn't really know anything. Film school ignited me, and I realized that film-making was something for which I had a natural talent. Three weeks after I got there I was on my way.

JF: If you hadn't applied to USC, do you think you would have found your way into film?

GL: Eventually I would have stumbled onto my talent in film because I love photography. Once I did discover it, nothing could stop me because, for me and, I think for many people like me, once you discover your thing you become obsessed with it—have a passion for it. It's an addiction; it pulls you without any reason or logic, and you cannot undo it. I couldn't not make movies!

JF: Is video a valid training tool?

GL: I believe in video as a learning tool. I have pushed very hard for film students to abandon film for video. I prefer 8mm video to 8mm film any day. Forget about learning the technology. You don't need to have a class in equipment operation. You don't need a separate class in technology. You should be doing still photography, video, film, art—it doesn't make any difference what the medium is. You can draw the images and do storyboards. Film schools should be teaching how to communicate using sound and images and the juxtaposition of sound and images rather than worry about technology. Communication is not something you're born with though you may have a talent for it. Some people are geniuses, but in most areas, you need a well-rounded education. How do you teach great writers how to write? You don't, but you do give them insight into what great writing is and how to recognize it. Going through one of the better schools for writing doesn't mean you're going to become a great writer. There's talent, and then there's training, and the training is to give you that background—the exposure to how the great masters have used words or, in this case, the image, and how to put the elements together. There's so much involved in the aesthetic and cinematic side of filmmaking that doesn't have anything to do with technology. Filmmaking deals with how you put several images together and produce emotion.

JF: How much is instinctive?

GL: Part of it is instinctive, but you have to know why, so it requires analysis. I think this is true with all art. There are your intuitive, creative urges, and then there's just discipline. Modern thought about art seems to be that you do your thing and whatever it is is art, but I don't think that's really true. A really great artist is someone who knows how to draw well, knows the basics, knows color, and the vocabulary. Anybody can write a novel, but somebody who has a better background, better vocabulary, and better word usage, and has had more experience is more likely to become a good writer.

JF: Any other valuable characteristics?

GL: You also have to have discipline. You have to meet certain perpetual requirements, and you have to meet deadlines. And then you have to be creative and innovative. There are some very practical things that one needs to know for directing, for producing, and for writing. If you have a lot of talent, you can overcome almost anything. If you know the techniques of writing, how a screenplay is put together, how a story works . . . then you can deviate from the accepted if you want to, as long as you know the basic principles and how they work. Ultimately, filmmaking is a form of applied psychology—more psychology than applied. This is especially true with lighting. Film deals with images and sound and juxtaposition. It comes down to telling a story and getting true responses—very pragmatic work. I have to know that if I use this, then people do that; if I say this, then they laugh, and if I say this, then they jump. There are tricks to it, that's all. Anyone who connects with an audience or with a reader in a certain kind of way, either consciously or unconsciously, is using these techniques or tricks. Young people are very impatient, yet at some point you'll find yourself *knowing how* to make movies, but not knowing what to make them about. I strongly believe that the whole educational system should be accelerated. Kids are smarter younger. And kids can learn faster than most people assume.

JF: Let's discuss your statement, "The first film is easy. It's the second film that's hard."

GL: Well, I don't know who first said it, but I heard it when I got out of film school. I was struggling to get my first film made, and I thought, Boy, this is impossible. If I can just get this film made, I'll be on the gravy train after that. But that's not the way it works. The first one was relatively easy to get off the ground, because you can sort of con somebody into believing you're a great filmmaker, a genius, that you're going to make this really amazing film. It's rare for anybody's first film to be good, and then you have to spend a lot of time convincing people that the first film was an accident, that you're better than that and given a second chance, you will be successful. That's why it's so hard to do a second film. So you struggle for a while, do a lot of "learning process" movies, until you finally get it together and connect. You can learn a lot in film school, but there's no way you can really learn on the grand scale. Each film is unique, and you might be able to do one genre but not necessarily another. The skills transfer but it's like a writer who writes short stories and then tries to write a novel. They're different forms, and they operate in different ways. It takes you a while to learn a medium. You can have a lot of skills, talent, but when you move into an area, it's going to take you time to figure out this form. What you get in film school is breadth of knowledge; you're learning how to communicate using visuals, how people have done it in the past. Sometimes you get the basics of storytelling in film school, and sometimes it's better to go to a college that teaches literature or creative writing. You have to learn the art of acting, directing, working with actors, and the whole art of theater and drama. You need to know architecture and a little bit of science. And music, I almost forgot music, but music especially is important. There's so much that a filmmaker needs to know in order to be good, and it's hard to get it all in one place. You really need that range in order to be able to communicate adequately.

JF: Can you define the role of the producer?

GL: That's impossible. People always ask me that question. There are as many definitions as there are producers.

JF: What is your definition?

GL: I don't even know what I am, but I can describe certain different categories of producers. One is an individual called the line producer; I would call him the real producer. That person manages the movie. He's the real nuts and bolts guy. He sees that checks are cut, people get hired and paid, and that the film comes in on budget. He's there to help the director achieve his vision economically and creatively. It's a very complicated job, very difficult and very stressful. On the other hand, I've always put myself in the role of executive producer—the breed of person who does everything. There are some people who put deals together and make movies. Others come up from the ranks of production managers and assistant directors and may not know the world of agents and Hollywood parties, literary agents, how and where you get a property and a literary agent, or how to put it together.

JF: Is there another name we can give you?

GL: As an executive producer, I fall into the dealmaker category. However, there is a difference between sitting down and writing something, and directing and overseeing something on the set. Now I oversee it more than do it. I'll come up with a story idea, then hire a writer and a director. Sometimes a friend of mine will come to me and say there's a problem getting a picture off the ground, and ask if I'll put my name on it. So that's another category. Today my procedure is to sit down, work up a story, and at that point I have a choice. When I was a writer/director, I would simply start writing the screenplay, which could take me six months, a year, or two years, and then I would make a deal with somebody to direct it. Doing the sequels to *Star Wars*, I realized that I couldn't operate that close to the ground anymore. I had to be able to step back, have a larger view of it, and handle it on a bigger level.

JF: What followed that decision?

GL: Once I had made that decision, I took projects that I had been trying unsuccessfully to get others to do, mentioned it to Steve (Spielberg), who said, "Let's do them," and found myself producing two movies. Ideas excite me. Once I get an idea, I want to see it on film, and it's a lot easier not to do it myself. An idea can sit in my brain for years and years and eventually it will become something concrete. You can't get them to disappear.

JF: How are they retrieved?

GL: Randomly. They're like love affairs. You see somebody, get a crush on that person, and then can't forget them. It may have been a glimpse for a brief moment on a street in Paris, something that happened in three seconds, but it somehow connects, stays in your brain. The advantage to the filmmaker is that eventually it finds its way into a movie. Then it's out of your system but part of your life forever.

JF: What process converts the idea into reality?

GL: That process is the "crush" that happens, and the writing process is the love affair. You go through the love affair and the shooting is the marriage; you have kids, and at the end of it, you have a family up there, one way or the other. There are all sorts of practical sides to making a movie. Making a film is like making the impossible happen every day. It's the job. Whether you're the director, the producer, or the actor, that's what you do for a living. The level of intensity is so much higher than in normal life—like surgery.

JF: As executive producer, what is your relationship to the process?

GL: You can compare it to football. There's a difference between being the coach and the quarterback. It's fun being the quarterback, being really focused on the play, but he's the one getting hit. When you're the coach, you also feel pain, but it's more abstract. You're not getting punched, maybe, but you're in there looking at the whole game, not just the play. The producer is like the coach. He's looking at the bigger view at any given moment. The quarterback is focused on the nitty-gritty . . . he's got to keep his eye on the ball all the time, so he doesn't have time to look around and see the overall picture. There's also teamwork that comes into play in filmmaking as in football. That's what I try to do with the directors that work for me. I've always had good directors and had good relationships with them.

JF: Has the business, which is also an art, changed significantly?

GL: It's changed dramatically! It's changed dramatically, I think, because of the influence of Wall Street and the executives who read the *Wall Street Journal*. The amazing thing about film, as far as I'm concerned, is that it is the art form of the 20th, possibly even the 21st century, and the United States is its Florence. The 20th century will be this amazing point of light in the birth of film.

JF: What is your plan for the nineties?

GL: Well, I'm going on a five-year plan that will involve making a lot of movies. I'm not planning to direct in these five years, but I probably will again. I'm going to do a lot of television. I've never done television before. There are two other things I'll be involved in—Lucasfilm Learning is the first. Then there's another foundation I'm starting to develop, which is a prototype on how hypermedia works in the educational system, how the schools will have to adjust to fit that, and what technology will have to be advanced in order to make it happen. A lot of people are working in this new field, and I figure I have a chance to put some ideas out there that might influence a lot of people. Things are beginning to happen, and I hope to see education move out of the textbook era.

Peggy Rajski

■ ■ ■ ■ ■ ■ ■ ■ ■ ■ ■ ■ ■

Peggy Rajski attended the University of Wisconsin, where she received her undergraduate and graduate degrees in Communication. Relocating to New York, she began producing industrial films, documentaries, and feature films. In 1983 she began an association with director John Sayles, producing *Brother From Another Planet,* the critically acclaimed *Matewan,* and co-producing *Eight Men Out.* She also produced three music videos for Bruce Springsteen, which Sayles also directed. In 1989, she co-produced *The Grifters* with Martin Scorsese, and recently served as producer for *Little Man Tate,* directed by and starring Jodie Foster. Ms. Rajski is also currently developing Michael Dorris' novel *A Yellow Raft In Blue Water* for the screen.

EL: Could you briefly explain how you got started?

PR: My first real break into feature films came with *Lianna.* I had met John Sayles, Maggie Renzi, and Jeffrey Nelson at a party (this was after they had done *Secaucus Seven*). They were going to do another film. I offered to do anything. They needed a production manager, but didn't really know what one was. I said I could do it and they hired me. That began my association with John Sayles. After we finished *Lianna,* Maggie Renzi asked me if I wanted to produce with her another project of John's called *Matewan.* Of course I said yes. After two years, we were very close on the financing, but it fell through at the last minute. John brought up an idea for another movie he had written about a black extraterrestrial who winds up in Harlem (*Brother From Another Planet*). He had about $250,000 saved from writing screenplays that he would use to make the movie. He gave Maggie and me a three-page outline for the script and we prepped the movie in six weeks and shot it in four. It came together very quickly, and it was hard, really hard, but I also had a lot of fun and it resulted in a movie I'm very proud of. It ultimately cost about $400,000 to make. After *Brother*, we made another attempt to raise the money for *Matewan*. It took four more years to raise the money, but we finally did, and I've continued producing since then.

EL: Discuss your studies at Madison. How did they prepare you?

PR: I earned an undergraduate degree from the University of Wisconsin at Stevens Point where I was born and raised. Then I went to Madison and got a Master's Degree in Communications. Communications there covered radio, TV, and film. My emphasis at school was more in television than in film simply because you had to pay for the film stock and processing, etc., in the film classes, and I was too broke to swing it. With television production, the camera and videotape were free. We created programming that ran on the local cable channel. It was mostly documentary-style programming. I learned a lot about hands-on production then, and it was fun. When I went on to graduate school in Madison, I continued in television production. As part of the program, I got to direct and produce some narrative pieces that aired on the local Public Television affiliate. It was very good practice, though I'd be embarrassed to look at the stuff now. My school experience seemed to combine hands-on practice with critical theory. I think that combination served me well. In film, I came up as a production manager, which is very nuts-and-bolts, and then got to combine that with producing where your concerns are not only about money, but how to best realize the story you want to tell. I didn't go to school because I thought it would lead to a job. I didn't really have a grand plan for getting in the film business. I just followed my instincts about where to go and when, and things seem to have worked out all right.

EL: How would you characterize the role of the producer?

PR: Producing is a very individual thing. You see so many people taking credit on movies these days. It's hard to sort out what the executive producer does as compared to the producer, the co-producer, the line producer, or the associate producer. But ideally, the producer's role (no matter how many people fill it) is to find good material, sound financing, a great cast and crew suited to the project at hand, innovative marketing and distributing, and all the things in between. You need to be a salesman, motivator, negotiator, hand-holder and occasional tyrant. Once the director is on board, the dynamic shifts a bit, and a big part of the producer's role is to support and enhance what the director is trying to do and also to keep the film on track.

EL: When you shoot, are you on the set/location all the time?

PR: Yes. Because filmmaking is a collaborative and fluid process, you have to be there to both absorb and influence what's going on. Everyone's needs and priorities shift constantly, and I wouldn't know how to assess those needs without being there. And since part of your role as producer is to be a facilitator (making sure everyone is talking to whom they need to when they need to) and putting out fires, you must be there. I also think an important function of the producer is to be the one person people can talk to if they're having problems with the director.

EL: How big a psychological burden is the financial aspect of producing?

PR: Since I take it quite seriously when I say we'll deliver a picture for X amount of money (as does every director I've worked with), you do wind up sweating it out a bit throughout the process. The truth is you never feel like you have enough time or money to do what you want, so the real challenge is how you still make something great under the particular budget/time/manpower constraints you're working with.

EL: What has been the range of budgets you've worked in?

PR: $350 thousand to $10 million.

EL: Does more money make the process easier or are there just bigger plans for bigger money?

PR: Oh, of course, it makes it easier in some respects. I'm always happy when I can pay people a little bit more money. But it's always a struggle. None of the movies I have been involved with have been high-concept, blatantly commercial films (if anyone even knows how to define those). But they've all been very ambitious for their budgets. We made *Matewan* for three and a half million dollars. A lot of people can't

believe it was made for that price, given how it looks. I've always taken a certain pride in knowing how to stretch a buck. But you know what? Nobody really cares if a movie came in on budget if it isn't any good. Conversely, if it came in on budget *and* it's good, everyone's delighted.

EL: Can you describe your relationship with some of the key folks such as production designers or actors during shooting? How do you interact with them on a day-to-day basis?

PR: I talk to department heads (D.P., production designer, costume designer, etc.) quite a bit during shooting. The production designer is often responsible for how a great deal of the money required on the picture is spent. A lot falls under their domain—construction, props, and dressing. It's an area that can easily go over budget, so it's important to stay in close touch. But more important, your department heads control the look of the picture. And if you're concerned about that—which you should, be—you have to talk with them often. I'll talk with the actors about a character and story if they want to, but for the most part actors prefer to, and really should, have those discussions with the director. (All my comments about directors, by the way, presume you've got a good one). But if there's a strong difference of opinion between an actor and the director, your job is to try and resolve it. Sometimes it's just about smoothing ruffled feathers. You're there if someone is angry about something. An actor's been called to the set too early, or they're not happy with their accommodations, or their costumes, whatever. Your job is to listen and do your best to correct what you can.

EL: What about the cinematographer?

PR: You talk to the cinematographer a lot. Though the specifics may vary, the modus operandi is the same with your other department heads. In preproduction you discuss how the movie should look, and those thoughts get changed and refined throughout shooting. You test fabric swatches, lighting set-ups, background colors, make-up, etc. How pretty or gritty should the movie or each scene look? You look at dailies and try to assess where you've succeeded and where you could be better; can you do better by the leading lady or the leading man?

EL: Taking all that into consideration, what are some of the personal attributes someone should have in considering producing?

PR: Producers come in all shapes and sizes. But you have to be incredibly driven and like working very, very hard. You have to have passion and conviction. You have to believe that your movie needs to be made more than any other movie in the world, and be able to convince other people of that. Stamina is important, and integrity doesn't hurt. And most important, you've got to like working with other people. When I'm producing a movie, I try to have things run as smoothly as possible so I'm free to troubleshoot, to anticipate problems rather than react to them. I like to be direct and honest about where things stand; people know when I say something I mean it. I like things to be clear about who's responsible for what. I rely on the people I bring in to work with me, and I don't try to do their jobs for them. I don't like to yell but will if someone's messing up.

EL: You've worked with a partner and you've worked alone. What are the differences?

PR: Filmmaking is interesting to me because it's so collaborative. There have been other producers involved in every film I've done. I've partnered with people to produce my own projects, and I've been asked to line produce for other people. In all these situations you have people, myself included, who believe they're right, although we don't always agree. So you have to learn to resolve conflict about creative issues. There's always a certain amount of conflict, anxiety, and stress in any creative process. The challenge is always to deal with that and stay on an even keel.

EL: Do you think being a woman producer creates additional difficulty?

PR: I wish it weren't true, but I do think you have to work harder and be better at your job if you're a woman. But one of the great things about producing is that to a great extent, you can choose your crew. And you're certainly not going to pick people who are going to give you a hard time because you're a female.

EL: What kind of balance do you seek between being a hired gun and developing your own material?

PR: In both cases, I try to make the best movie possible. In terms of how I allot my time, it is a real struggle. Development and line producing are almost mutually exclusive. If I'm hired to line produce, I'm asked to commit my time exclusively to that one particular project. Developing material is also time intensive. I turned down a lot of production work in the year preceding *The Grifters* so I could devote my time to finding and developing material. But when Stephen Frears comes along and asks you to produce a movie for him, it's a hard gig to pass up. The truth is, I like doing both and want to continue doing both, so somehow I will.

EL: What's the most frustrating thing about being a producer?

PR: Trying to raise money. It took us almost seven years with *Matewan*. Sometimes you feel you're beating your head against a wall, and it can get very depressing.

EL: What's the best thing?

PR: The best is seeing the finished movie at the end. It's a wonderful thing.

EL: How important is film school for somebody who wants to produce?

PR: I guess I don't think film school is essential. I never went to school with the idea that it was going to help my career. I went to school because I liked learning about lots of different things. School provided the structure for that, and I really enjoyed it tremendously. I still remember my political science courses, my constitutional law courses. These things supposedly don't have anything to do with making movies, but have something to do with shaping you as an individual, and that's what's most important. To succeed in the film business, you need imagination and drive; that will get you through more than anything else. There are many people in the business who didn't go to film school and they're doing just fine, but so are others who did. I don't think there's any right way.

EL: Any other advice that you'd give to a young person who wants to pursue producing?

PR: You just have to go for it. Try to learn anything you can about how films are made. I went from being a producer/director on industrials to being a production assistant on After School Specials. You have to know where you have gaps in knowledge and do what you can to fill those gaps.

EL: Would you reflect briefly on the state of independent film?

PR: It seems to me it's what it always was—difficult. Sometimes it's a little less so and sometimes it's a little more so, but it's always difficult. That fact hasn't stopped people from making independent films. I don't think it will now.

EL: Discuss your participation in getting the distribution and promotion set up.

PR: The producer is the first one in and the last one out on a movie, and when it's ready to be released, you get involved in how the movie will break and how you want it positioned in the public's mind through your marketing and publicity. Will it be platformed? How wide should it break? What theaters should it be in? What's the one sheet going to look like? All those things. Like the process of making movies, you try and make sure everyone is in synch about how to release and promote it. You're the one who's also got to make sure everyone's paying attention. At release, it's also crucial for the director and the lead actors to go out and do publicity, particularly on independent films. Some "event" movies like *Batman* sell themselves, but all the movies I've been involved with have required special handling and strong word-of-mouth to succeed. Independent movies are review-driven, and it's really crippling if you get a bad or mediocre one. That's where your actors and directors can help. Sometimes they can help counteract negative reviews and position your film more positively in people's minds. All this is critical if your movie's going to succeed. Making it is great fun, but you have to want to make sure it gets seen by as many people as possible.

Gale Anne Hurd

■ ■ ■ ■ ■ ■ ■ ■ ■ ■ ■ ■ ■ ■ ■ ■

Gale Anne Hurd graduated Phi Beta Kappa from Stanford University with a combined degree in economics and communications. She began her film career at New World Pictures as an assistant to Roger Corman, eventually serving as Assistant Production Manager on such features as *Battle Beyond The Stars* and *Smokey Bites The Dust*. In 1982 she formed Pacific Western Productions, an independent production and development company that made its debut with *The Terminator*. Her producing credits include *Aliens, Alien Nation, The Abyss, Downtown* and *Tremors*. Most recently, she produced *Terminator 2*, the upcoming film *The Water Dance,* and is in production with *Raising Cain.* A member of the Board of Trustees of The American Film Institute, she has been a frequent lecturer at the Center for Advanced Film and Television Studies and has served as a judge for the U.S. Film Festival, the Focus Student Film Awards, and the Academy of Motion Picture Arts and Sciences' Nicholl Fellowship competition.

JF: In what ways did your formal education prepare you for the role of producer?

GH: Without a good grounding in academics you're really not prepared to think on the level this industry requires.

JF: Didn't you major in economics?

GH: Economics and communications with a minor in political science.

JF: To what extent were they helpful?

GH: I learned how to analyze. Whenever you're being pitched a project, either an idea or a screenplay, you have to be able to analyze it and decide whether it's something with which you should be involved. A project can take up to two or three years of your life, so it's very important to have the tools necessary to judge projects with a great deal of wisdom.

JF: When you talk to young people, do you suggest that they study certain subjects?

GH: I think the classics are extremely important. Filmmaking boils down to narrative storytelling, and a grounding in the classics can provide excellent models.

JF: How do you define or characterize the role of a producer?

GH: It's the glue that holds the project together. The producer is responsible for all elements of the film: selecting the director, the completion of the screenplay, casting, crewing the film, and, ultimately, the marketing and distribution.

JF: Which part interests you the most?

GH: I really enjoy collaborating with writers and directors and making the day-to-day decisions that are required during production. I love the excitement and the challenge of making the right decision because you simply don't have time to do it over if you're wrong.

JF: What advice would you offer to someone getting started?

GH: I think that you have to start at the bottom. Those who feel that they can make a lateral move from another industry to filmmaking are making a mistake. I began by being an apprentice to another producer. I went to work for Roger Corman, who was an excellent role model. He does it all: a real mentor.

JF: What did your apprenticeship involve?

GH: When I worked for Roger, he was running New World Pictures, which involved development, production, distribution, and marketing—not only of his motion pictures but also certain art films that he'd pick up for distribution. I was involved in every area—from answering his telephone and writing letters on his behalf, to making notes in rough-cut screenings as to how the picture should be re-edited, critiquing screenplays, making deals with agents for actors, location scouting—all that in the first three months!

JF: How much did you know about most of those areas?

GH: Nothing. I thought that was a bigger obstacle than Roger did. Roger believes that if you're smart, ambitious, and have a modicum of talent, you can succeed in this business. He emphasized intelligence, which is why he tended to hire Phi Beta Kappas from some of the finer colleges.

JF: Describe the most essential skills.

GH: The ability to tell a cohesive and interesting story. The ability to work with actors. The ability to visualize how the picture should look. And the ability to achieve all that through artful editing. Then there's the whole post-production process of determining how the picture should sound—both sound effects and music.

JF: You have been involved with each one of those processes. Do you think you have more talent for one than another?

GH: I think I'm a good organizer, which is an extremely important skill for a producer to have. And I like to collaborate. Someone once called it "holographic vision," which means you can see things three-dimensionally.

JF: Do you have a system of organization?

GH: I tend to operate on a worst-case scenario basis, which means that with every project I'm involved, I imagine on each level what is the worst thing that can happen as a result of a meeting or of a particular change in the screenplay. From that point I make what I consider to be an informed decision. That approach works extremely well when you're on the set. I used to dream about possible problems every night. I would imagine the next day's shooting and what could possibly go wrong, and come up with A, B, and C plans.

JF: What specific skills are most helpful in post-production?

GH: Post-production is the area in which a producer can truly excel. The director is very much in charge of running the set. I've found that in post-production there are more subtleties. A scene can turn out any number of different ways based in part on how it's edited. I generally get very involved in post-production. I've been responsible for re-editing films, bringing in new composers, activities that have considerable effect on the final film.

JF: Distribution and marketing—how are you specifically involved in those areas?

GH: I think that studios often have objectives other than those of the filmmaker in terms of getting the audience into the theater, and I don't blame them. In this day and age you may have one weekend in which to establish a film as a hit, and if you don't have big numbers, you may not have a second chance. Consequently, the important thing is to

get moviegoers into the theaters. I've discovered through frequent attendance at marketing and research screenings that if you misrepresent a
film to an audience, they may enjoy it, but they won't like it if they
feel they were deceived.

JF: As a producer, how much input do you have into marketing and
distribution?

GH: Much less than I would like, but I've found that you can at least
state your point of view, and there are times when the studio will
embrace it. Other times the studio simply says, "Thank you very much,
but we're going to do it our way." At least you have an opportunity to
offer creative ideas for marketing.

JF: Is this cycle of the big first weekend going to last?

GH: I think that when a picture that does $10 million over a weekend
is viewed as a failure, we're living in very competitive times. Today
$20 million is the average price tag for a feature film made by a major
studio. I'm trying to change that. I've made more films under $10
million than I've made over $10 million. But I'm at a disadvantage.
People would rather spend $40 to $60 million on a potential blockbuster
(with a cast that represents perhaps $10 or $15 million of the budget)
than $10 million on a film that has a great screenplay but perhaps
doesn't have a blockbuster star on the marquee.

JF: How many blockbusters are made in an average year?

GH: All of the summer pictures tend to be programmed as blockbusters.
At Christmas, you alternate between serious dramas vying for Academy
Award consideration and films that people perceive as cash cows. That's
why we're seeing so many sequels and remakes. The studios want a
sure thing.

JF: What kinds of films would you like to make in the next three years?

GH: It's impossible to say. However, I think it's important to make
responsible films; it's important not to perpetuate stereotypes.

JF: Do other filmmakers talk about this sense of responsibility?

GH: A lot of filmmakers are responsible and very well respected, but their films aren't always number one at the box office. There are people like Jim Brooks who feel it's important to go against the grain. He has succeeded with films that aren't high concept. They sometimes defy standard patterns of successful marketing in the sense that they're challenging; yet people respond to them. I think that *Aliens* was certainly an unusual film in that there was a woman in the lead who succeeded in an action role. One of the reasons we were able to do that film was because it was a sequel. It was considered pre-sold, because *Alien* had been a very successful film.

JF: How do you see the relationship of television in our society vis à vis feature filmmaking?

GH: I think that we will see audiences returning to dramas, as they've done with *Presumed Innocent* because high quality drama is not available on TV. We have to compete with pay cable and with free television, so we have to provide alternative programming.

JF: Do you think that you'll have to make different films from what we see on the small screen?

GH: It takes a lot more to get someone out of the house these days. That's a partial explanation of why big-budget extravaganzas continue to succeed.

JF: What other advice would you give to young people coming into this profession?

GH: I'd say that you can never learn too much. The people who enter this business under-prepared and unwilling to learn are at a serious disadvantage. It's very competitive out there. The success that you've had in another field may be your passport into this business, but it does not guarantee your success.

JF: At what point do you bring in the director?

GH: Once I have a first draft of a screenplay I try to bring in the director to be involved in any revisions and to start pre-production.

JF: How do you select a director?

GH: I try to look at everything that they've done; I meet with them; I call the people they worked with previously; contact them if I know any of them; producers, writers, crew, actors. I don't hire someone based on how closely their last picture is related to what I want to do next. Directors can get pigeonholed, but someone who's talented in one genre may very well be able to handle another. This way they might have the opportunity to do something they haven't done before.

JF: Are you heavily involved with casting?

GH: Absolutely! I work with a number of casting directors. I've found that among them there's a great difference, not only in techniques, but in skills.

JF: Can you characterize some of those skills?

GH: Anyone can come up with lists of actors and let the producers and directors make the decisions. They are like traffic controllers. Some casting directors, I think, have intuition and know when a particular actor is perfect for a role and will fight to the death to secure that part for them. Personally I prefer to use casting people who live by their instincts rather than the people who absolutely defer to the director. Auditioning is a very difficult process. Some people are excellent at auditioning, but not particularly great on film.

JF: How do you find that out?

GH: You have to rely upon casting directors. They'll tell you this person is terrible at cold readings; he will come in and stumble over the words, but when he gets the part, he delivers better than anyone else. On the other hand, some people can deliver a performance that will make you cry the first time they pick up a script. Mary Elizabeth Mastrantonio did that when she read for *The Abyss*. After she had finished reading, we couldn't talk. Our casting director had said Mary Elizabeth not only would deliver at the reading, but she'd be able to do that day in and day out on the picture. Other people are terrible at cold readings. Some people don't read. There are people who become engines for the picture in a certain way. You're not going to call Mel Gibson and ask him to come in and read for your film. You have to decide ahead of time if, based on his body of work, he's right. Sigourney (Weaver) did not audition; she'd already done that. She had an entire movie as an audition!

JF: Any other problems you care to discuss?

GH: I think you have to plug away. One thing you can't do in this industry is over-analyze. Then there's the problem of changing world events, and other factors as to whether or not a film is successful. Then there's the lag between the time that you embark on a film and the time it's projected in a theater. There are times, especially if you're dealing with a political thriller, when you have to project a lot further ahead than if you're dealing with a romantic comedy. On the other hand if you had to second-guess every judgment made in the development process, you'd never get anything done.

JF: What are your greatest satisfactions? Do they come with seeing that film on the screen?

GH: Absolutely. The satisfaction is seeing the film with an audience. Of course, it can also be the absolute ultimate horror. The first screening is usually held before the movie is released, and that can generate a lot of anxiety. After the film has opened and you've survived the litmus test, which is audience reaction, I find it difficult to see the film again. In fact I often find it painful because I see things I wish I could have done differently, and I see compromises that shouldn't have been made. However, home video as a secondary market has opened up the opportunity for different or extended versions of a film.

JF: Is there any further advice that you would like to give to young people interested in filmmaking today?

GH: I'd like to think that the new filmmakers will usher in a new age of responsibility so films once again have a voice in our destiny. Right now we're seeing the product of short-term thinking in politics, the economy, and the media, and I think it's important that people re-examine ideas and ideals and project them into our future.

THREE

■■■■■■■■■

★ The Director

The director is the artistic leader of the production team and is ultimately responsible for every decision that shapes the film. Usually hired by the producer, he/she determines the style of the film and translates the script from the written page into moving images. The director is the center of the creative team which includes the producer, screenwriter, cinematographer, editor, production and costume designers; he/she is involved in hiring these key creative collaborators. The director guides the actors and assists them in achieving performances that suit each character and best serve the story.

According to the Director's Guild of America (DGA) (213-289-2000), the salary of a director is heavily dependent upon the budget of the film. If the budget is $500,000 or less, and the director will work a minimum of eleven weeks, the salary is $5,038.00 per week. A feature that employs a director for a minimum of thirteen weeks and has a budget between $500,000 and 1.5 million will pay a salary of $5,726.00 per week. Any budget over 1.5 million dollars, employing a director for a minimum of thirteen weeks, will pay $8,017.00 per week. There are also numerous variations of this scale. Any directors employed by a DGA company are required, through their employment agreements, to join the DGA, and only those employed by a company affiliated with the DGA can join. The DGA currently has 9100 members.

Lawrence Kasdan

....

Lawrence Kasdan was born in 1949 in Miami Beach, Florida, and raised in Wheeling and Morgantown, West Virginia. He attended the University of Michigan, graduating with a Master's Degree in education. Working as an advertising copywriter, he wrote screenplays hoping they would lead to a career in directing feature films. In 1977 he sold his first screenplay, *The Bodyguard*. The rights to his script *Continental Divide* were then purchased by Steven Spielberg, who signed Mr. Kasdan to write the screenplay that later became *Raiders of the Lost Ark*. In 1980, Mr. Kasdan wrote and directed *Body Heat* for the Ladd Company. The success of *Body Heat* led to *The Big Chill*, which was nominated for three Academy Awards, including Best Picture. He has since directed *Silverado*, *The Accidental Tourist*, and *I Love You to Death*, *Grand Canyon*, and produced *Cross My Heart* and *Immediate Family*. He has been nominated for three Academy Awards and five Writer's Guild of America Awards. In 1983 he won the WGA Award for *The Big Chill*.

JF: You started as a writer, but now you work primarily as a director. In which role do you primarily see yourself?

LK: I don't think I'll ever be just a writer again because I enjoy directing so much. Writing is the more difficult part, though. It's not as physically demanding or stressful as directing, but it's far more difficult. It's lonely, hard, it takes such skill, and then you don't get any of the fun of the filmmaking. There are deep-seated satisfactions that come with writing. There's the old joke, "Do you like writing?" "No, but I like having written." It doesn't compare, however, to the pleasure of directing, which is the most stimulating, exciting, best job I can think of.

I'm sure I will continue to write, but I will continue to look for other people's scripts to direct as well.

JF: Do you feel differently about your words as opposed to those of someone else?

LK: Yes. To direct someone else's screenplay is a challenge, a little analogous to being an actor. You're trying to understand what the writer meant. I never had that experience until this last picture because the first four pictures I directed I had also written, though sometimes with collaborators. With the fifth picture—a difficult picture in terms of tone and potential—I felt like an actor trying to understand the script, trying to understand the nature of the scenes, trying to establish the tone. That is a completely different experience than coming in with your own script and having imagined the movie clearly as you wrote it, having creating the structure and hearing the voices.

JF: How did your education prepare you or spark your interest in writing?

LK: I was writing in elementary school and got reinforcement for my writing in high school. I chose a college where the writing contests would help support me. I decided very early during college that I wanted to direct movies. At that time a lot of screenwriters were getting opportunities to direct movies—Francis Coppola, John Milius, Paul Schrader, among others. So it seemed screenwriting was the best way to get to direct. I was already a writer; I had written fiction and plays. I started writing screenplays and nothing else. It took me seven years to sell something, but then I started selling a lot, and things happened very quickly. I worked for George Lucas for almost two years writing two different movies. During that time I was asked to write a lot, but I turned down all writing offers. Finally, in frustration, the people in the industry asked what it was I wanted. I told them I wanted to direct. So I came to directing using screenwriting as a way in. I was influenced by reading good literature, the theater, and all the great films that I had seen for the first time at the University of Michigan. When I was growing up in West Virginia, those films hadn't been available to me. But the Hollywood films we did see made a tremendous impact on me.

When I went to Michigan I was able to see what the rest of the world had been seeing—old movies and foreign films. And they just blew me away. Most of those films had come out of a literary, dramatic tradition of narrative. My orientation and enthusiasm were for those films which obeyed those disciplines. The movies that I didn't like very much were the ones that seemed to come out of the television age and not the Golden Age. Character didn't seem to matter. Everything had to be immediately apparent; and there was very little interest in the complexity of life. Television tended to look for the simple understanding of characters, the simple resolution of conflict. I was interested in all the opposite things which came from these other traditions of theater and literature. I was reacting to a disregard for those traditions. However, reaction is not the most useful creative impetus. One must understand what form is and how it works. I think some of the films I was resisting were actually quite good. Their makers understood that movies and their audiences did not require the same kind of structure, set up, and development at this moment in the history of the medium as they had in the thirties and forties, even 1960.

JF: What is the difference?

LK: I think *Lawrence of Arabia* may be the greatest screenplay ever written, beautifully constructed, the writing so elegant and evocative. The tiniest detail evokes the greatest feelings. Great screenwriting. You don't find much screenwriting like that now. There have been some good screenplays, but you rarely see something so delicately, so finely wrought, and then given the full treatment of great filmmaking on top of that. I consider it the ideal. Those who have grown up watching TV and commercials and MTV have a visual sophistication that has benefited from the work of people of the thirties, the forties and the fifties. It's possible for them to understand visual information very quickly. In fact, other kinds of pace and development will not do; they won't work in certain ways.

JF: What kind of background do you think that young people need to have to work in films today?

© 1988 Warner Brothers, Inc.

LK: This is an interesting question. The best thing that was said to me about directing when I was about to do *Body Heat* came from George Lucas. He had helped me a lot. I said, "I don't know much about the technical aspects of film. I didn't go to film school, but I have lived and breathed and thought about movies and art and drama for a long time now." George said, "Directing movies has nothing to do with the technical side." (This came from George Lucas, the techno-king of the film world). "It has to do with what kind of person you are." I think that's the best thing anybody ever said to me. If the movies are any good, you will see the personality of the director in that movie. I'm talking about the way the characters change, the way the stories unfold, the selection of the details used. They reveal what kind of person the director is. The way a woman is shown in a movie tells you a lot about how the director feels about women. The way people treat each other tells you what that director's personality is like, what has been his life experience. It is absolutely apparent because the director's fingerprints are all over that movie. Critics mistakenly think it's camera movement, and it's not. Style is important, but it doesn't reveal the personality of the director. So how do you prepare to be a director? Elia Kazan once wrote this endless list of things you should do. It sounded almost egomaniacal because he seemed to be implying that he was all those things: "Be a lover of music and art, and a student of philosophy and religion"; ideally all of us would have all those skills and all that knowledge, but we don't. We can try to have a rounded view of the world and be interested in all things great and small instead of just last week's biggest hit. We can watch the news and be amazed and disturbed by it, have a reaction to all that and turn it into art. I tell students to study everything else; don't study film. You can spend the rest of your life working on film so spend this time seeing how complex and interesting and strange and unexpected the world is and how different people have thought about different things.

JF: When did you decide that film was art?

LK: I never had any doubt about that. Art is reality that has been shaped by someone and moves you and touches you and puts you through different kinds of feelings. Sometimes it touches you intellectually; sometimes it touches you emotionally. It is shaped reality; someone has had a hand in it. Someone has said, "I'll take those elements, and I'll put them into some kind of frame." That's art—someone managing the world. Sometimes art takes on a surreal kind of vision, and sometimes it's very realistic. For me movies were always art because they thrill and delight and are clearly constructions of life.

JF: How would you characterize the role of the director?

LK: The director has to guide the thing from beginning to end. If he hasn't written the work, it begins at the point at which there's a screenplay. He must bring together a group of collaborators, people he respects and whose opinions he respects, and guide them toward a clear goal. That involves taking their ideas and putting them up against his own, adding what's new, choosing among good and appropriate ideas for this movie. He needs to channel all the assembled talent toward his goal, which he must hold steady in the rush of making a picture.

JF: Other than empirical knowledge such as film history or technical knowledge, what skills must a good director have?

LK: First, an ability to see the whole clearly, to remember what you're doing. Everyone looks to you for guidance. These people are very skilled and are ready to serve the director, but the director must know *how* they can serve. A large part of directing has to do with the management of people. I favor having a harmonious, happy experience in which people feel they're being respected and their ideas are welcome. Not every director sees it that way. I don't want to imply that the only thing a director needs is management skills. That's terribly important. Getting a job directing is really hard, and sometimes the things that get you the job, such as ambition and drive and personality, are not the things that will help you do the job. And I believe a director has to be an artist. He has to see himself as an artist and have an idea about what art is. The crew is looking for guidance about what to do next, why it is being done and what is the best way to do it. Only a person who has some sort of artistic impulse can have those answers. Anyone can get a movie made because the machinery works, but to make a good movie is very difficult and comes only from a clear vision.

JF: When you are trying to elicit the cooperation of your team, do you discuss the movie in artistic terms as a team or with individuals?

LK: I try to do both. The most valuable communication occurs on an individual basis with someone like your cameraman or a particular actor. One of the skills of directing is finding a language that works between both you and the person who is listening. That language is different for each person. It's helpful if the director is genuinely interested in people and recognizes their differences. There's a tendency among people serving directors to want to be agreeable, and it requires some perception on the part of the director to know when he's getting through. Some of the people are on a need-to-know basis. There are others who need to know why and fully understand your overall scheme for the film. So there's a sorting out of those who need to know, when, and how much they need to know.

JF: How do you communicate in visual terms with your cinematographer? What kind of references do you make?

LK: I think you can make references to other films as well as your own. You can make references to the cinematographer's work in other films, assuming that you've admired it and that's why he's working for you. I've often referred to painting and theater. I often speak in literary terms to a cinematographer. I've worked with three different cameramen, and they've all been willing to talk in such terms about what we're trying to achieve. Then you have some common material to discuss when you see the dailies.

JF: Describe your approach to rehearsal.

LK: I've always had extensive rehearsals for my movies, and it's been a very valuable and useful part of the process. The relationships a director has seem to separate into three areas. In the rehearsal period, it's a relationship with the actors. You have the freedom without time pressure, without a crew standing around, to discuss what the movie is about and to hear their ideas, since no two people read the script the same way. So there's room for discussion in this less-pressured atmosphere of rehearsal. Rehearsal is not focused on getting a finished performance. It's an exploration of everything that the movie can be.

JF: Do the actors read around a table, or do you stage some scenes?

LK: I have not staged much. It's talking and talking and reading and talking—going through the script a lot, doing some readings very fast and then very slowly. Sometimes we'll switch parts to see it in as many ways as we can. So the rehearsal stage produces a very intimate kind of relationship with the actors. During the production your primary relationship is with the cinematographer. While you never want the actors to feel that they are second, in fact, your cameraman is the focus of your concentration. There's an enormous amount of time spent with your cinematographer trying to get the thing on film. The third type of relationship is with the editor in post-production. Everybody is gone, and sitting in a dark room you get to rethink the movie. One hopes it doesn't require too much rethinking, but there are times when it does. Carol Littleton used to say to me (she denies this) that "everything before me is theory." In some sense she's right. She was referring to the trucks and the cast and the script and everything else. It's just a theory until you actually start to bump the frames up against each other.

JF: How much of your job is cerebral, and how much is instinctive as a director?

LK: It's really hard to quantify that. I compare directing to athletics. I like sports, and directing is very much like a sport. When you start to play a sport you think about every move; you try to repeat it and repeat it until it is habitual and almost instinctual. Then you don't have to think, "Well, gee, the tennis ball is going over there. I'd better run over there." You just go. When you are first learning, you think about everything. The better you get, the less you think about it. It means that you've totally integrated what you've learned and can now start to improvise. To me that is the ideal way to direct. You want to take everything you've ever known and not think about it, but use it.

JF: What kind of adjustments do you make when you shift genres?

LK: I've made some genre films. I think I approach each as a separate problem. It is less about genres and more about what we do in this genre—how to tell this story most effectively. You try to bring a style to it that is appropriate rather than impose upon it a specific style. I want the camera to be where it should be. That sounds simple, but it's really hard. Are we seeing what we want to see at that moment? Is the camera focused on someone who's not talking, someone who's listening, something lying on the table? Or the camera can be moving. That decision is very instinctual; it's very musical; it's a sense of where you want to be. Sometimes you want to go against that sense; you want to use the tension that the viewers will feel because they can't see something they want to see. Being aware of all those forces at work is the difficult part. That's the aspect no one ever totally masters.

JF: I've heard editors describe sitting at the editing table and seeing the film take on a life of its own.

LK: Well, writing is very much like that too, and often the characters will start talking to you. That's what you hope for. When they don't, you're forcing words onto them. The same way with scenes. I've sat in front of a pad for hours trying to make something work. Other times I've sat down and the pen started writing. Before you know it, here's this scene and you don't know where it came from. You pray for such moments when something greater than your intellectual idea of it takes over.

JF: What's the most frustrating thing about being a director?

LK: There's always this sense that you don't have enough time. Time is money, and money is always limited. No matter how big your budget, you never feel you have too much money. The money is only good for the time it buys to do things right: to light it well enough, to work with the actors long enough, to move the camera (which is time consuming), to wait for the light—all these things that you can rarely afford to do. So you're always running ahead of the train, and that's a frustrating feeling after a while, because in your mind—when you were dealing with just the script—you had the perfect movie in your head. Sometimes, however, there are things that are much better than you imagined that life and production offer up to you. You hope for those things. But a lot of time you feel that somehow you've fallen short of your ideal. That's frustrating. It's frustrating that so much focus is put on the product and so little on the process. The bulk of my life is involved with process, but the community we work in is focused on product. And things are judged on that. Who can say what's good and bad? Certainly not the reviewers operating in this country. Certainly not the audience because, in fact, there are many, many kinds of audiences, and some will love it and some will hate it. Most people, fairly and rightly, go to movies to escape from their lives. They want to be transported to somewhere easy, pleasant, with happy endings, and so on. That is often in direct conflict with an attempt to record life in some interesting way. People want movies to be a certain length which is absurd; they don't ask that of novels. Somehow they're offended if it is longer than they expected. The most frequent criticism of movies is that they're too slow as though that were the only criteria for judging things! Yet people will always respond to the good stuff, and that's what you want. You want to transport them in your own way.

JF: What's the most exciting thing about being a director?

LK: For me, it's going out there every day and facing a specific challenge with a group of people you respect. Again, I'll use an athletic analogy. It's like being on a very good basketball team. You may be the point guard and be directing the play, but you can't play center as well as the center. You can't act the way actors act. You can't shoot the way the cameraman does. You can't even prop the thing as well as the prop man. It's really delightful when true professionals are all serving one goal—and very stimulating. As hard as the process is physically, what keeps you going and what invigorates you is this temporary community that is set up. That's why I've never understood directors who flourish on conflict and on putting people down. The crew doesn't have to be happy every minute, but they must feel that their work is respected and that they bring some skill to it that no one else on the team can.

JF: Any other advice for a young person?

LK: I believe in reading. I believe in seeing theater. I believe in being aware when you listen to music of what you feel and why. I believe in being aware of your history—your personal history—trying to understand a little bit about it and why it affects everything you do. I believe that movies are not outside of the political situations in the world and in this country. I hate to see directors act as though they don't come from somewhere and don't impact on something, because they do. I believe in a "connectedness" to the world. I think it enriches the work.

David Lynch

Known primarily for his avant-garde and surrealist approach to film, David Lynch had originally planned a career as a painter, and attended both the School of the Museum of Fine Arts in Boston and the Pennsylvania Academy of Fine Arts. He soon began to use film for creative expression, and in 1970 he moved to Los Angeles to attend the American Film Institute's Center for Advanced Film Studies. In 1972, Mr. Lynch began work on *Eraserhead*, which was released by the AFI in 1977. Although it was not widely distributed until a year later, it has since become one of the most successful "cult classics." In 1978 Mel Brooks chose Mr. Lynch to direct *The Elephant Man*, which received eight Oscar nominations, including one for Best Director. Following that success, Dino de Laurentiis offered Mr. Lynch the task of directing *Dune*, and later offered another directing opportunity with *Blue Velvet*, which earned Lynch another Best Director nomination. His most recent films include 1990's *Wild at Heart* and the upcoming *Twin Peaks: Come Fire Walk with Me*. Lynch brought his unique vision to the small screen with his television series "Twin Peaks," and he is currently busy with other television ventures.

EL: Would you briefly describe your education and how it affected your career development?

DL: At first I was setting off to be a painter. While in high school I studied painting at the Corcoran School of Art in Washington, D.C. After graduating from high school, I studied at the Boston Museum School for one year and the Pennsylvania Academy of the Fine Arts for two years. While in art school, I became interested in film, made two short films, and in 1968 I used one of them to help me get an Indepen-

dent Filmmakers Grant from the American Film Institute for a film called *The Grandmother*. In 1970, I finished *The Grandmother* and was accepted at the Center for Advanced Film Studies in Los Angeles. In those days that was a two-year program, but I stayed there for about five years and made *Eraserhead*.

EL: What was the most helpful thing about the film school experience?

DL: Two things were very helpful. One was the opportunity to make a film utilizing all of the Center's contacts, resources, and equipment. The other was Frank Daniel, who had just come over from Czechoslovakia where he was the head of the Prague Film Academy. He was a great teacher and a great inspiration.

EL: Did you work on a lot of films during that period, or did you concentrate on one project?

DL: The first year I was working on a feature script entitled *Gardenback*. It was through script meetings on *Gardenback* that I learned so much from Frank Daniel. The second year I got the green light to make *Eraserhead*, and like I said, it took quite some time to finish.

EL: What elements of your painting experience transferred to filmmaking?

DL: I think film can be very abstract, so film without words and telling stories in pictures and moods came from painting.

EL: What was least helpful about going to film school?

DL: There was nothing unhelpful about it; without AFI I wouldn't be anywhere.

EL: How would you characterize the role of the director? Everybody has given it a slightly different definition.

DL: I always say it's like a filter through which all things have to pass. The director has the final say on everything. There are twenty-five trillion decisions that have to be made, and if all pass through this one filter, then the picture has a chance of becoming a whole that's held together in a certain good way.

EL: What skills, professionally and personally, are important for a director?

DL: The more skills you have, the better. I like to be involved with every single aspect of filmmaking. I love to build things; I love to paint things; I like to get in on the design and the look of the film; and the more feeling you have for these things the better off you are. You can talk with the heads of departments and discuss things with them in a better way. My weakness was writing, but now I love to write, and I've gotten into music. I was very interested in sound effects at first, and then I met Angelo Badalamenti, who brought me into the world of music. Every single offshoot of film is another whole world, and whatever you know about it reflects back and helps the films too. You've got to be involved with everything, and the deeper the better.

EL: What is your relationship with the cinematographer? Your painting background must give you a great advantage.

DL: Yes, sometimes we talk abstractly. Everybody working on a picture, cast and crew, has to tune into the material—it's a magical thing. With much of the crew it comes out of lots of talking. With actors you get there by rehearsing and talking.

EL: How much do you rehearse?

DL: The more the better, but, unfortunately, there usually isn't a whole lot of time for it. With the larger roles you try to rehearse for at least a couple of weeks before the picture starts. A lot of roles are important, but they don't get that much time. During shooting, usually in the morning, we clear the set, have a rehearsal, get everything worked out, bring in the key people, show it to them, and away we go.

EL: Is the film editor there every day?

DL: My editor is not on the set with me. He's working in the editing room. Sometimes for fun he visits.

EL: Did you have a mentor?

DL: I suppose Frank Daniel, Tony Vellani, and George Stevens.

EL: What's the most frustrating thing about filmmaking?

DL: There are lots of traps in this business, and it would take a while to discuss them all. What goes on the screen is the only thing that's really important, and of course to have fun doing it.

EL: How much of your job is cerebral and how much is instinctive?

DL: I think intuitive is the better word. It's the emotional and mental working together, you just "know" certain things, and that's what I trust. As long as that "thing" is operating, I can make decisions.

EL: Has your work on "Twin Peaks" impacted on the way you look at filmmaking?

DL: Yes. The speed of television is not a bad thing; it's a beautiful thing, and it doesn't mean you go shallow because you're going fast. It means that this automatic pilot can be allowed to function as fast as it can. Many times you settle into a slow pace on a feature film, and everyone is depressed about it—the producers especially. The knowledge that good things can come from working faster came from my experience on "Twin Peaks."

EL: Do you think film school is important to a young person who wants to pursue film?

DL: There are no rules. I think that some people would be better off getting a camera and some film and shooting something. They should try to make it ninety minutes long if at all possible in order to get some return on their investment and master the structure of a feature. It's tricky to keep people entertained for two hours. If you do go to school and get a teacher like Frank Daniel or Tony Vellani, then you can learn a lot. I loved being with the students I met in school; they were a very inspiring good group. We helped each other because we were all so excited about the whole thing.

EL: How about entering film festivals as an activity for beginners?

DL: That may give you the reason you need to get out and do something. It also gives you a deadline. It can help if you win some festivals, sometimes money, or some recognition. Someone could take notice and help you with your next picture.

EL: Do you have any other advice you would give to young people?

DL: Don't put lima beans or beans of any type up your nose. Refrain from putting objects, especially metal objects, into electrical outlets. Look *both* ways before crossing a street. Do not take any medication unless it is prescribed for you by a physician. Never look directly into the sun. Do not dive into any water unless you are certain it is devoid of harmful material. For further information on safety one can consult the local library.

Martha Coolidge

Born and raised in New Haven, Connecticut, Martha Coolidge made her first film during her first year at the Rhode Island School of Design. Since the school did not have a film department, Ms. Coolidge left after her second year to study independently. Moving to New York, she worked in commercials and documentaries and attended night school at New York University, the School of Visual Arts, and Columbia Graduate School. After working steadily and winning numerous festival awards she made her first independent feature, *Not A Pretty Picture*, in 1975. Following a move to Los Angeles, she worked on a project for Francis Ford Coppola, but it was never completed due to the collapse of Coppola's Zoetrope Studios. Her second feature, *The City Girl*, was never released commercially, but she struck critical and box office success with her next film, 1983's *Valley Girl*. She has since directed *Real Genius, Plain Clothes, Rambling Rose*, the pilot of "Sledge Hammer," and several episodes of the television series "Twilight Zone."

EL: Summarize your education as it applies to filmmaking.

MC: I concentrated on theater all through high school, where I also directed and acted. I had started with singing and performing. Theater acting led me to directing in high school, which I immediately enjoyed highly. I did summer stock, and all through college I participated in theater. Later I went to Rhode Island School of Design; in my first year I took a class in which you did a film as a project in two-dimensional design. This was animated film, and I just fell in love with it. Filmmaking seemed to combine my interest in drama and art. The next year I made three films, little tiny movies, which were exercises in a school program that was not a film program.

71

EL: They were narrative films?

MC: One or two of them were narrative. I knew people who had dropped out of school to make movies or had made them in school. I had thought it so competitive that I would never want to go into this field. In the end I fell so in love with it that filmmaking is all I've thought about doing ever since. It gave me the opportunity to control the overall picture, to use my abstract thinking ability and my attention to detail. When I direct movies I'm able to use my visual ability and my interest in photography, time, and place. It just seemed more suitable than theater. It never occurred to me that I couldn't do this because I was a woman. The filmmakers that I loved were all men. I looked desperately for a role model and did in fact go to see a couple of Agnes Varda films. At least I knew that there was one woman director out there, but I never felt alienated by the fact that all of my idols were men.

I did, however, drop out of school and go to New York. At first I got jobs in commercials, gopher jobs at first, then as an assistant editor, script supervisor on commercials—they weren't easy jobs to get. It took me a long time to break in, and at first I worked for free. Once I found a producer who liked me, and he started moving me up. He advised me not to tell people that I wanted to be a director; he said that that wouldn't be a good idea.

EL: What did you learn specifically from your experience in commercials?

MC: I did get some very lucrative commercial jobs occasionally, and that was great. This is not an easy business to get into, and you really have to have some money behind you. When people ask, "Shall I go to college?" I tell them it depends on how much money you have because you're going to need money once you graduate and try to get into this business. If you're blowing every dime on college, and you don't even make a movie there, then I think college is highly questionable. When I was in New York, a $340 stipend a month was enough for me to live on. I could pay my rent and buy myself food so that anything I made was used for equipment, clothing, or whatever.

EL: What were you picking up from watching the production of those commercials that has served you later?

MC: I learned how a set works, and I learned all the crew positions. I also took night classes, and they were terrific. Carefully selected continuing education classes are excellent and New York is a hotbed of such offerings. I took two classes at the School of Visual Arts and one class at NYU Continuing Education. Finally I went to Columbia Graduate School as a "special student," based on my film work (I hadn't graduated from undergraduate school). Their graduate school in film is like a continuing education program. It was an evening program and very interesting. I learned more in those classes than in most I've taken since then. One was in music composition and sound editing. I took another one in which you cast actors in a scene you wrote, directed, filmed them on videotape, and then analyzed it all, and then the next week you did it again. That's something that AFI, UCLA, and many schools in the main film centers do. However, what you fail to get that way is the community you develop when you spend four years at one school. That is one of the reasons I went back to school after I'd been out in the working world.

EL: I once heard Jill Robb, an Australian producer, say that she thought women made remarkable filmmakers, (she was speaking in particular about producers), because women come from a tradition of having to balance multiple roles in life, and that compromise, patience, and nurturing are part of a woman's life, and all of these attributes really suit filmmaking. Do you subscribe to that?

MC: I don't know if I can generalize, but I think that those are qualities that I have that make me a good filmmaker.

EL: What other qualities do you have that make you a good filmmaker, particularly a good director?

MC: I was the oldest in a family of five, and when my father died I wanted to run the family. I did run it in a certain way. I was bossy. Now I'm not a bossy boss, but I did get used to the idea of being a leader. Some people, both men and women (but I've heard particularly women), have a hard time delegating. I'm not great at delegating, but I've certainly gotten better at it, and I'm very good at bringing talent out in other people. I really like to see the talent in other people, encourage it and let it flourish. I think the best directors, such as Francis Coppola with whom I worked for so long, are people who really do that.

EL: Have you ever recognized resistance to you as a woman director on the set, and if so, how did you handle it?

MC: Well, you don't see it so much face to face. When you're busy making a movie, you have more important things to think about than whether somebody's resentful because you're a woman. The more secure I am, the older I am, the more I'm able to see the sexism that is around me and that has probably always been there. At the same time, you don't see it overtly because you're hired by people who *want* to hire you. It's one of the difficult things about sexism; like racism, it's not something you can confront. People just say, "Well, she's not artistically right for this film." And that's it. You might get an executive that comes into the studio who wasn't there when you were hired and that person has got a problem. Or it might be a production manager who's hired by the studio. I've had that happen. With crews that's unusual, because you usually hire the keys and they hire their people. The people who work for the keys don't answer to you.

EL: You're known as being very good with actors. Can you just describe how you work with actors, how much you rehearse them, and how you've learned the actor's language?

MC: I think the most important thing a director can understand is acting. Probably the best way to learn is to act, and if that is not possible, to direct actors a lot. I acted; I worked for directors; I had a lot of scene work, both in acting classes and in a video class. The film schools I attended did not have many acting classes, and I believe that that's still a basic problem in film schools. This is one of the greatest gaps there can be in a film school. Most of what the director does involves working with actors. When I went to RISD, which is a Bauhaus designed art program, every single week I had a minimum of nine hours of life drawing with another minimum of six hours of some other kind of drawing. We learned the basics. Actors are the director's basic tool. Yes, you should understand writing, lighting, and camera, etc., but the technical stuff is not what tells the story. You can hire a great cameraman, and you can learn that on the set. You don't even need to study it, although the greatest teacher I had in film school was my cinematography teacher, and I learned more about actors and filmmaking from him than from anybody else.

EL: How much of your job is instinctual and how much cerebral?

MC: Now it's instinctual, but from my early twenties to thirty-six or seven, it was a very cerebral process for me. The older I get, the more instinctual it gets. I have such an overpowering calling for filmmaking it's hard to describe. I couldn't live without doing it. I still go back to the rules, but less often. I used to be a religious shot-list maker, and I found that on this last movie, I didn't always make a shot-list, and I never counted how many set-ups I did in a day. It was the most fun, relaxed time I've ever had. As a director, you ask, "What are the emotions that this story arouses in you?" because you need to arouse the audience. Your tools are the script and the actors. The secondary tools are the cinematography. You respond to the material emotionally, instinctively. Then you cerebrally say, "OK, is there something wrong with why I love this or is it right for me now?" or "Fine, artistically it appeals to me, who's the producer?" That's the cerebral part.

EL: Do you see your images immediately upon reading the script or do you get a few and then research?

MC: I've found that many of the scripts I read appeal to me because of the conflict within the story and the way the drama and the characters interrelate. That makes me want to do the film. When someone says to me, "Well who do you see in that part? What is the look of the picture?" I have to sit and think, but eventually I have to go back to my feeling. Now how do I convert that feeling into a look? I always do some research, and it's always the details of real life that provide me detail for the movie. That's something I learned in documentaries. I think detail and specifics are the key to good drama.

EL: You are a wife, mother, and filmmaker. You're active at the DGA, you're active at the AFI, and you teach. How in the world do you find the energy to do all of it?

MC: One of the reasons I can do this now is that when I was younger I exhausted every filmmaking possibility. Now when I think of how I'm going to shoot a scene, I can automatically cross out five options because I instinctively or experientially know that those choices won't work. I can settle on one or two. The same thing is true of every aspect of filmmaking. I know how to approach a rewrite, how to select a writer, and so on. I just know more.

I am also a workaholic; I got married at thirty-seven, had my baby when I was forty-two—with great desire, but also great hesitation. I was very worried that it would interfere with my work. Now that I have a baby, I understand a whole other side of life; I think it's wonderful to have a family and something to cut into this constant work. When I was thirty-eight years old I was a judge at the U.S. Film Festival and got on a pair of skis for the first time in twenty years. I had been a really good skier, and as I went up that lift and experienced the silence on the ski slopes and the feeling of going down those slopes, the dance-like invigoration of skiing, I thought, What an idiot! What have I done to myself? All my prime skiing years lost to what? It wasn't that I was making films all those years, but that I felt I couldn't leave town or couldn't spend the couple hundred bucks it would cost to go skiing because I had to spend it on movies. This is a deep regret because I now know I could have gone skiing and still have been a filmmaker. So, yes, I can do the family thing and still be a filmmaker. There is a tremendous price and I have to be very careful about my time. It's hard. Yet I also love to do all those other things and for many reasons. I felt that as a young woman I had no role models, and I know how important they are, so I do enjoy going out speaking or teaching. I love working at the DGA because nothing has taught me more about being a director in Hollywood than hanging out and working on committees with a lot of directors. Most are men, although there are some women that are active in the Guild who are directors as well. You get a picture of the history of being a director. It's been a very important role for me because I was out there alone for a long time with no organization protecting me. I had to negotiate my own contracts, and I really appreciate the fact that there is an organization that gets things that I could never get for myself and also protects my interests. So I am willing to give back to that.

EL: Even though directors never really work together, do you think there is a fraternity of directors?

MC: Yes there is, but as a rule young directors don't participate in it. There's no natural fraternity outside of the DGA, and it isn't until you get to a point in your life where you have a body of work, a little leisure, a little time or a little money, that you can express any interest and commit your time.

EL: Does directing ever feel lonely? I know film is a collaborative art form on the one hand, but you often stand alone in making final decisions.

MC: Totally lonely. It is a very lonely position, and you can't be a director if you're not willing to be lonely. You have to be willing to make people angry with you. You have to be willing to do certain things to get results. I've learned these lessons along the way. The people that work for you aren't necessarily going to like you, but your job is to make the best movie you can.

EL: How do you characterize the role of a director?

MC: I think you have to be a visionary on some level. Not every director is Woody Allen, or Peckinpah, or Coppola, or David Lynch, but you can be a director who recognizes a good idea. You have to be able to own those ideas and exercise leadership. Once you do that, you can work in a very collaborative way. It is a collaborative medium, but it is not a collaborative job. In addition, you answer to enormous numbers of important people creating bigger and bigger pressures; the amounts of money are greater and greater. There are more executives, more corporations on top of those executives, and more interests all saying, "You have to do this and you have to do that and you have to cast so and so, and you have to have this in your movie and do it this way." The result is that you are a lone visionary in a room full of fifty people telling you what to do. It's a very odd job.

EL: What advice would you give to future directors?

MC: It's important to realize that you need to know a lot of things, a lot about people, including actors. When you're ready, you should make a movie. Whatever it takes to make that movie, you do; it may take you one year, and it may take you ten years. It's very hard to convince people you're a director if you haven't directed. It may take $10,000 or $100,000 or a million dollars, but you need to do it. Right now, it's so expensive that if you blow your first shot, it will be hard to get it together a second time because money is hard to get. It also means having patience, collecting favors, collecting knowledge, waiting until you have a worthy piece of material, and making it as personal as you can. It doesn't have to be a personal story, but rather designed to move you personally.

Robert Wise
....

Robert Wise was born on September 10, 1914 in Winchester, Indiana. Forced to drop out of college because of the Depression, he landed a job as a messenger in the film-editing department at RKO. He soon became an apprentice editor, where his editing assignments included Orson Welles' *Citizen Kane* and *The Magnificent Ambersons*. When the original director of the film *Curse of the Cat People* was removed, Mr. Wise stepped in to complete the film, establishing himself as a director. He has since directed numerous films including *The Day the Earth Stood Still* and *Somebody Up There Likes Me*. He directed the Oscar-winning films *West Side Story* (with Jerome Robbins) and *The Sound of Music*, both of which he also produced. Mr. Wise is on the Board of Directors of the American Film Institute, the Board of Governors of the Academy of Motion Picture Arts and Sciences, and has served on the National Council on the Arts.

EL: Could you summarize your formal education and indicate if it had any great bearing on your becoming a filmmaker?

RW: It had no direct bearing. I was from Indiana; I had a year of college after getting out of high school in '32. This was the height of the Depression, and I had no money to go back to second year. My parents decided that I should go out to Los Angeles and visit an older brother who'd come out here five years before and started in the studios. I had no thought of being in films; I was going to be a journalist. And this was before film schools were even thought of. That was the circumstance that brought me into movies. Since my brother Dave was working at RKO Studios, he arranged some appointments, and one of them happened to be with the head of their film-editing department.

Roads to directing originate from many directions. We've had many fine directors come from the stage who had had no previous movie experience. George Cukor is one case in point, and also Garson Kanin with whom I worked years ago. Certainly film editing isn't the only way, but it's certainly one of the best routes for someone starting from scratch to learn the whole process of filmmaking. Here you're surrounded by people who know all the technical aspects of film—you're not going to be set adrift. Many writers have become good directors; actors too.

EL: How would you characterize the role of a director?

RW: The director is often compared to the conductor of an orchestra. True, he has got a lot of help, and he has certainly had strong input from his writer and producer, but once he's on that set at that location, he's conducting the whole thing and running the whole show. He has to be on top of everything. He has to not only direct the actors, but also the crew and the staff, and, as the boss, be in charge of countless fast and ready decisions during the day. I have two words that I always pass on to would-be directors when I go to film schools (and I do that very often): anticipation and communication. To anticipate day-to-day things that are going to be needed on the set that maybe haven't been planned. You get an idea in the morning and you say, "Gee, it'd be marvelous at this point if the leading lady had a white scarf that she rips off," or some other such business that hadn't been planned. However, I've got to be sure to tell the wardrobe lady, "Have a white scarf this afternoon." If I forget, then in the afternoon I've got to sit and wait while someone gets it. Anticipation gives you more time to spend with your actors in getting the scenes right. So that and communication are a couple of key operational words.

EL: Can you identify a couple of mentors?

RW: You pick up a lot of things by osmosis, but I did learn from Dieterle and some of the others whose films I worked on, the value of preparation and planning. I learned many things from Orson Welles. One was about keeping the dynamics in the film; he always had such energy in his films. Also the use of sound because he was marvelous at that having come from radio. From others, I learned the value of evaluating scenes in terms of timing. You can often have a sequence that you think is just right in terms of the pacing and tempo, but when it is placed in the continuity of the film, you find it's a little slow. I don't think I've ever had a scene that I wish I had played slower.

EL: I read one of your quotes that I thought was profound. You said: "Mine is a prepared approach with ample room for improvisation."

RW: Well, that is true. I understand certain directors and particularly some of the European directors are reputed to start shooting with a bare outline of a script and make up the scene as they go. That seems to work well for them, but from my experience, I feel that if you've anticipated everything you possibly can, if you have things laid out, then you have the freedom to move away, reach out, try new things, and yet know you have that solid base of preparation to fall back on. I remember Julie Andrews saying much the same thing—she felt that only after she was totally organized for whatever was happening on the set could she fly. I always prepare; I usually have storyboards for everything except action sequences and dance numbers. When a scene is finally brought to life on the stage with the actors, new dimensions and values are found. The actors bring things that you can't anticipate in advance. If incorporating these things into the roles makes it necessary to move away from your original plans and change your camera set-up, then you do it.

EL: That kind of preparation must be very reassuring to your crew and also to your actors.

RW: Right, I think that is true. The director has to be the boss. You're forced to defend this role by answering questions from your staff, your crew, your actors; you have to make decisions constantly. The more prepared and organized you are going in, the more they know they can count on you. It's very reassuring. There's a limit, however. I'm not very heavy on giving a lot of direction to actors. Before shooting we explore a character's relation to the other characters, to the story and the plot, so that we see eye-to-eye on most of the material. Then on a day-to-day basis, I work with them and help develop their performances.

EL: I understand you were heavily involved with the story and script of *I Want to Live*. How did that work?

RW: This was a real-life story about a woman (Barbara Graham) who was sent to the gas chamber back in the mid-fifties—fascinating story. We had a long, unwieldy first draft. So we decided to get a new writer, and we chose Nelson Gidding who did the screenplay. We were under the gun schedulewise, so while Nelson was working on the script, I interviewed people who were real characters in the story and got all the information I could. Part of the director's job is research since you have to know what you're dealing with. I research every film I do. I immerse myself in first-hand research if I can. So, part of the process with *I Want to Live* was going to San Quentin to see the gas chamber. Then I felt I needed to see an execution. I felt a bit like a ghoul asking but I wanted to be able to say, "That's the way it is." I didn't want the critics to say, "That's Hollywood's version of what it's like to go to the gas chamber." Interestingly enough when I went to the warden to ask for this privilege I said, "I want this for my own knowledge, but I'll not use it for publicity purposes." He surprisingly said, "Mr. Wise, I understand where you're coming from and I agree with you. Capital punishment is the law in the state of California, and I think it's well for the citizens of the state to see just how it works." So I was called a couple of weeks later to come up on a Friday morning, and I saw an execution. I was with the warden and the doctor. I didn't know whether I would really be able to watch. Fortunately, it was a very calm scene. But for the film I didn't know how to structure the last act, and during my interviews, I had the chance to talk to the priest who had been at the prison when Barbara was there, but had left. During my conversation with him I said, "Father, how did it happen that you left the prison?" He said, "Well I don't suppose you have any idea, Mr. Wise, of the terrible pall, the awful atmosphere that settles on a whole prison the day before an execution, when everyone in the prison knows that preparations are being made to take a human life. It's just dreadful. I couldn't stand it anymore and I left." After I had been to the prison, had seen the gas chamber, had my art director photograph it, knew all the areas of the death cell and had taken measurements so we could reproduce it, I realized I hadn't thought about the procedures. So I went right back to the prison and said, "I want you to show me everything you do to prepare for an execution so when I show the film you see exactly the process that goes on." That's how things happen sometimes.

EL: When you read a script, how do you visualize certain things? After you have read the script, chosen to do it, done your research, how do you find your images? Do you find some of them immediately and stay with those that are strong, or do you have to let go of those initial ones as you do the research?

RW: Well, I think primary images are pulled out of thin air, particularly if you're dealing with a subject that you're not overly familiar with. You imagine the background look and the feeling, and then as you go to the reality of things, you make adjustments and work from there.

EL: How do you find the balance between reality, authenticity, and what works dramatically?

RW: I think reality often leads very strongly, very directly, and very effectively into the dramatic. Certainly in these instances of real-life stories such as *I Want to Live*, there are dramatic life stories. If you put these into the right frame and the reality of the places these lives were lived, you have the drama and the authenticity.

EL: What is your relationship to the cinematographer?

RW: I've been a director who has not always used the same cinematographer. Many directors like to use the same one, but I try to cast my cinematographers for the quality, the look, and feeling that I want for a given picture. So I haven't had the same cinematographer for more than two films. If I want a really hard, gritty, documentary feeling and look, I look for a certain person. I usually cast my cinematographers. In a meeting I give my view and the cinematographer adds his. You must have a meeting of the minds, whether it be in the characterization of an actor, the look of the cinematography, or the look and feeling of the sets and costumes. In bringing all those together, one has a sense of how each aspect will fit into the whole. That is a major responsibility of the director.

EL: Do you communicate verbally with your cinematographer, or do you share images, pictures, paintings?

RW: Yes, very often we'll share and I'll ask, "Do you like this feeling?" I don't do this to excess, but Val Lewton, who was a very, very creative producer of small psychological horror pictures back in the early forties, was the first one to make me understand what to use. He used to bring in prints of the Old Masters to study. When I did a Franco-Prussian War film called *Mademoiselle Fifi* from a De Maupassant story set in 1870, Val brought in Daumier sketches, which provided the looks of the people, the faces, the costumes and the types of carriages, the villages of the period. We copied a lot of that for the film. Of course, you need a good relationship between the cinematographer and the production designer. The production designer is as important to the cinematographer in producing the look of a film. A solid rapport between them is an asset.

EL: The choreographer of a film in many ways is a storyteller also, and you've worked with choreographers. What is it like to share a directorial role for dance scenes?

RW: I worked on *West Side Story* with Jerome Robbins as choreographer and co-director. He felt he had to do more with it than just handle choreography. So we worked out our modus operandi, and I wouldn't take a moment's credit away from Jerry for all those marvelous dance sequences and numbers. I was there; but he directed everything, including the camera. I helped him get extra cameras, saw that everything was covered, and offered ideas and suggestions. It was agreed Jerry would do the music sequences while I would do the book scenes. So I was there when he was shooting the musicals, and he was with me when I did the book, and it worked out quite successfully. Then I worked with Mark Breaux and DeDe Wood, who were the choreographers for *The Sound of Music*, and later with Michael Kidd who was so marvelous for *Star!*.

EL: Is it hard for you to give up some control to your film editor?

RW: No, I'm not of the school that says to the editor, "Don't cut anything until I finish shooting and I'll do it with you." I've always worked with my editors in the way in which I was accustomed when I was an editor. I finish running dailies on a sequence, make my selection of takes, and give them to the editor who goes away, cuts the first edit, and runs it for me, and I say, "Yes, I like this," or "That close-up's no good there, try this." If you don't allow the editor to do his own first cuts, then you deprive yourself of his creative instincts. I've put sequences together myself not quite the way the director planned and they've worked. Billy Hamilton, the old-time editor I broke in with, gave me this piece of advice: "Bob, the thing the director expects from you as editor is to make the scene play." Of course, everybody should understand that the final edited version is something that has got to be approved by the director. Some people seem to have the idea that we shoot our film and turn it over to the editor. He then puts the film together and that's that. It doesn't work that way, but certainly the final version often reflects a very large amount of creative input from the film editor. I think my whole editing experience enriched my knowledge of what's possible, what's impossible, what can be improved, and what can be better.

EL: You are so versatile; you have done horror pictures, sci-fi, musicals, period pieces, suspense pieces, and drama. As you approach each genre do you think that you're putting on a slightly different hat?

RW: I've been asked many times if I prefer one thing to another, one genre to another. I have a couple of no-no's I've had for years. I haven't done a Western since the mid-fifties, and I found I just didn't enjoy doing them. I did a big spectacle in the fifties, and I found that genre wasn't something I enjoyed very much. What's important is that script. When in the late sixties, I realized I had done *The Sound of Music*, *Sand Pebbles*, and *Star!*, all period pieces. I suddenly felt the need to do something very contemporary; I'd had enough period work. At that point Universal sent me a galley copy of *The Andromeda Strain*, which I liked very much, but it also filled a need that I had at that time.

EL: How much do you rehearse your actors on the set? I've heard directors say some actors are good in the first take and other actors aren't good until the third take or so.

RW: Films, and particularly Hollywood films, are very difficult in terms of rehearsals. Many people don't understand why, but it's a matter of economics. When I've had the luck of having some rehearsal time, I've used the set in the morning or maybe gotten the actors together in one of the dressing rooms and read through the script. When we know where we are in the story, we go into the set, start to block out the action, and get the scene up on its feet. A lot depends on how difficult the scene is. Often you rehearse a simple scene for twenty–thirty minutes, and you're ready to go ahead with the lighting. Other times you have a very difficult scene, very complicated scene, very emotional scene; in such a case I may spend one to three hours, or a whole morning. In such a situation I have sent the crew off the set, just had the cameraman in the back watching from the shadows, the soundman off someplace with the script clerk taking notes.

EL: What would you say is the most frustrating and then the most satisfying part of being a director?

RW: I've often said that directing films would be the greatest fun in the world, if it weren't for schedules and budgets. Of course, I started doing eighteen-day pictures when you worked under tremendous pressure, but there is always a feeling that the clock is ticking, time is passing, you're getting behind schedule, you don't want to slough, you need an extra take and you want to take another angle. I think that's the biggest frustration—the constant pressure of schedule and budget. On the other hand, the greatest joy is when you've got that picture done, you take it out, and the audience eats it up. That's its own form of joy.

EL: Do you think that today film school attendance is important for young people?

RW: I think it's very helpful. I believe in film schools, and if young people have the means to go, I recommend it highly. They will learn a lot, experience aspects of filmmaking, make some of their own films, do some writing, directing, whatever. I hope they understand that coming out with a degree isn't "Open, Sesame," and that the gates of the studio will not automatically open and say, "Come on in; here's your picture; do it." They have to understand that they are not going to automatically walk into something professional, but once they finish film school they have that advantage over the young person starting without any experience at all.

EL: In addition to film school preparation for a career as a director, what other activities are valuable?

RW: It's very important to get as broad an education as possible in all aspects of life, society, arts, and government. The more depth one has, the better filmmaker one is going to be. I always encourage students to do that while they're in college, not just solely concentrate on learning filmwork. Another thing that is valuable (for writers as well and directors particularly) is to do some acting. I didn't have any experience in that. When I was doing school plays I was always backstage or stage manager, so when I started directing I had to learn how to deal with actors. One of the most important things that should be learned in film school is how to collaborate. Filmmaking is a collaborative art, and it's often very difficult for young people to understand. They all want to do their own thing, and I think the sooner they learn that they have to work with, deal with, talk with, and handle other people who are writers, cinematographers, assistants, or actors, the sooner they will become good filmmakers.

EL: What would you single out as the most significant change or changes in the process of filmmaking over your career?

RW: It's changed so much since I came here in the thirties and started directing in the forties. Then the studios had contracts with actors, directors, cinematographers, and writers. The major studios made fifty or sixty films a year, maybe forty of them B pictures. You went from one film to another, and it was normal to have ten–twelve films shooting at the same time. Even RKO, one of the smaller majors, could have three or four films in the last two or three days of shooting and four or five others just starting. Since the fifties the studios haven't had contract lists, although they might have a commitment with a few directors and actors for two or three films. Today there's a whole different administrative operation up front and far fewer films being made. There's so much more money, time, and effort going into each film. Of course, it's always been a business and an art, but it seems that the B in business is a big, big, big capital B with a big need to make those blockbusters. I'm very happy to say that the thing that hasn't changed is the day-to-day shooting on the set, with the actors, the staff, and the crew. That is much the same now as it was in the old days. There is more equipment, better equipment, lighter equipment and all that, but the motion picture crews and the technicians really know their stuff, work hard, and do it with great humor. That hasn't changed, and I hope it never will.

EL: What kind of stories would you like to see being made into films?

RW: I would like to see more films that deal in depth with human relationships with less emphasis on backgrounds, special effects, and locations. Not enough emphasis is placed on the foreground, which to me is the story, the characters, the plot, the premise that is going to involve the audience—that's what's important. To be more thoughtful, more adult, doesn't mean that a film has to be less entertaining or involving.

FOUR

✪ The Cinematographer

The cinematographer (or director of photography) is charged with literally setting the vision of the director onto film. Cinematographers need to balance an aesthetic sensibility with a solid background and grounding in technology. A cinematographer must be concerned with framing, lighting, style, composition, continuity, and exposure. There must be clear communication between the cinematographer, the director, and the production designer. Often a cinematographer and director will form a close association and work on several projects together.

Salaries for this position range widely. According to the union, scale begins at approximately $420 for an eight-hour day, but a renowned cinematographer may make as much as $15,000 per week. Cinematographers may belong to the American Society of Cinematographers (213-876-5050), which has close to 300 members.

Haskell Wexler

....

Haskell Wexler has spent more than three decades in Hollywood as a cinematographer for both documentaries and feature films. Born in Chicago, he left for California on the day of his high school graduation. He spent a year at UC Berkeley and then joined the Merchant Marines during World War II. Following the end of the war, he began making documentaries and moved to Hollywood in the fifties, quickly catching the eye of some of Hollywood's finest directors. He was soon photographing films for such directors as Elia Kazan and Norman Jewison. Mr. Wexler has photographed over twenty-five films, including *In the Heat of the Night, The Thomas Crown Affair, American Graffiti, Coming Home,* and *Blaze.* He has won Academy Awards for cinematography for his work on *Who's Afraid of Virginia Woolf?* and *Bound for Glory,* and has received Oscar nominations for *One Flew over the Cuckoo's Nest* and *Matewan.* Mr. Wexler has directed and photographed numerous documentaries, including *Medium Cool* and *Interviews with My Lai Veterans,* which earned him the Academy Award for Best Documentary.

EL: You once said the magic tool is your eye, and to some extent you're born with that. Are cinematographers born or are they made?

HW: I don't know. Certainly there are levels. You can study hard and become a good professional. If you have certain innate and undiscoverable, unmentionable, or unknown feelings, tendencies or trends that are part of your psyche, I'm sure that they can feed a professional dedication. So where one begins and where one ends, nobody knows. You could take a concert violinist who worked his ass off to learn to play from the time he was six years old. It could be said he's wonderful;

on the other hand there might be someone who didn't work so hard technically and professionally but who exhibited certain proclivities or certain aspects that allowed him to play as beautifully.

EL: How would you characterize what a cinematographer does, both from a functional and an artistic point of view?

HW: A cinematographer is in charge of the crew and of bringing images together on motion picture film. In the course of doing that he helps the director with framing, camera movement, and telling the story through images. The status of the cinematographer has changed in so-called Hollywood films because he is "below-the-line" and considered interchangeable. Unlike directors, cinematographers have been fired from films for various unimportant reasons. The position of cinematographer has changed partly because of the attitude that the people who make films have toward the public. I have heard it said overtly and covertly, "They won't know the difference" or "Look, as long as they see the actors clearly as they say their lines, that's all that matters." The subjective factors that images interestingly done present to an audience are not quantifiable, and most people in charge of films are interested in quantifiable results because that's the world they live in. So the position of cinematographer has not been enhanced in recent times. What he does and what he's able to do have changed over the years, and changed with the way and the reasons why pictures are being made. Most people see pictures on television, and television is there for one purpose—to reach the widest audience able to buy what is being sold. It's called different things, but the purpose of television is to feed a consumer society. To get people to consume, purchase things that they may or may not need, that may or may not be healthy, that may or may not be good for the world or for them; but those issues are set aside— that's television. Because images are brought forward for those purposes, what the cinematographer does is *ipso facto* part of that system.

EL: How do you develop a language with a director? You are the person that has to put the director's vision on the screen. How do you develop a language to communicate and achieve that vision?

HW: That really is one of the key challenges to the cinematographer. The director is the captain of the ship, but the navigational language of photography is imprecise.

EL: But you are the navigator.

HW: True, but sometimes you have to alter course to fit where the skipper wants the ship to go even if you don't want to go there at all, and so you do have to develop a language. The easiest way is to see films together, to talk together, maybe even see some films that your actors have been in so you can learn something about how they best project their image, in what angles, what attitudes, what kind of shots. We are literally talking about two languages, about grammatical English and abstraction. If you've ever read music criticism, the music critics discuss colors, emotions, mostly untranslatable words, in an effort to write about music. Though it is an almost impossible task, it is a requirement, so you do the best you can. So it is by seeing things together, and discussing, going to the locations and saying, "God, I love the way the light comes in through this window. When we do the scene, let's get it like that."

EL: Do you ever use still photographs?

HW: Yes, still photographs are very helpful. I used still photographs on a picture I did a long time ago called *America, America*. I used still photographs on *Matewan*. On *Days Of Heaven*, Terry Malick had a lot of old photographs which Nestor Alemandros and I both examined. Again, that is a good way to bridge the language obstacle into the image.

EL: Is there a kind of director towards whom you really gravitate? Or do you gravitate toward the story? What makes you want to take on a project?

HW: Well, there have been a number of things. Number one, there have been directors whom I like who want to make films not because they want to direct, or see their name up there, but rather because they feel a certain way about the world around them, about people, about human expression. They don't focus solely on what a film will do at the box

© 1988 Mark Harmel

office or how popular it will be with the studio. It's one of the reasons I enjoyed my association with Hal Ashby. Hal had edited *In The Heat of the Night* and *The Thomas Crown Affair*. I found him to be a person who loved films, a very principled person. I worked on some dogs with Hal, but all the time I learned something from him; I respected him and felt honored to be with him. Not all the time—we fought, but I always respected him. Other times you do pictures with certain directors because of the script; sometimes I do pictures because if I don't, I'll lose my crew. Over the years I've developed some great guys, of course, some of them move up. A lot of the guys who were operators for me are now great D.P.'s. I love the guys, and part of what I like about filmmaking is the camaraderie, the feeling that a good crew has for one another and for what they're doing.

EL: You've done documentaries, commercials, and features. What translates between the three, what doesn't translate, and is there one route that is a better one to take? Is the documentary experience a good place to start for young people?

HW: I think it's excellent. I think that documentary gives you a chance to be out amongst them. One of the things I see with a lot of younger film students is that their whole world is films, their frames of reference are films, their knowledge of history is films, and the way people act and react to others is film acting and reacting. Of course, real people also act like film characters. So documentaries are an excellent way to be out amongst them, to learn, to be a student, and also to learn certain technical things, to learn such things as how conventional framing may hurt the urgency of a scene. When you're shooting a documentary, you can't put the camera in the ideal place, and you can't light in an ideal way. So when you're doing a scene and you have forty guys on the crew, you're also going to have the assurance of the remembrance of that scene that looked pretty damn good when you did less than you're capable of doing. Documentary filmmaking brings you closer to the total filmmaking process. You're there; you have to think for yourself as a director would think. You learn a lot about filmmaking and your decisions have to be immediate and instinctual. In addition, most documentary filmmakers spend time in the cutting room. Overall, the closeness to the total filmmaking process is an excellent background for any kind of filmmaking.

EL: How important is film school?

HW: I think it totally depends on the person. Some can go to film school and get fantastic elevation in their abilities to be filmmakers, and I think others can come away with nothing. How you evaluate the importance or success is something that deserves discussing, because if it only means that you go on to become a George Lucas, then I think that's a narrow evaluation of how successful the school is. I think film school can enhance your overall education in the fullest meaning of the word "education." Film schools have to work more seriously on *what* we're doing as well as *how* we're doing it. You have to truly examine films—not just how they're done, or their box office success—but what they're saying. And even why they're saying it. What needs do they feed? How do they reflect certain things in our culture? In other words, we need to look at films the way anthropologists might look at films and to imagine (if the world lasts for another forty years) what people would say when they'd look back at this summer's films. What were these films telling people? We have to look carefully at what we're seeing, and decide what we want to see. It is important to be good professionals, to know about lenses, to know about cameras, to know about films, to know about movement, but that's not the beginning or the end of the world. It's also important to know ourselves, our values, and what we would like to do with the magic that is our profession *and* our art.

EL: Some film professions lend themselves toward mentorships. A writer can have a mentor, yet it's tough for an actor to have a mentor. What about the cinematographer?

HW: Well, the film school offers the cinematographer tools that he can't afford for one thing. It also offers a cinematographer people who can help him do his work. There are a lot of things you can learn about filmmaking on your own. You can do a lot with still cameras because cinematography is still photography. There's a lot being done with the video camera in terms of storytelling. There's more to be learned doing it with other people. You learn from one another, you learn from mistakes and so forth. So film school offers that. But the overall philosophy of the film school is its biggest message and, unfortunately, it has become vocational. Will it help me get a job? Will I meet the right people? Do I like the kind of stories that they're buying? So schools, which should be the area of experimentation, of new ways of looking at things, have become more or less factories for employment. If you can't experiment when you're a student, forget it, because for the rest of your life you're going to have to be practical; you're going to have to get a job; you can't leave the system. But instead at that point if imaginations could be enhanced, at least some of it would stick and maybe it would make a better world.

EL: Is working on video valid?

HW: Definitely, because many of the things that work in film are pertinent to video. You have to edit, know how to frame, and think about camera movement. However, lighting is different. The video screen is different emotionally for a number of reasons. I'll just mention one or two. We're conditioned to feel a certain way when we sit in front of the video screen. That glass thing says it's going to do everything it can to keep you sitting there until the commercials are complete. There's no interaction. There's an action. Otherwise I might flip the channel, leave the room, I might even talk to my child or my wife. Television is a force to keep you there for the commercial. That is the obligation. Motion pictures and all of drama traditionally function with an interaction. They say, "We want to draw you into the screen; we want you to discover things that we plant there. We want you to empathize. We want to have you as part of an interactive creative process."

EL: Describe your relationship with the producer during the film.

HW: Well, producers are different now. Walter Mirisch was the producer of the film *In the Heat of the Night*. He wanted to make this film because he believed in the script and what it said about black-white relationships in the South. He also believed that there was an audience out there that would believe in it; he was not a total dreamer. So he worked on getting Norman Jewison, the director; he talked to Sidney Poitier; he dealt with United Artists to get the money. When we were a few days behind schedule he helped protect the director by calling and telling United Artists that they'd make it up. In other words, the producer was an active participant in seeing that the picture got made. Nowadays, you see pictures that have eight producers' credits on it. You don't know what the hell they do. I don't know how they pick producers. I don't. That doesn't mean there aren't good producers, but I believe that part of this new system has lost a lot of creative producers from that business.

EL: How much do you generally interact with actors?

HW: All depends on the people. Some actors are best left alone. Others will come to you and ask you things. I tell them simple things like the size of the shot so that they know how to temper their performance. I'll also tell them—half the time with the director present—how we're going to cover a scene so that they can pace themselves. I'm going to give an extreme example—so an actress knows not to summon up real tears when I only see a very small side of her face in the foreground. In general, actors are insecure people, and so when I see dailies and they look good, I like to tell them. I also learn some things about their faces and about their bodies, which, depending on the person, I'll tell them— little things that we may notice but which the person can't see. The camera is only as good as what's out in front of it, and that means art direction, that means actors, and so forth. So I like to make it comfortable for them.

EL: What about the art director and costume designer? Do you talk a lot with them?

HW: As much as I possibly can, and I learn a lot from them too, because, as I say, photography is only part of the image. The image is what's in front of the camera and what's in front of the camera, in feature film is what's in our control. Certainly the interiors—the color of the walls, the drapes, the kind of furniture, the wardrobe, the makeup—all those things are done by a group of people, not just a director of photography. The longer and more intensely you can work on those things together the better the picture, no question.

EL: You've worked on big budget films and on small budget films. *Matewan* looks like it cost a lot more than it did. How much does a small budget handicap you?

HW: Well, sometimes being able to do everything hurts you. I have certain opinions and decisions—I mean visually—which I can't defend when dealing with other people. If you didn't have to consider such things, you could act on your own. You could find a location—if it's a low-budget picture—and if you think the scene should have a certain type of background, you could say to the director, "Well, let's shoot it by that desk over there because . . ." and the "because" is often bullshit. The "because" is a rationalization developed to transmit ideas in verbal ways. The "because" might be that I looked over there and saw that the light came in in a beautiful way or that I could get a nice frame partly with the mountains outside and her sitting there. You can't say those things to a director because it may sound like you're trying to make a pretty picture for your own department, and directors are very sensitive to that, particularly with a cameraman like me. They figure he may try to feature himself rather than the picture. That is a danger which I have to deal with myself.

EL: A lot of your job is instinctive. Even though you have mountains of technical skill and knowledge, an eye is an instinctive thing. It's coming from your gut to your eye and brain and onto film.

HW: Yeah. But that's the magic of filmmaking. That's why I love to shoot and direct my own film. That's the ultimate. It's hard to compromise, but you have to learn to appreciate other people's ideas. All aspects of filmmaking are a series of immense compromises. Directors too make compromises because actors can't do something, or something that's been planned is impossible to do on location.

EL: But I would think that kind of creative problem-solving would sometimes yield some potentially better results.

HW: No question about it.

EL: What do you look for in a picture? When you look at a script (and I know that you're motivated by things that might have a humanistic basis), do you look for a story that is visually interesting to you?

HW: Less so now than earlier in my career. Right now I view my photography the way I do my life. I want to do things that—I hate to use the word—that fuel relevance in me. The selectivity of the relevance is higher now that I'm older. Once when someone asked me to shoot a picture—any kind of picture—I'd shoot it! Now I feel differently. It's not just because I'm more successful, it's because I think differently about life.

EL: What advice would you give to a young person? Would you say, "Go out and shoot everything you can?"

HW: I don't give advice—particularly to young people. I do think that they should keep in touch with the real world. How you do that in modern times is rough, but they should realize that this job is a privileged job, and with privilege comes a responsibility as a human being on this planet. They should not close their eyes to the people not seen on television, those we don't see in our everyday life. They should realize that they are part of every other human being, every other living thing on this planet, and they should think about that and work around that while they're sharpening their tools, while they're expressing themselves. This is vital; then in my definition they'd be "good" filmmakers. It is time now for artistic aggression to reassert positive human values that will go hand in hand with better films and create a planet both peaceful and livable.

Caleb Deschanel

....

Caleb Deschanel began his studies at the Johns Hopkins School of Medicine, but soon transferred to the University of Southern California's film school where he began shooting educational films. After graduating from USC in 1969 he became the first Cinematography Fellow at the AFI's Center for Advanced Film Studies. His first feature film was *More American Graffiti*. He went on to photograph *The Black Stallion, Being There, The Right Stuff* and *The Natural*. As a director, his credits include *The Escape Artist, Crusoe* and an episode of the television series "Twin Peaks." In 1979 he was named Best Cinematographer by the Los Angeles Film Critics Association for *The Black Stallion.*

EL: What kind of films did you see as a student at USC?

CD: I saw all the old ones, you know, the Murnau films and the old D.W. Griffith films, but the ones that I really loved were the French New Wave films. Those were the ones that first really impressed me. People like Renoir influenced the New Wave; but at the time it was really the work of Jean-Luc Godard and Truffaut and all those people that influenced me.

EL: When you got to USC, did you know you were going to go into the cinematography program?

CD: No, I went there just interested in film without having any idea what I wanted to do. Because I had worked for a still photographer, I knew how to use a light meter that nobody else knew how to use, and so I started shooting as soon as I got there. Partly because I knew Matt and Walter, I started working with them shooting their movies, and because I did that, other people would say, " Well, why don't you shoot my film?" So I shot a lot of student films, and that's kind of how it happened. I really fell into it, though when I was at USC, I did direct a couple of films. But ultimately cinematography was the area where I had really the biggest impact.

EL: What was the least helpful about the USC program and what was the most helpful?

CD: The least helpful was the formal training and the most helpful was the informal, sort of revolutionary units who would sneak into the place at night, mix films, and use the movieolas from midnight until 5:00 in the morning. In that sense it was a kind of microcosm of what you found on the outside; you never had enough film, or enough time. You were under certain restrictions in terms of the amount of film you could use. This meant finding ways of getting more film, processing it on the outside, sneaking it back into the movies, and doing all the things you would if you were making a feature and didn't have the budget. That underground aspect of it was, I think, the most helpful. At the same time there were people at USC who were really terrific teachers and imparted knowledge in a less academic sort of way. People like Dave Johnson, who would tell you things like, "As a production manager, the only thing I can tell you is not to make excuses." You suddenly realized that that's as important as knowing the details of budgeting. It's probably the most important thing you can know—don't make excuses, just do the job. Cinematography takes a certain talent, and if you take advantage of that and have a guy who enthuses you to the point where you don't care how hard you work or how much time it takes, you'll make it. If you don't have an absolute passion for it, then you really aren't going to do anything. There are plenty of people who are potential brilliant cinematographers or artists but because of their situation or circumstance they are discovered too late or are forced to be something else. If there was a way of analyzing whether one had an eye or not, you could probably go out and find thirty million people in the United States with the same eye that Haskell Wexler has, or Connie Hall, or Vittorio Storaro. But discovering that passion and that desire in themselves, I think, is the biggest problem.

© Carl Studna

EL: As a director, what language do you use (other than technical language) when you're trying to communicate cinematographer to director? Do you use still photographs? Do you make film references?

CD: As a director or as a cameraman you use everything you possibly can. It's even more evident as a director working with actors because different actors need different kinds of input. You just have to keep feeling the actor out until you find the right language that communicates successfully. It may not be in words; it may be a shrug of the shoulder if it gives the kind of emotion that is supposed to be in a scene. It gives the actor something to go on. There's no limitation to what you should use to communicate. Whether it's a drawing, a photograph, a scene from an old movie, or sitting in a restaurant having lunch with someone and noticing the light across the way and saying, "That's what I'm talking about—the light coming in the window like that." Whatever you need to communicate, you utilize.

EL: You once said that in cinematography you try to visually create the kind of emotion the characters are experiencing. How do you do that?

CD: Well, you have to understand the script. There's a really wonderful film that Renoir made about what he calls the Italian method of acting. The actress takes a scene and reads it dry, like reading a catalogue; there is no emotion in it. Renoir sits there and he won't let this girl put any emotion into it for a inordinately long amount of time and then finally he feels that she understands it. The same is true in cinematography. Most movies that are comedies are brightly lit. Look at a Jerry Lewis movie, everything is lit with a 10K over the camera. You can see into all the shadows, you can see everything on the screen. Conceptually, that's what most people think of as comedies, and to some extent it works. But if you look at a film like *Being There*, which is a comedy, it doesn't utilize any of those visual cues at all. There are no visual clues in that movie that it is a comedy. Visually, the art direction is as if it were a film about power and politics; the lighting is as if it were about the great emotions and conflicts between people of power and wealth. The humor is ironic humor that comes from the fact that this man is in a situation that is totally absurd. That is the source of the humor. The humor comes from the contradiction of the visual images; they contradict everything that you know and that your funny bone is telling you. How do you express these things, the emotions of the scene? First of all, you have to understand them, you have to read the script and understand it just the way Renoir makes the actors understand. For example, you say here's a scene: this woman's best friend has just been killed, so she cries, right? Well, not necessarily. If you really think about what people go through, maybe she laughs, maybe she goes through some other emotion. You've got to really find something in the depth of your understanding of your own emotions. Sometimes you play against the emotions, other times you go with it. You have to start with a real understanding of the drama. Otherwise every film would be photographed or acted exactly the same.

EL: Did you have a mentor?

CD: Yeah, Haskell Wexler and Gordon Willis.

EL: Were those working relationships, or did you choose to model your work after them?

CD: I studied Gordon's work on a film. That was helpful; it built my confidence and confirmed that I knew what I was doing. Also, when I saw what he was doing, I realized it really was what I wanted to do.

EL: How has directing changed your perspective?

CD: Now that I mostly direct—though a lot of things I direct I also shoot—I find I really don't like the technical aspect of shooting anymore. I tend to be contemptuous of light meters and labs and everything. I like to look at something, take one light meter reading, and judging from that one meter reading, interpolate everything else. I used to read this and then I'd read that shadow and then I'd read there in the corner. I don't do that anymore. It's probably confidence, but it's also recognizing that the reality is in the creative part of it; it's not the technical side that's important. I worked with Haskell sometimes doing second camera on commercials, and when I did a documentary about passenger trains he let me have all his black-and-white floaters because he said he didn't need them anymore. I was able to use those in the film. One of the reasons I did the training film in black and white was because both Haskell and Gordon told me, "Oh, you guys coming up now, you don't know what it's like to shoot black and white. Black and white's really tough and color's so easy." So I got a grant from the Corporation for Public Broadcasting and shot it all in black and white, and I learned the truth of what they were talking about, but I also *loved* shooting it in black and white; it was great.

EL: What do you learn as a young cinematographer doing commercials and documentaries?

CD: There are several things you learn doing commercials. One important thing was how to work with crews because the kind of films I was doing were educational films. I couldn't get in the union, I could do commercials. I got to work with gaffers and with grips and art directors. From that point of view, it was good training in learning to cooperate, getting along with people, and learning to express your view in terms of light or camera movement or whatever. That was valuable. Because they're so short, they last anywhere from a day to two weeks, you're changing visual concepts all the time, so you get to try lots of different things. In a feature, even though visually the style changes from scene to scene, you're still working within the structure of an overall visual style that's consistent throughout the film.

EL: How about documentaries?

CD: Documentaries are amazing because you really have to think on your feet. Documentaries are like Zen. I would get to a point in shooting documentaries where I would know what somebody was going to do before they did it; I would know when they were going to get up and walk out of the room or take a drink of water. It's really uncanny, but you actually become so attuned to people's body language and the kind of things that they do to telegraph their intentions that you're prepared to pan with them, or tilt with them, or whatever. Documentaries also force you to think in a really economic way—much more so than in a feature. In a feature you block people so that things cut together, but in a documentary, you have to follow what happens, and then after the fact, figure out how you can find the elements to make it cut together. You're thinking backwards in a documentary, which can be really valuable. Lots of times in documentaries I couldn't afford to use real paper, diffusion paper, and I discovered I could buy rolls of wax paper at the store and use those instead, and it cost about 1/50th as much as buying the same thing from Rosco or Lee.

EL: Since the tools of a cinematographer are pretty expensive, is film school one of the few options for training in order to get your hands on the equipment?

CD: Well, there certainly are advantages in film school in that you have the opportunity to use the equipment.

EL: How would you characterize the role of the cinematographer?

CD: Most cinematographers, Haskell and Connie Hall and Bill Fraker, John Bailey, John Hora, consider themselves filmmakers dealing with that particular aspect of filmmaking. Honestly, the best cinematographers really are filmmakers in that they aren't dealing with one small, limited aspect of making the movie. It doesn't mean they intrude on other people's jobs, but the fact that most of the best cinematographers have a true understanding of moviemaking makes them very valuable to a director. As far as what the job is, it really ultimately depends on who the director is and who the cinematographer is. There are directors who like to control every aspect of the film. Carroll Ballard even makes sure you eat the same kind of food he wants to eat on the set. Carroll is one of these total filmmaking madmen. But Carroll and I had a good relationship. We just sort of worked with grunts and groans and never had to communicate on any kind of sophisticated level at all. We really saw eye-to-eye so there was rarely a problem. It really depends on the director, but directors I've worked with have generally given me a lot of freedom. If you're allowed the freedom to choose the project and you choose the wrong film, then you're not going to see eye-to-eye, you're going to be in conflict and you'll be miserable. So you want to make sure that you have enough discussions with the director in advance so that you understand each other and agree about the style, whether it involves total agreement, compromise, or arguing it out. Ultimately the most important thing is the story, and that dictates what gets put on the screen, whether it involves the actors or the camera.

EL: Can you describe your relationship with the art director and production designer?

CD: Again, it varies but they're really the most important relationships, second only to that with the director. It's really important to be in synch because you need to know what the sets and the locations are going to be like. I've always been involved in films early; about the same time as the art director. This doesn't happen anymore. One of the things that has made me lose a lot of interest in cinematography is that they put the art director on and then bring a cameraman in a week or two before the film starts. Then you're stuck with what the art director's created without any consideration for the input of the cinematographer. It doesn't happen on the best films, but it happens more and more now.

EL: Is that a financial consideration?

CD: Of course it's financial.

EL: Haskell spoke about a diminished regard for cinematographers.

CD: I think that's true. It's definitely true.

EL: What's your feeling about young people working in video?

CD: I think it's great. People should work with everything. As with documentaries or commercials, it gives people a lot of opportunity to experiment. Gordon Willis said to me when I was starting, "Shoot as much as you can." I don't think it matters what you shoot. If you've got the talent, you're going to learn from every experience you have. It may be that what you learn is never to work with the same people again, or it may be something very obscure, but you're going to learn something, even if it just tunes in your radar to figure out if people are lying to you or not.

EL: What's the most frustrating thing about the profession of cinematography?

CD: The most frustrating thing is that, ultimately, the director's in charge and there are times of conflict where you aren't going to win the battle.

EL: What's the most exciting thing about the art of cinematography?

CD: The most exciting thing for me is to not know enough technically so I will be surprised in dailies. That means taking chances. It's lighting to extremes of contrast, or underexposing something, or overexposing something or playing around to the extent that you don't quite know what's going to happen. When you get good enough, your mistakes are never going to be terrible, and you get good enough so you have an educated guess as to what is going to be right when you burn out the film five stops or ten stops or whatever it is. The ultimate excitement is having something end up on the screen that is more than what was expected and more than what you think you're capable of. It's having something that's been drawn from inside you and from inside the writer, director, and the actors that somehow in its combination is more remarkable than you could ever imagine. That's the ultimate. The greatest experience of the cinematographer is to suddenly realize the incredible emotional impact within a scene that comes from the actors and the visual images and the music and sound all combined. It rises above anything you ever imagined, and that's what's great. It's to go to a movie, watch it, get involved, and forget you worked on it.

EL: What kind of advice would you give to a young person who wants to enter filmmaking?

CD: You have to have an absolute passion for it and the determination to get truly involved because it's a field in which there's so much competition and so much frustration that if you don't have absolute determination, you're not going to survive. I think that people just know within themselves whether that's what they want to do. I used to read these same things about artists, that they *had* to get something on canvas; I think that's the way you have to be in film as well. Something inside you has to escape that way. Otherwise, I don't think you're going to have what it ultimately takes to live out a life in movies.

Allen Daviau

■■■■■■■■■■■

Allen Daviau is a director of photography who has worked in both film and television. He has received three Academy Award nominations for his work on the Steven Spielberg films *E.T. The Extraterrestrial, The Color Purple,* and *Empire of the Sun,* and recently received his fourth nomination for Barry Levinson's *Avalon.* Other film credits include *The Falcon and the Snowman* and *Harry and the Hendersons.* Mr. Daviau has also worked on the television productions "The Boy Who Drank Too Much" and "Streets of L.A." Most recently, he served as cinematographer on Albert Brooks' *Defending Your Life* and *Bugsy.*

EL: Would you summarize your formal education and indicate how it did or didn't prepare you for what you're doing now?

AD: My formal education, for all practical purposes, ended when I crawled out of high school getting a diploma from a very benevolent principal who could very easily have chosen to flunk me. This was a Jesuit high school, Loyola High School, and the only college that I could be accepted at with the grades that I had was Loyola University. They kindly took me in for one glorious semester where I spent a very, very creative time lighting all the stage productions.

EL: Where did you go?

AD: Well, I went to work. I worked at an audio-visual house in the shipping department; it was a company that was making educational materials. I worked in labs and camera shops. I spent one summer at a dye transfer laboratory. In those three months I learned more about color than I could have ever learned from any book or in any other formal or informal setting. I took a course in color techniques, and it basically encouraged me to get my hands in the chemicals. It was one of my great unfulfilled desires to do a picture in Technicolor so I could use dye transfer in motion, but the process ended before I ever got a chance to do it. I worked in other laboratories, large and small, and decided that there were certain aspects of the work that I liked. I really liked being around people more than machinery and I wound up working in camera stores.

I worked in other areas and did stage lighting, which I think is a very important part of my background. Working in theater is a very rewarding thing. I think the idea of associating light with drama and the use of light in dramatic situations is important. I was bringing a more cinematic approach to stage lighting. I also did a lot of still photography on my own. Those two activities kept me involved in the related processes. At the time there were only two film schools available out here—USC and UCLA. I didn't have the money for USC or the grades for UCLA. Basically, I had to conduct my own courses and continue to gate crash and look for my "in." Around 1965, I'd saved enough money to buy a 16-millimeter camera.

At this time I was doing things for a friend, Ron Jacobs, who had become program director of radio station KHJ here in Los Angeles and who supervised its transition from middle-of-the-road radio to rock and roll. I would go out with a 16-millimeter camera and shoot a couple hundred feet of Kodachrome on the various disc jockey promotions, *Summer of the Big Kahuna*, *Big Kahuna's Luau*, *Boss Jocks at Ontario Speedway*, these kinds of radio station promos. The radio station became so successful that RKO General offered them an hour of television time to produce a music-oriented show. My friend Ron brought a friend of his out from New York named Peter Gardiner; Peter wanted to use a lot of film on this show and needed a cameraman. I showed my work to Peter, and he said, "You're quitting the camera store," and I said, "Thank God." I had to take a $50 a week cut in pay to work on the TV show. The nice thing was having all this knowledge, all this desire and having a 16-millimeter camera. When we started *Boss City*, every week was the same. Monday morning we would have nothing; by Saturday night I would have shot and edited three three-minute pieces to be on the air. We'd be putting something together out of thin air from whatever the hit record of the week was, what personality was in town, what promotion the radio station was running—all of these different things, but it had that wonderful deadline pressure that can't be beat. You can't buy that kind of education. I was shooting, editing, and running all the lab stuff through, getting the pieces on the air, and still managing to get into the camera store to work on Saturday because I had to have a few extra bucks to be able to make it.

EL: You were making hundreds of mini-films then.

AD: We made quite a few, I doubt if we made a hundred, but we made a lot of them. I know that in our peak period (which was probably from the peak of summer '67 to peak of summer '68) we probably made at least a film a week. I had invested in a 16-millimeter camera on the theory that, as in a neighborhood game the kid who has the football gets to be the quarterback; I had the camera and I got to be the cameraman. I remember showing up at places and volunteering my photographic services. A year later this nineteen-year-old guy named Steven Spielberg decided to make his first 35-mm film; he wanted to have a real cameraman do it and he was asking around about available, young, very inexpensive cameramen. We talked and Steven told me, "Well, this film is going to be in 35 mm." I said "Gee, other than one day of special effects footage for Roger Corman's *The Trip* (which, by the way, was my first screen credit) I have really never gotten to use 35-mm equipment and am not truly slick with it. I don't know if I've got the experience." I introduced him to a cameraman who had worked a lot in 35 mm. I volunteered to be B-camera operative, and, thank heavens, that was a smart move. Later Steven called me up to do *Amblin*. It was a very slow period in the business, and the union was not at all interested in letting me in. So after hitting a number of stone walls I said, "Don't worry, Steven. Now that I've got 35-mm film experience, I'm going to get into commercials and I'll get a commercial company to get me in the union. Then I'll be able to shoot for you." That is what I did; but it took eleven years more of all kinds of fighting. I finally decided to get into commercials. That timing was very good because commercials were very interested in quality and in visuals. They shot in 35 mm, they had good crews and there was a whole community of commercial production companies. I was able to show the film I had, get into NABET as a director of photography, and thus work in commercials. While I was trying to get established I worked a lot in documentary for David Wolper. I also worked in industrials and educational films. Those films not only provided me with work, but they also gave me the opportunity to keep shooting things of a dramatic nature. You can get into commercials and shoot wonderful visuals, but if you're not getting any experience on ways to cover a dialogue scene or how to see dramatic progression in something that lasts longer than sixty seconds, you're not learning.

EL: Can you discuss your agent's role in your career development?

AD: I'd gotten an agent, a wonderful guy named Randy Herron. The role of the agent for a cinematographer or designer can be really pivotal. The story goes: "As ye enter so shall ye stay." How you get started and how you're first perceived is extremely crucial. When anybody goes in and sits down with an agent, you have to give the agent something to sell about yourself. An agent isn't going to take anybody from ground zero; an agent must have something to show and something to sell. In the world of feature films particularly, what you say no to is every bit, if not more important as what you say yes to. You want to have your name on something automatically associated with quality or uniqueness; you decide how you want your name to ring when it's said. If you go out and say, "I've just got to work; I'll do anything," then you're being stupid.

EL: How do you communicate with your director?

AD: When I began working on *E.T. The Extraterrestrial*, I spent many evenings up at Steven's house watching movies together. It was one of the best experiences I've ever had in my life. We would look at the work of cinematographers like Vittorio Storaro, Gordon Willis, and Caleb Deschanel. I would look at his films, show him some commercials I had done and we would bounce things off each other. He would ask wonderful questions like, "What is that? Is that a filter, or is it smoke, what do you think is doing that?" We had a chance to get a visual vocabulary going, and by shooting little tests of the E.T. creature, we were able to get this more and more refined. Another real important factor is that Jim Bissell came on the picture as production designer. I worked with Jim closely from the very beginning, and he and I are still great friends to this day. Jim and I had a chance to go out together and explore the neighborhood where Elliot lived. We could see how things would cut together. By the time we were ready to shoot, we had a handle on what we were after. The other relationship that is extremely crucial for a cinematographer is with laboratory people. I said to Steven, "Give me one thing; give me my lab; give me Deluxe." A cinematographer has to have a close association with several laboratories; you have to be known and conversant at several different laboratories. It's a relationship you start early in your career. During the shooting of *E.T.*, every possible day I went to the laboratory first thing in the morning and saw the previous day's rushes and then I would go to the stage or to the location. I always saw the film before Steven. This had a two-fold benefit: 1) the dailies were right for him to see, and 2) I had a very good grasp on what we had just done the day before. I was cutting with a very fine blade in terms of lighting, exposure, the amount of smoke, the amount of diffusion, and everything else used to create the illusion of this creature being alive. Cinematographers who can't communicate with their laboratory people are not going to last long.

EL: Let's talk about period pieces. How and to what extent do you research and find a common vocabulary with your director?

AD: I love period films; I think they're just wonderful. An American cinematographer once said, "Until we really get a time machine, making a period film is the best thing we've got." Looking through that finder and being able to say "I'm looking back in time, and there's nothing that doesn't belong there," is the goal. A good relationship with the production designer is absolutely essential. People ask, "How does the look of the picture come about?" Certain things are just your preferences. I love looking through old magazines; it goes back to my spending all that time with *Life* magazine back in college. I interpret while looking at pictures of the forties because I know what color film they used to shoot those pictures; I know what it meant to take that picture, why they lit it as they did, and what the film was good at doing as well as what it wasn't. There's a certain technological filtering going on that has nothing at all and yet everything in the world to do with aesthetic response. I may remember going over to my neighbor's grandmother's house that had green wallpaper, and you don't see that color of green anymore. What makes something look different? You just remember things from your own life, from a time you lived through. If your research is for a time you didn't live through, you use illustrations, magazines of the period, also paintings and old photographs. You immerse yourself in a lot of material from the time: Sears catalogs, magazines, contemporary movies.

EL: Do you have a visual encyclopedia inside your head?

AD: You just carry so much stuff around. It's really true. A lot of people provide you with inspirations. I may have to imitate the light coming out of a fixture that somebody designed in 1936. A light on screen gives you the excuse to do something wonderful, something scary, or to create any emotion. The sources that you put in help you get a context of reality or naturalism. I like the term "naturalism" more than "realism" because you can bend it more; it gives you a way to get out into a different aspect of clarity.

EL: Do you enjoy portraiture?

AD: Yes. I'm so inspired by the idea of dealing with a great face. Great faces aren't necessarily beautiful faces, although sometimes they are. A great face has eyes that take light; eyes that just reach out, drink the light in, and reflect it back. Actors who come from a background in stage work understand how they are related to the light and how the light is related to the audience and to the lens. It's less a concern of how they look, rather an awareness of the fact that they're putting themselves in a relationship to the light and to the camera. They feel the drama in that. In my days in stage lighting, there were actors who absolutely had a sense of where that light was, and you couldn't keep them out of it if you tried. I feel the same thing in film. What you do as a cinematographer is communicate with your actors. They have to know you're there to aid in their performance. If they think you're getting in the way of their performance or that you're simply there to record their performance, the quality of the relationship will not be the same as if they feel we're all collaborators. It is essential to like actors and respect what they do. If you don't, you won't be able to achieve the same kind of result or accentuate it in the right ways. The look of a film is a combination of design and discovery. Certain things that are designed from the beginning and other things are discovered as you go along. Unfortunately, people writing M.A. and Ph.D dissertations like to think it was all planned from the very beginning, but often it wasn't. Half the time somebody runs in with a substitute for something that was supposed to be there in the first place, or it didn't show up, or they didn't have time to get it. Perhaps you didn't have high-speed film stock so you underexposed the low-speed film stock and, guess what? It came out looking brilliant anyway. You stand there and take the credit for it. People don't understand the chaos of the creative process of making a film. We're trying to do this thing in a short period of time, and we're always fighting the conditions. No matter how much money you have, the light is going to end at a certain hour of the day; the weather is going to change; the actor is going to leave town because his contract's up. You will shoot something, whether it's your original grand design or not in accordance with your plan, but you'll shoot, you'll get something done because it's your job and you're contracted to do that. Within those confines, you do something as creative and wonderful and as designed as you can, but it may not be what you started out to do at all. That's why I burst out laughing at so many learned dissertations on films. I really feel that film critics or anybody who writes a piece of film criticism for an audience of over 2,500 needs to be licensed. In order to be licensed, a film critic should have to stand next to a director when he/she announces a film and then show up everyday for pre-production (particularly negotiations), the entire period of shooting, post-production (editing, dubbing, scrolling, lab, publicity meetings), and everything else, be there the morning the reviews come out, and then go to the theater and see the film a few times with an audience—the real paying audiences. Then they get their license. The miracle is that any film ever gets made at all. If you look at the potential for chaos with all the people, the egos, the logistics, and the creative and technical elements, it's amazing that there ever is a final product.

EL: Shooting must involve both spontaneous creativity and planning.

AD: Yes, and sometimes it's a creative accident, and we all better own up to that. Sometimes you have to admit, "It was really a mistake, but you know, it's not bad."

EL: What advice would you give to a young person considering cinematography as a profession?

AD: Be interested in a lot of things. Obviously you're already interested in film; you do all the things that people with madness about film do. You see a lot of movies; you see the movies you really love over and over; you talk about films, you study all the works of the people that interest you. If there are cinematographers whose works are particularly interesting, discover what it is that captivates you about their work. I really believe that film schools are of the greatest value because they bring film students together. With the guidance and inspiration of good instructors and with your own passion, you can be successful. You're going to need that passion. Remember this business is set up to discourage you, make you give up and go away. It's geared to make you say, "I can't do this. Oh gosh, I'll never get in here." You need the passion that can only be maintained by being with people who are as enthusiastic as you are. Study a lot of things that don't seem to be directly related to film. Anybody interested in being a cinematographer should be forced to take a course in architecture and the history of architecture. Any and every art form is worthy of your time and attention. You've heard about cinematographers going to museums to look at paintings and look at sculptures in certain kinds of light; all this is true. Listen to music, go to the theater; all the art forms in the world are about people expressing themselves through some medium. Understand there are going to be many more new technologies. If you're not studying electronics, or if you're not learning a lot about video right now, you're going to be in real trouble because video goes hand-in-hand with film. People will be shooting film at the front end a lot longer than people anticipate, but they in turn will be interfacing with video technology. Digital video will come to mean a completely different thing than it does now. Learn about electronic distribution, a far more sophisticated system than we know now. We're also going to be involved in delivering and processing a lot of information in the next century. If you prepare yourself by understanding, not just the technologies but the philosophy of choice, you're going to have a tremendous advantage over people working today. The other important thing is how you work with people, how you are able to establish working relationships. You may have to walk onto a set completely composed of strangers before you have a really established reputation. It will be up to you to convince those people that you're an asset, that they want to be on your side, and that you're on theirs. That's something that only can come from your sincere enthusiasm about what you do and your faith in yourself. A director of photography really spends a third of the time being director of photography and the rest of it in communication, tact, diplomacy, honing the ability to respond to less-than-ideal circumstances, and pulling something out of the situation while maintaining creative integrity. It's not easy. As we say in the business, "If it was easy, they would have hired a relative." You're going to be tested early to see how well you can produce under circumstances that are less than ideal, because, I promise you, the first chance you get to do something will probably not be your dream assignment. You have to take it on as though it were your dream assignment, and you've got to know how to respond to your own failures and not let them drown you. The ability to make decisions is the other key quality. You have to be able to juggle a number of possibilities and pick one—you cannot be indecisive. You may regret your choice, but you've got to pick one and do something with it. You develop confidence through experience. Finally, the way you evaluate your own first performances will help you to prove how well you communicate, how well you make decisions, and how well you seek to achieve your aesthetic dream.

FIVE
······

★ The Production Designer

The production designer is responsible for the overall "look" and design of the film. Working closely with the director and integrating the ideas of the cinematographer and the costume designer, the production designer must translate the director's vision into a reality into which the film can be set. Because this task can be monumental in scope, the production designer often has a large staff and budget and therefore has direct responsibilities to the producer as well. The production designer is one of the first on the creative team to begin work. He/she and the design team create drawings, models, and plans for the director that are ultimately translated into sets and locations under his/her direct supervision.

Union minimum for art directors (also referred to as production designers) is $1,826.48 for five days' work. In Los Angeles, the art directors' union is Local #876 (818-762-9995). Membership is permitted if one has worked for a minimum of thirty days for a union company. The union has approximately 420 members.

Jim Bissell

■■■■■■■■■■

James Dougal Bissell, III was born in Charleston, South Carolina. He earned a BFA in Theatre at the University of North Carolina in 1973. From 1976 to 1981 he served as art director on various television movies, making the transition to feature film and production design with Steven Spielberg's *E.T. The Extra Terrestrial* in 1981. Since that time, he has served as production designer for such films as *Twilight Zone—the Movie, The Falcon and the Snowman, Harry and the Hendersons, Someone to Watch Over Me, Twins,* and *The Rocketeer.* He has also held the positions of second unit director (*The Boy Who Could Fly*), production manager (*Kentucky Fried Movie*), and art director (*The Last Starfighter*). In 1982 the British Academy of Film Arts nominated him for a Production Design award, and the Academy of Television Arts and Sciences presented him with an Emmy Award in 1980.

EL: You went to the University of North Carolina at Chapel Hill, right? Can you just briefly summarize your education there as it pertains to what you do now?

JB: Yes, I worked on a Fine Arts degree in Theater. It was the best introduction to the art of theater that I could have had. It was an intense four-year program with acting as its core. Theatrical experience is a lot different from architectural, which is another route to production design. I think theater, or people with a theatrical background, tend to approach the problems of production design with more of an ensemble approach. Consider, for example, the needs of actors, lighting, and theatrical effect above the structural reality of buildings. Also, your instincts usually revolve around dramatic imagery and the number of different ways a set can function and evoke images that resonate with dramatic truth. If the script says, "They meet and have a cup of coffee in the living room . . ." it's not as simple as just going off to a fashion magazine and seeing what kind of interesting living rooms you can create. Instead, you look at the kind of imagery you want to evoke, how you create the image, and how you give those images a good geographical excuse.

EL: Can you contrast the work that the production designer would do in theater with film or television? What's the biggest difference for you?

JB: Television is like doing stock theater, you're basically hammering out stuff. It's very good experience because it teaches you that, no matter how large the project, you're never going to have enough time, and you're never going to have enough money. Television teaches you to prioritize, to determine which visual elements you are going to develop and which you are going to ignore. It also forces you to paint with very broad strokes. It is great, except that I wouldn't recommend doing it exclusively. You lose your sense for nuance and subtlety. If commercial television is a popular entertainment comparable to popular musical forms, then theatrical features could be comparable to symphonic forms. Time and resources allow you more of an opportunity to exploit color, texture, volume, and form to a far greater degree. Also, the fact that a theatrical feature is a continuous event allows you to build contrast and create rich harmonies between images as well as design subtle visual transitions. Television is far too fragmented for that.

EL: When you sit down with your director, who goes first? Who gets to say, "This is what I see," and then once you both put it on the table, what's the language with which you can translate those images in your head for the director?

JB: It doesn't matter who goes first, as long as the process begins immediately. It's great for me to begin by listening. That way I can be more sensitive to the director's preliminary thoughts and intentions. Then when things start happening in my imagination, hopefully my point of departure will be closely aligned with his. As the process continues we grope for common metaphors—art, music, sports—sketch a lot, look at

photos and continue exploring in whatever way possible the problem of "What is the scene all about?" And my job is to continue to explore that question visually and offer the results of that exploration to the director right up until the time that the scene is shot.

EL: Can you describe your creative team?

JB: My art director is a key element in the way that the department is structured. Sometimes the size of the show will necessitate having more than one, but I prefer just one. As I wrestle with a multitude of amorphous forms that are trying to congeal into an overall vision of the film, he helps to solve all the problems that arise as a result of schedule, budget, or engineering constraints. He's right there with me understanding my intent and helping me to discover methods of executing all this stuff. He directly supervises the set designers and makes sure that the flow of information regarding the visual elements of the film goes unclogged to all the right people. He works closely with me in evolving the design schedule (when designs have to be turned out and put into the hands of construction), the construction schedules, and the set dressing and rigging schedules. All, of course, are coordinated to meet the requirements of the shooting schedule. He's there monitoring the progress on an hourly basis where I may have to go out on a two-day location survey, or be in a creative meeting with the director until all hours of the night. I can't emphasize how important he or she is to me. In my case it turns out to be a fellow I've worked with for five years. Often, he will have an assistant art director working with him. Nearly as crucial to the film are the set decorator and construction coordinator. The set decorator has to round up all the furnishings, draperies, carpets and props for the sets. Obviously, this is someone whose taste I have to trust. By being extremely sensitive to the nature of a set, he or she can breathe life into it by detailing with the eye of a still-life master. The construction coordinator can make or break both the construction schedule as well as the budget and can affect the look of the set by the team he assembles as well as by his mastery at coordinating the efforts of carpenters, plasterers, painters, etc., who are all trying to function at once in the same space. Set designers and model builders are also integral members of the creative team. In the course of preparing drawings for construction personnel, they can enhance the design by suggesting appropriate detail and finishes as well as assisting in working out the more complicated problems of wielding pieces of the set for camera and lighting. Models are invaluable as visualization tools for directors, producers, cinematographers, and construction people alike. During pre-production we may also have one or more illustrators.

These artists help give focus to the visualization of the film by story-boarding complicated sequences as well as set illustrations. Last but not least, I have an art department coordinator. This is the person who functions as a research assistant, librarian, cataloguer of the vast amount of material that we wind up generating, and expert tracker, who can find any one of us in the department no matter how desperately we are trying to hide.

EL: Have things changed within the industry of filmmaking? Are you more involved in the post-production process?

JB: The pendulum swing now is to bring production designers in earlier because post-production effects work is so expensive. Visualization progress in pre-production helps you pick the images that you'll need to do post-production effects more effectively and efficiently. There's always the hazard of having visual effects be an afterthought. That's dangerous to the budget and to the visual integrity of the film. Having a designer on earlier helps the director and the producing team effectively determine the best use in camera effects and post-production effects.

EL: Do you think that production designers tend to get characterized and categorized by the films that they've made? Is it difficult to break out of a genre?

JB: Oh, yes there's no question about that. That is that very, very unnerving marriage of art and commerce. Production designers can be responsible for tremendous amounts of money. Essentially producers or producing studios are businessmen and nothing reassures a businessman more about committing a lot of his money to the hands of a strange person—which most production designers are—than to be able to see what they've done before. It's just like typecasting. There's nothing wrong with it. Many people can make a great career out of being a wonderful futurist and concentrating on that kind of design. There's a lot of fantasy designers that would prefer to be just that—they like being typecast, they like doing shows like that. I don't, but the only way to make sure that I don't get typecast is to make sure that I have a diverse design portfolio; some of the films I've done are period films, some are very elegant, and some are fantasy. Fortunately, I have a really good range of work, so I don't feel like I could get typecast at this point unless I wanted to go out and exploit one aspect.

EL: What's the most frustrating part of your profession?

JB: It just changes constantly. The most frustrating part actually is the schedule, the amount of work that has to be done in a very short amount of time. That turns the whole production process into an emotional form of madness because you become so unbalanced. You don't have time for children. It becomes very difficult.

EL: Is there any way in which you can combat that other than great preparation?

JB: I don't know, I'm working on it. Now I tend to really draw the line at a ten-hour day. In the past if I had tickets to go to the opera and I was in a creative meeting with the director, I would just skip it and keep on going with the meeting. Now I can just say, "I have somewhere else to go, I'll see you later." There are times when you just can't do that, when it will really affect the work, affect what gets out in front of the camera—then it takes its toll. It also takes its toll mentally. I still haven't learned how to deal with the many images floating through your brain that you can't purge yourself of. There are going to be sleepless nights when images pop and dance around in your head that you can't sort out and give them a place to tuck them away for the night.

EL: Did you have a mentor? Or were there people whose work you admired and inspired you as a young man?

JB: It wasn't so much their work as it was how to deal with the industry. I love being around people who seem to have an angle, an emotional angle on how to deal with the chaos of making a motion picture. In terms of emotional mentors, music is where I really found much of my inspiration. I would say probably my greatest mentor musically would be Mahler. The work is very cinematic in that there's so much going on at the same time; there's that wonderful and constant and relentless juxtaposition of images, profound with profane, and that's what I meet on a daily basis here. Just listening to his music helps me put it in perspective and also helps me in looking for richness in everything, how to keep looking for a unique approach or a unique angle on something. That leads me on to another problem I have, which is looking to films for inspiration about making films. To me that's not healthy. It's far healthier to find inspiration from reality if you can find it. Otherwise you start making films about films.

EL: How much of your job is instinctual and how much is cerebral, or has it shifted as you've gotten older?

JB: Yes, it shifts every minute. For instance, the production manager just called and wanted to know how much money I had left in the picture's visual account and how much more I was going to spend. There's one way that I set myself up to relate to a department and another way in which I relate to the other members of the production team, especially the fiscal people like the production manager and the line producer. I place a great deal of emphasis on being a responsible designer. Eventually what I always try to do is to make sure everyone understands what I think it's going to take and that I'll be responsible to do it that way. That keeps a lot of people off my back. That also is a lot of work; that's why I have to have a computer. I monitor cost reports very carefully, I put it against my visual priorities, what I hope to be able to do with the set and accomplish with the set, how much personnel we're going to need to make sure that it's executed properly, and that sort of thing. So that's very cerebral, and that never stops; you can't do that instinctually. In the beginning you can; you can instinctually say you have a one-hour conversation with the director and a one-hour conversation with the producer and you know whether they're on the same track or not. The actual monitoring, guiding this whole thing, is very cerebral. On the other hand the design process is far more visceral and gets more so as I get older which makes it fun, more interesting.

EL: Thinking back on all that you've said so far, what are the characteristics that a production designer needs; it sounds like they need to be an accountant and an artist and counselor . . .

JB: Everybody does it differently; this is one of the fun things about doing the seminars for AFI. I only worked with one production designer, and I'm completely different than he is. I'm fascinated to see how other guys do it. I'm absolutely fascinated. In the seminars, I usually try to have other production designers come in as individuals and say, "I want to talk about this film." They discuss what happened when they first got the script, how they first broke it down, what their reactions were, how they evolved their relationships with the director and what the problems were during production. I'm fascinated with the process. Everybody does it differently. I doubt that there is any common denominator except that you have to put together a system for delivering intricate imagery to producers and directors and appease both the creative and the fiscal sides. How you get that experience, how you instill confidence in a producer and a director is half the game; that's Hollywood.

EL: Do you work as much with the producer as you do with the director?

JB: It depends on the show. Most of the time I'll work very closely with both. I'll probably see the producer more because so many of the physical aspects of the director's vision come down through me via the producer. In other words, if I'm talking to him and I understand what he wants then I will be his liaison to the grips and the gaffers and the guys who build the models of the sets. We'll show all those guys what the shot is and what they should be prepared for. He'll want me to be there to make sure that everyone is prepared for what the director expects.

EL: What kind of advice would you give to a young person who was considering a career as a production designer in terms of their education and opportunities that they might initially pursue?

JB: I'm a great believer in a liberal arts education. Learn as much as you can about art; if you draw a lot and find expression through drawing and painting, fine. If you don't, it doesn't matter. Find expression through model building, and I mean real model building, not plastic kits. Explore your mind and the world around you. The rest is technique. Accounting is a technique; it doesn't take that long to learn it. If you have a good liberal arts background, you can do it. If you have traveled around the world and you know how to put the logistics of travel together you can probably put the logistics of an art department together. Experience is very important.

EL: How important is film school?

JB: I would say of no importance. That's my limited perspective. I work also on the production side; I'm not the director.

Richard Sylbert

....

Born in 1928 in Brooklyn, New York, Richard Sylbert attended the Tyler School of Fine Arts at Temple University to study painting. After some early work on television and on Broadway, he moved into motion pictures in the mid-fifties, where he worked mostly on black and white films for the next ten years. He won the Academy Award as Art Director for *Who's Afraid of Virginia Woolf?*, and has garnered three Academy Award nominations for his work on *Chinatown*, *Shampoo*, and *Reds*. Mr. Sylbert's credits also include *The Graduate*, *The Cotton Club*, *Tequila Sunrise*, and *Dick Tracy*, the latter of which earned him a 1990 Academy Award for Best Art Direction. Most recently, he designed the film *Mobsters*. Mr. Sylbert has also served as production chief for Paramount Pictures and has worked as an independent producer.

EL: How do you define production design?

RS: Production design is a title that has no definition. I got my definition for production design by making all the necessary changes in what director William Cameron Menzies had done. What Menzies had done was quite simple—storyboards and big sketches. He would do big sketches and then put them on glass. When I started, the idea of doing storyboards was a joke. It was a joke because I started working with directors like (Elia) Kazan, (Sidney) Lumet, and (Martin) Ritt, and nobody cared about storyboards; they cared about drama. They came from backgrounds in theater and early television. I translated Menzies' idea of production design (in his case, storyboards) as a way of structuring a movie, but I did it with visual ideas that connected. You can't write a book without structuring it, you can't write music without structuring it, you can't write a play without structuring it—why should you

© 1991 Universal City Studios, Inc./Bruce McBroom

be able to design a movie without structuring it? It's slightly different in one sense. Although a playwright, director, and actors in a theater are doing a structured proposition, the movies have so many people involved, the main ones being cinematographers, directors, costume designers, production designers, and editors. I believe that the phrase "production design" does not mean, "I'll do this set and then we'll shoot here because it looks great," and "This looks pretty, why don't we shoot over here?" I've always understood production design to mean that you can structure a movie visually before you shoot it.

EL: How did you get to Hollywood?

RS: I went to Hollywood under the best possible conditions. Charles K. Feldman brought me to Hollywood. My first Hollywood picture was *Walk on the Wild Side* directed by Eddie Dimytryk. I learned a lot of things about Hollywood. So I went back to New York and did *The Pawnbroker* with Sidney just so I could feel better. I returned to Hollywood to do *Manchurian Candidate,* my second Hollywood movie. In 1963 *The Pawnbroker* was the last film that I designed entirely in New York. I had accomplished what I wanted to accomplish—incorporating realism. I knew all that other stuff. I could file it away any time I needed it. From then on, for a very long time, I went to Europe. I came back to Hollywood and went to Europe, came back to Hollywood and went to Europe.

EL: What kind of director do you like to work with?

RS: Directors who are directing the emotional dynamic of the narrative. That's what's important to them whether they fail or they get it right. The whole focus is on the emotional dynamic of the narrative. In order to translate that into images you have to have control. If you think about movies, they're much more related to music than they are to paintings. They begin here and they go to there. In between you're trying to dramatize. To dramatize you must have structure which means form. You give it form the same way a musician gives anything form. He has a choice of themes, variations on themes, repetitions, patterns, architectural space. Frozen music is architecture, so melted architecture is movies. So you structure the film. When you look at a picture like *Chinatown* you can see it. It has a tone all its own. It doesn't look like *Shampoo*. It doesn't look like anything else. That's what I'm interested in doing. I try to translate a sense of wholeness—make everything relate. A movie is in time. Not in real time, like music, but it's in time. It goes from here to there. A novel and a play do the same thing. It could be thirty years for all you know, but it only takes a few seconds. Yet it does move. As soon as you say to yourself, "Oh, yeah, I get it," you begin to think more about music than you do about paintings. Paintings are not helpful unless you're running a boutique. They can give you a tone, but they can't give you a movie. They can't give you a series of connected sequences that mean anything to anybody.

With designing, you get another painter every time you make a picture, and that's you. Because every movie is a different problem emotionally. Music has in it things that are very important, and it has structure, it is a series of ideas. Music has a theme, it has patterns, repetition is used, like in the sonata form that Mozart invented. In the

18th century it was structured like this: "A" was home or the home idea; "B" you went away (and) then you came back to "A"; "C" (you) went away again, developed something, and came back; and "D," then you come back again to "A." If you couldn't get back to "A" you made a coda, which was the summing up of these other little musical ideas, and you put it all together. That's the way Mozart structured music. Before that, in the Baroque period, it was very simple. It was A-B-A, but you went back home. "A" was always home.

Now, home and getting back home are very serious ideas in American sensibilities. They have always been, and you'll see it everywhere you look. It goes further back than American, but in America it's especially strong. Homer's *Ulysses* is a story about getting back home. So is *Moby Dick*. There is something satisfying about getting back home, which is the way musicians always thought about it. It satisfies the mind, it closes the circle.

EL: How do you use the screenplay as a platform for design?

RS: In playwriting, novel writing, and in all dramatic literature, the trick is to immediately unbalance things. The trick is to unbalance it right away. The fun is to set something up right away that looks stable and then knock it over, but you know the story so you know what's going to happen. The audience doesn't realize that what they're watching suggests that everything is going to be fine and then the next scene is a total madhouse. The movie *Reds* is very simple—it was a four-part tone poem where the rules were very clear and simple. Anytime you're in America, the people look large and they stay in small rooms with low ceilings; every time they're in Russia, the rooms are huge and they look small. It suggests the idea of innocence abroad.

EL: Describe how you reflect the structure of the narrative.

RS: The framework of the building is what structure is, which comes before the windows, or the plot. Boy meets girl, boy loses girl, boy finds girl is why, how, when, and where these events took place. How did he lose? That's all the plot really means. You've managed to make a series of events that give you the structure that you already have.

They make the basic action into flesh and bone. It's like a house before windows are added and the windows are the plot.

You can do the same thing when you're designing. You can say to yourself, "O.K., let's begin with the problem," which is always the script. You make up rules, just like musician's rules. That's how you structure. You say to yourself, "O.K. *Chinatown* is about a drought. So all the colors in this picture are going to be related to the idea of a drought, and the only time you're going to see green is when somebody has water for the grass. It's not about a drought alone; it's about a drought in 1938 in southern California." You say to yourself, "Okay, all the buildings in this picture will be Spanish except one. It will be generic to the area, but it won't be Spanish. And they'll all be white because the heat bounces off them. Not only will they all be white but they'll be above the eye level of the private eye." "Above the eye level" means, for the private eye that he has to walk uphill, like the old expression, "Man, is this really uphill?"

Then you decide what the colors are going to be, why they're going to be that way, and what the range will be. Let's say from burnt grass (which is a terrific color) to white (which you know you're already going to deal with) to umber. Umber is an interesting color because it's the color of a shadow, and in a movie like *Chinatown*, the more shadowy, the better. Then you're going to repeat certain images in the film, like the predominance of Spanish buildings. Although they're not the same style, it's definitely repetition. It's just like a keyboard on a piano, it's just there for you to use. Symmetry is important in architecture, as it is in all art forms. It means that everything is balanced and stable, therefore everything is O.K.

EL: How big is your crew now?

RS: Right now? At one point I can have as many as three hundred people. I had four hundred people on *Dick Tracy*. I've got about seventy-five people now. We're just beginning the next picture. There are two groups of carpenters. I have about forty carpenters, twenty in the studio and another twenty out in another location. I have only five painters now. They're just beginning.

EL: What do you still do yourself?

RS: When I do a picture I design the sets myself and do all the research. If there are conceptual sketches to do, I do them. You need to be a good technician. I draw all the sets and turn them over to the draftsman because they all belong to this idea. You don't tell people this idea, you just give them the drawing and say "Make it nice." Tell them where the doors and windows are, why there are narrow passages, why people walk into a corner, why there's nothing outside a window or something outside the window is all part of the game. Why each exterior belongs to the last one in some way, why there's an echo, why you take a set like the Department of Water and Power in *Chinatown* and suggest a police station as effectively as possible by making the colors very similar. A writer, a director, and a designer all should be structuring the movie, that's the important difference. I'm not talking about rent-a-palace movies, for which there's nothing you can do but rent the palace and everybody thinks it's wonderful, but it's not. If I thought all there was to production designing was renting palaces or going to some apartment and changing the cushions, I never would have done it.

EL: What advice would you give to a person who wanted to pursue production design?

RS: This is a complicated answer. There are two schools of thinking. There's mine and then there is theirs. Mine is based on a very simple observation. The more you know, the more you're going to be able to do. The more you know technically, the more you're going to be able to accomplish and for less money and sooner. The more you technically know, the more you can do yourself. You're more likely to get the picture you want because you're not at anybody's mercy. The other school is composed of what I call the "hummers." There are more of them than you think. Some of them have been very lucky. If you could, imagine Mozart, just to pick an example, saying to somebody, "Listen, I've got this idea, but I don't know how to play the piano. You play the piano, I'll hum." There are people walking around out there with clipboards humming and getting through movies. Many of the movies are "rent-a-palace" pictures, you know, "rent-a-country" or "rent-a-tent." Many of them are real estate. They're not production design. But who is to say what it is? Who is to say—they've had careers. You can always tell when there's a set in their movies because it's obvious. It's why Paul Newman and Warren Beatty and Robert Redford direct. Acting isn't enough. Real estate isn't enough, either. Decorating is not what it's about. It doesn't mean there isn't a place for everything. There is. The best thing to do if you're doing *The Last Emperor* in China is to go to the palace in Peking. It's not interesting, but it's the right place to be. It's going to take perseverance. It's not the way it was when I was a kid. When I came out of the Army there wasn't a line for every job opportunity. It's been untrue for a very long time. Next to guitar-playing in England, being in the movie business is what every kid who comes out of college wants to do. Everybody wants to be in the movie business. Designing is starting to come into its own, as you know. The best thing you can do is learn to talk to a director. The best thing you can tell a director is that it's going to be all right. That, in a nutshell, is really what it's all about.

EL: And be able to deliver the goods.

RS: You'd better be able to deliver the goods. The more technically capable you are the surer you're going to be able to do that. A lot of people get in trouble saying one thing and delivering something else. You must make them understand that you're a better designer than they are. Eventually if you're really very good you help them so much that they never forget. There's nobody who has ever done a picture with me that wouldn't want to do another one. It's my choice. Perhaps my theory is something not worth doing is certainly not worth doing well. That's my family motto.

Patrizia Von Brandenstein

Patrizia von Brandenstein grew up in Arizona and spent her school years in Paris and Germany when her father, an Army officer, was transferred. Following marriage and a short time in Alaska, she moved to San Francisco, where she began working at the American Conservatory Theatre. Her first major movie assignment as a costume designer was *Saturday Night Fever*, for which she gained wide recognition for the white suit she designed for John Travolta. She got her first break as a production designer on the film *Breaking Away*. Her husband, Stuart Wurtzel, introduced her to Milos Forman, who hired her first as the art director on *Ragtime* and later as the production designer for *Amadeus*. She has since designed such films as *Working Girl*, *Postcards from the Edge*, and *Billy Bathgate*.

EL: How do you choose and execute your projects?

PVB: Every project is different; everything is different. One may be a small film; another film is a big period play with fifty-three sets and four different locations, two in North Carolina, another in Saratoga with a huge sequence involving hundreds of extras, and then the last here in New York City in a big street. It's a sizeable undertaking, so you need lots of people to organize. My colleague and I will come to some sort of primary idea about different things, but other folks will take those ideas and put them on paper in relationship to the places themselves, because after all, in films on locations you have to fit this stuff into a certain space. That space has to be surveyed; notes have to be taken about all the air conditioners, all the bedroom windows, and all the fire escapes; it goes on forever. Those spatial ideas wind up on paper, and then we take it to the director and start working to find out what he needs. Sometimes this is very direct, very simple, but at other times it needs a lot of moaning to get it done. Finally, it will come back to me for the selection of patterns, finishes, and colors, and I will then deal directly with my scenic artist. I get stuff like fabric swatches each day. Colors or finishes of some sort come to me and we look at them for the director and choose what they should be. The shop is two blocks away. By the time the film comes about, all the colors of this elaborate color wheel will be used.

EL: Where do your ideas come from?

PVB: Sometimes it's simple. Maybe a research assistant has found a greeting card picturing a candy store. She brings this in, so I take the idea with all of its labels, cans, and boxes, and so forth. All of that stuff eventually will be reproduced with the magic of color xerox and will wind up in the film, bit by bit. Imagine a huge mosaic or some kind of game like pick-up sticks, where each piece is put together. We round up all these books and all these photographs, xeroxes, and pieces of this and that that are impressions of an idea that we have about this film. This can be so subtle, so obscure. But there can be something about a certain photograph, a certain painting, or a quality of light that is very right for what we're trying to do. The whole is constructed so that each little stick is a bit of film, and you build it up until you make a world, and then the world is photographed. When I work with the cinematographer we discuss the colors of light, the directions of light, and whether the light is filtered or whether it's warm, cool, or whatever.

EL: Do you work with the same people over and over?

PVB: I have a tendency to do that. I tend to get long projects, so it just works out that way as you spend so much time with people. Of course, people do move up and move on. I'm pleased when someone who has worked with me goes on and makes something great. I still keep in touch with them. I have a very, very good team; they are wonderful. Everybody on my current team has done work on their own. The film we're working on is so special they just want to do it. They've all been art directors on their own. I am fortunate that they will come and work with me.

EL: Is your job solely design or do you have to be a bit of a businesswoman?

PVB: I wish it weren't true, but I have to be a lot of a businesswoman.

EL: Can you describe why?

PVB: It's the economics of the business. The art director absorbs an enormous amount of that pressure because his task is to seek and properly schedule so that things can be achieved with the time and resources we have. My colleague happens to have enormous talent for budgeting and estimating; he's good. That is, in fact, his job. He expedites all this work in an hour. He pushes me to get stuff done. After a while a movie takes on a life of its own, it's like a locomotive. Once it starts, you just get on and ride; there is simply no getting ahead of it. You can't step off because you've just got to get there in time.

EL: What proportion of your creative decision is made in pre-production and how much as you go day-to-day?

PVB: At the beginning we work on conceptual stuff. I do that right away, actually. I see things such as patterns when I read the scripts; there is a pattern that merges visual images. You choose elements out of that; you just let yourself go, and you see these elements and start putting them together. Sometimes it's a particular photograph or something that hits you. Other times it's not so obvious; you need to dig. It is important in the beginning not to make up your mind too quickly and not to close off—try to be free and it usually comes. On this particular film the source is not so much photography, but rather the films of the thirties. The people in our film have their images defined by movies. The escapism, even the gangsters in the film have their idea of how a gangster should act.

EL: You must have an encyclopedic mind to store all these details.

PVB: Some people would call it trivia, I don't know. I think the most important qualities that you could possibly have for this work are a curiosity—a kind of memory for the curious—and observatory powers—the ability to see and remember things. The mind is like a bank; put in, take out, but be very careful what you put in. So I don't put in things that are ugly. I see things selectively; I remember things and I bring them out ten years later, twenty years later, fifty years later. It's not so different from what a painter does. It's a way of life. You take what is inside you and express it.

EL: What advice would you give to young people who want to pursue this career?

PVB: Be careful what you store in your head. I think the best people come from a developed background. They are people who have observed carefully and have original ideas. It doesn't matter if you know exactly what the color or shape was; it doesn't matter if you know precisely what the width of the fabric was. All of that is not important. What really matters is how you take the physical elements of times and places, those imaginary worlds and organize all the details into the reality of the story, into the film that you are making. You're expressing something, and the "holy triumvirate," the director and the cinematographer and you, can draw on those things—can use those skills that you have developed. In practical terms, the very best thing is to attain knowledge, know something of social life, the social intercourse, the relationships of families—what exactly was served at that pancake breakfast. Be observant and experience life but not in a superficial or trivial way. Try to understand things, the relationships between people, the qualities of lives, etc. An appreciation of the arts is never a bad place to start. A mastery of some kind of physical skill—painting, drawing, the understanding of colors—is very helpful. The creation of clothing is another place from which to start. There's room enough for lots of different skills, but coming from only one place with one skill is not enough. It's a craft that encompasses a very wide spectrum. Do you like to read? Can you appreciate qualities of poetry, music, and the fine arts? Write, paint, draw, express yourself in whatever ways God gave you.

SIX

- - - - -

⬛ The Costume Designer

Working with the director, cinematographer, and the production designer, the costume designer outfits all actors—from lead characters to extras. Costumes can be the result of original designs or can be purchased or rented. Costumes are often subtle reflections of film's characters and, as such, are a critical element to the thoughtful execution of the concept of any movie. The costume designer begins work early in the pre-production phase and is usually on the set every day in order to check costumes and deal with any last-minute changes. The size and composition of his/her creative team depends on the number and type of costumes that need to be built.

According to the union IATSE Local #892 (818-905-1557), hourly salaries for costume designers depend on such factors as the union to which the designer belongs, the day of the job, etc. On occasion, an assistant may make $1,031.31 per week. General salary for a costume designer is $1,300.82. In order to be eligible for membership in the union, one must have at least one credit as a costume designer in a film, television program, or stage program. Portfolios must be submitted, and costume designers must submit a complete project within their portfolios. Letters of recommendation are also required. Initiation fees for a costume designer are $4,040.00.

Jeffrey Kurland

■ ■ ■ ■ ■ ■ ■ ■ ■ ■ ■ ■ ■ ■ ■

A graduate of Northwestern University, Jeffrey Kurland has been a work-ing costume designer in New York City since 1975. In 1978 he was assistant to costume designer Patricia Zipprodt for the musical *King of Hearts*. He then became costume assistant to Santo Loquasto for musi-cals, several ballets, and a string of feature films, including *The Fan, So Fine, A Midsummer Night's Sex Comedy*, and *Zelig*, on which he served as Associate Costume Designer. After *Zelig*, Mr. Kurland designed the costumes for Woody Allen's *Broadway Danny Rose*, and has continued to design the costumes for Mr. Allen's films ever since, including *The Purple Rose of Cairo, Hannah and Her Sisters, Radio Days*, for which he won the British Academy Award, *Crimes and Misdemeanors*, and *Alice*. In addition to his work with Woody Allen, Mr. Kurland has designed the costumes for *Streets of Gold, Quick Change*, and the upcoming films *Shadow and Fog* and *This Is My Life*.

EL: How did you get interested in film?

JK: I've always been interested in film simply because I love going to the movies. Even when designing for the theater I was looking at old films and seeing what those designers did. But I always thought of myself as a theater designer. It wasn't until I did my first film as an assistant that I fell in love with the way you make a film.

EL: What are the advantages of working in film over theater or vice versa?

JK: I don't think there are advantages. I think it's a matter of where your heart lies—what you love to do the most. I think a designer is a designer; a costume designer is a costume designer. Technically, it's different working on film as compared to theater because you just have to learn different things. Every day is the opening night of a film. A part has to be there that morning and shot that day, and at the end of the day that part is over and you go on to the next thing. You don't get that in the theater. There is a series of dress rehearsals there at which you can decide, "Well, I can change that tomorrow." In film immediacy is far more important. But a good designer is a good designer; you still have to study a character, understand what that character is all about, and create visually through costumes what and who that character is. Basically, it's the same process. You alter the way you do it and the way you present it. Then you follow through according to the medium that you're dealing with.

EL: Could you describe the process from the time you come on? What is the hardest part or the most time-intensive period? How long are you generally on a film?

JK: Usually you get pre-production time on a film, dependent on the film—if it's a period film or a contemporary film, or if it has six people in it or four thousand people in it. All this determines the pre-production time. Usually the set designer is one of the first people brought in as is, of course, the cinematographer. It takes longer to deal with sets than with the costumes. But, yes, I'm there pretty early on because of the construction process.

EL: Then you stay on for the entire term of the production?

JK: Yes, I'm on for the whole term of the production. Certain people come in and have a cut-off date, other people are on through the entire thing. It depends how you set it up with your director and your producer.

EL: If you make your choices fairly early, what's the nature of your day-to-day work?

JK: You can't make all your choices early. Things get changed; people are added; people are subtracted; ideas come up in the middle. A movie is generally not cast within two weeks and you have everybody there. Sometimes you're working with cast members who start two days before they shoot. You can spend hours and hours fitting people and creating costumes in the fitting room at your place of work, but what happens in front of the lens is what's important. If you're not on set to see what's going on in front of that camera, you're not going to achieve the look you want.

EL: Can you describe your relationship with the director? With the production designer? What vocabulary do you use to talk with your director? Do you show him sketches or photos?

JK: I do everything. I use every single way I possibly can to bring them close to what I want to show them. I will bring in research books; I will bring in photos; I will describe things; I will do sketches. Basically, we talk about the characters. I deal with the characters in the film from the principal, to the star, to the extra in the 96th row in the back of my auditorium. I try to get from the director first the feeling to be conveyed to an audience. What is the emotion of the film? How do they want to do it? Do they want it to be a warm film? Do they want it be a cool film? And, of course, color is all involved in that. How do they want to portray these people? I talk to them about character .nd atmosphere. It's the same with the production designer. Many of these meetings bring all of us together because then we can pool our ideas. At least we're all talking about the same thing, so we understand one another. Though we're all there, it comes from the standpoint of one mind. It is the director's mind, as in the theater, making a film is not a democracy. The director is the leader who tells you what the film is going to be about. Then you go about creating that person's vision.

EL: Can you describe what would be considered your average staff?

JK: It's so different. On certain films I've had one assistant and that was enough because the film was small, but on something like *Radio Days* I had twenty-six people working for me, each with a specific role. I had a first assistant and two second assistants who did a lot of the shopping and a lot of the gathering of things. I had a permanent milliner, and in the work room a shop foreman and her assistant plus eight men and women who did alterations and eight other men and women who did fittings on extras. You've got all these people but you have to keep it all together. Very long days. I would be up at 4:30 in the morning and I was on the set by 5:00. Extras were dressed, the principals were dressed and the shooting would begin. Once shooting began, I would leave, go to my loft and supervise whatever fittings needed to be done. Then I would leave there and my assistants would continue with the fittings, taking Polaroids of everyone they fit that day (sometimes up to 175 people a day). I would go back to the set, and when the shooting day was over I would see dailies. At 8:30 p.m. I would go back to my loft, go through all the photos, change whatever had to be changed, and do whatever had to be done. I would be home by 11:00 or 11:30 p.m. to be up again at 4:00 in the morning. That's a long day. That's how I do it. I'm a very hands-on person.

EL: How do you choose your projects?

JK: You're talking to someone in a very unique situation; I've worked with the same director (Woody Allen) for eleven years, first as an assistant designer, and then, with *Broadway Danny Rose*, as the designer. I've been designing the costumes for his films ever since.

EL: Do you and Woody now have a shorthand for talking about projects or is the process always the same?

JK: It's basically always the same; there's a shorthand only in the fact that we know each other very well. The trust factor is there, and that's a nice thing. He doesn't have to start from scratch. But each script is different, and every single script has different kinds of characters and different people in it.

EL: What's the most frustrating thing about being a costume designer?

JK: The pressure is always vast. You never feel as if you have enough time—I guess that would be it. You always feel you could do something better or something different. A film has to start and eventually a film has to end, and you've got to do the best you can within that spectrum of time. It's a frustrating thing because you can always use more time and more money. You do have to work within a budget, and you're sometimes asked to do what you feel is the impossible, but you do it.

EL: Do you prefer contemporary pieces or period pieces?

JK: I prefer good pieces. It can be contemporary; it can be period; it doesn't matter. I want a good story; I want a good script; I want good characters, and I don't really care what period it is. They're all fun to do. Period costumes are always fun. Contemporary pieces are interesting as long as the script and the characters are interesting. There's one thing you don't like as a costume designer—and that's to have a director say to you, "Oh, they're New Yorkers, just dress them." Everybody has a character, whether it's set in 1990 or in 1812; everyone has a mind, a psyche, feelings and emotions, and that's what you've got to portray in a physical sense.

EL: At Northwestern, what courses other than your design classes helped you to become a good designer?

JK: I took all the courses I could. I took acting classes, directing classes, all the design courses, lighting, sets, costumes. I took them all. I worked on prop crews, scenery crews and, of course, on costume crews. I never acted in a play—I never went on stage—but I took all the classes, did my projects, and performed in classes simply to know what it was like.

EL: How much time do you spend simply researching? Does it decrease the older you get and the more knowledge you accumulate?

JK: There are certain things you just know, so you don't have to do them again. There's no way to convince yourself that you've seen everything, so with each project you do research. Today, my assistant asked me if I felt I had enough research for our current film and I said, "Anything you've got, anything you can think of, bring it in." In a 400-page book there may be one photo with one person in it that you've never seen before that could spark something that you never had thought of, and all of a sudden your mind starts to wander because of that one thing. You can never see enough paintings, and it's not just photos and people you're looking at, you're looking at painters—at artists for color schemes and different ways of using color, for different shapes, for different images. You look at films, old films, new films. You look at books, of course, actual photographs, painters, garments. You go to the museums and look at the garments themselves, how the fabric is treated, what fabric can do. I think I have good instincts when it comes to dealing with a character. I use my own experience—what I see on the streets, in my interpersonal relationships with friends, family, whatever. I'm a good observer, and I think you have to observe all the time, everywhere, on the subway, at the opera, anywhere you are, on the playground. You observe everything around you and it always is there, somewhere in the back of your mind, and you can draw on it. It's like a little card file in the back of your head in which you keep filing away information.

EL: What advice would you give to a young person who wants to pursue a career as a costume designer?

JK: Want to do it very badly. It's not fun and games—not an afternoon of shopping at Saks Fifth Avenue. Want to do it very badly because it's hard, it's difficult. You have to use all your powers of observation and all your talents. You have to be ready to start at the bottom. I fetched coffee for a long time. I fetched coffee for the best, that's important, and I learned a lot. I paid attention to everything. I was with the best designers in the best shops, and I saw what they did and tried to retain everything I possibly could, including how they dealt with certain difficult situations and tension-filled moments. It's hard for me to say, I started a long time ago, and I was very, very young.

EL: Do you think that costume designers get characterized by the films that they do? Is that a handicap?

JK: Yes, I think probably they do. The same way certain actors do, which is unfortunate. I've been fortunate to have done period films, contemporary films, stylized films, black-and-white films, and color films. I've done a broad spectrum of things in ten years that I didn't think I would ever be able to do. I've probably worked in different ways and done more different things for one person (Woody) than I would have had I worked individually for different people all over the place.

EL: Tell me about the production designer and your relationship with him.

JK: I am very close to our production designer because we work as a group of creative people trying to produce one goal. We talk about lots of things: the look of the film, the tone of the film. I worked once with a production designer who didn't want to know me, let alone what I was doing, but I find this is not the norm. Santo Loquasto and I always make a point of taking the time to see what the other is doing so that what you see on film is not coming from two separate minds; we're both creating the same thing, separately, of course. I do the costumes, he does the sets, but it has a unity, a coming together in one place. I think it's important to have that relationship with the production designer as it is to have a relationship with the cinematographer because the cinematographer is the one who is going to tell you what you're going to see and how you're going to see it and what colors they prefer and what they think about tone. That's why we do a lot of wardrobe tests. It may look great to the naked eye, but when it goes on film, it's a totally different thing.

EL: Do you have any aspirations to play a different role?

JK: I have no other aspirations at this point. I'm not saying that eventually I may not do something else, but right now this is what I do and I want to be the best that I possibly can. On each new project I try to be better, to improve my craft. I don't want to be the set designer or the cinematographer, or the director, but I want to be the best damn costume designer I can be. We all have a job to do and if we're good at it, we should be trusted to do it. In my situation, it's ideal and I think that's a great way to work. You must show the person that you trust what they do, so that they can go out and do it. That's not to say that you won't make a mistake. There are many times I do something, and the director says, "I can see what you're doing, but that's not what I'm getting at." Well, you throw it away and you do it again but *you* do it again. You will give them what they want because if you've got their trust, that will urge you to go ahead and deliver. You asked, "What do you find the most satisfying about being a costume designer?" It isn't so much creating a bunch of beautiful clothes (it's always nice to do beautiful clothes), but it's what that clothing says to an audience. When you do a film and someone sees it, walks out of that film and says to you, "I don't know, the feeling was just great, the way she or he was, I understood that person." But I don't care particularly for, "Oh, what a great dress!" or "Boy, that suit was really beautiful!" It's the first reaction that is extremely satisfying because then you've done something in a subtle way. You've aided that actor or actress and that director. I think we as costume designers can't be obvious. We're not there to show our wares, but to help the actor, the actress, the director. If our work becomes too obvious, if it becomes the first thing you see and the last thing you remember, in some way we've shortchanged them and overridden them. That's something one must be very careful not to do.

James Acheson
■ ■ ■ ■ ■ ■ ■ ■ ■ ■ ■ ■ ■ ■

James Acheson has won several awards for his costume design work in film and television. He received his B.A. Degree from the Wimbledon School of Art in England, and began designing for numerous television programs for the BBC, including "Dr. Who," "Isaac Bashevis Singer Short Stories," "The Chicago Conspiracy Trial," "War and Peace" (for which he designed the military costumes), and "Just Another Saturday," which earned him the Italia Prize. He has designed for *Time Bandits, The Meaning of Life, Brazil, Highlander,* and *The Sheltering Sky.* Mr. Acheson won an Academy Award, the David Di Donatello Award, and a BAFTA Award for *The Last Emperor,* and earned a second Academy Award and a BAFTA nomination for his work on *Dangerous Liaisons.* Most recently, he has designed for *Wuthering Heights.*

EL: How would you characterize your role as costume designer? Beyond designing the costumes, what is your contribution to the film?

JA: I think people do have this idea that we sit in a rather splendid office with a large drawing board and do delicate, interesting drawings that we then hand to minions to have them made up into costumes. In fact, in America you have something that we find very strange here in England; you have people called "sketch artists." I had an interview not long ago in America where a producer actually asked me if I would need sketch artists. This was to me a very strange idea, and I don't know what one would say to a sketch artist, "I see this character in green, with a fur collar?" I guess they're the ones that draw the pretty pictures. The job of the designer is to support the characters, then their clothes. I'm not very interested in the "look at me" school of design, which is about the designer's "label" being on the performer rather than the clothes supporting the character that the actor is playing. Few of us get the chance to work on what I call "coffeetable book movies" such as *The Last Emperor* or *Dangerous Liaisons*—the kind of movie in which one gets a very real chance to display clothes that a lot of people will not have seen before and that will produce a fairly strong response. A lot of one's best work is much more modest.

EL: How much time do you like to have in pre-production?

JA: It really depends on the film. I am one of those people who loves to do the research and loves to be a magpie but also does need the gun at my head, which is called a deadline. For instance, *The Last Emperor* took just under a year between my starting to work on it and the start of shooting of that movie. *Dangerous Liaisons* took only nine weeks, and two of those weeks were devoted to research. Strangely enough, you always think, "If only I had more time." I don't know whether there is an optimum time. There is a kind of momentum and an energy that happens when you know your deadlines.

EL: On a piece such as *The Last Emperor*, what were the difficulties of being in another country? I presume you were there during the shooting. What are the difficulties in being in a foreign land where you might not have the resources available near your shop? Did you run into any of that?

JA: I remember reading Milan Kundera's *The Unbearable Lightness of Being* while I was in Peking, and he compares being in a foreign country to being a tightrope walker; you don't have the safety net of familiarity beneath you. You can't just run down to the store and get another three meters of whatever you need. It was often very difficult. We did have quite an efficient system of flying needed items into China, and also we were very prepared. More than anything, it was very difficult in terms of communication. You can't pick up a phone in Peking because there aren't many of them, and because you wouldn't be able to make yourself understood. Physically it becomes very tiring. Obviously, you need a lot more manpower and the conditions are difficult. You would think in a country that has more silkworms per square mile than anywhere in the world that you could find good fabric! But much of the silk was mixed with synthetic thread, it was very difficult to find good silk. But you still got wonderful surprises, you'd walk into a shop in the middle of Chan Chung in Northern China where there are more horse-drawn carriages than cars in the middle of winter and you find cut velvet like you've never seen before.

EL: When you do something such as *The Last Emperor* or *Dangerous Liaisons*, you obviously have mounds of research material available to you. How did you approach something like *Time Bandits?* Where did all those ideas come from?

JA: Terry Gilliam is one of my favorite people to work for, you can tell from his films that he has a very fertile imagination. I was very surprised when we did *Time Bandits* that he gave me such a free hand. He gave me a lot of space. It was a great job—there were six little dwarfs who have been travelling through time for centuries and it was a very simple idea—as far as the costumes were concerned, they picked out the kind of garments that they thought they looked best in. One would be a pirate and the other would be in a bit of military uniform, and there was a kind of eclectic variety that was appropriate for the different characters. That was lovely because instead of having to work within the confines and discipline of a period, the world and its history was my oyster.

EL: Would you talk about your relationship with the production designer and then with your cinematographer?

JA: It depends on who they are. The great thing and also the frustrating thing about the job is that the process of making films is very much a collective art. I am quite surprised at how often the relationship with the production designer is fairly scanty. While you may have initial meetings and may be showing your production designer your design for certain sequences, often out of a different sense of logistics and geography, you may not be in the same place at the same time. I've often found that unless one has a lengthy pre-production period, the relationship with the production designer is quite limited. I usually have a very good relationship with the Director of Photography. Storaro and I disagree occasionally. Vittorio has a lot of complicated conceptual ideas about lighting; I think his lighting tends toward glamorization, and I tend to fight with him about that. Your work can obviously be enhanced or obliterated by the light and camera position. My favorite D.P.'s are people like Philippe Rousselot, Roger Pratt, and Vittorio Storaro, but for different reasons. They all bring a quality that is quite exceptional to the film.

EL: Let's say you're allotted minimal time with your production designer. What are the key elements that you need to work out in those first meetings so that as you go your separate ways you have established some parameters?

JA: The title "production designer" seems to suggest that the production designer is in overall control of the design of the film, which would include costume, make-up, hair, and even lighting in certain cases. In my experience, that is not the case. The production designer is really another name for the art director, i.e., he concerns himself almost exclusively with the set. In terms of the things that you actually discuss, again those vary. For instance, if we are doing the coronation scene from *The Last Emperor*, we're going to be talking logistics, where these crowds of people stand, what they're carrying, how many of them are there on horses, who's got a sword, which one's got an umbrella or a banner, and all this will be in connection with the property master as well as the production designer. Simple or smaller effects may have an important color scheme. Obviously the production designer will want to know about the color of the costume in the same way that I will want to know about the color of the set. Usually the big discussions are about color and logistics. Hopefully we'll meet on the set and slap each other on the back and be thankful it all arrived on time.

EL: Do you think that costume people get characterized by the films that they've made?

JA: Yes, I think we do tend to get pigeonholed. Most of the time no one even notices what we do. I'd been working away for eighteen years, and then I did a couple of movies that were recognized. It is tragic to hear people say sometimes, "We didn't even ring you up because we couldn't afford you," or "We didn't think you'd be interested because there aren't 4,000 extras in brilliant costumes." I think you do get characterized. I've noticed that you begin to be clearer about your strong areas as you get older, either out of experience or interest. There are certain periods about which you feel you're not particularly strong or you don't have any inclination towards. Only if you research a period very thoroughly can you start to design within it. You have to understand the period and then you can start to design. As Bertolucci would say, "You have to know the truth before you can be unfaithful."

EL: Is theater training such as you had the best preparation for film work? Is film school an option, or is straight art school preferable?

JA: I think art school is important because it allowed me to expand my ability to draw and paint but more importantly, how to break down a script, how to really think about characterization, how to imaginatively create characters and the ways that one could go about designing them. I don't know about film school courses. I know when I was a student I felt we were very much in some kind of ivory tower. I think in America you are much more interested in relating the world of the student to the world of the actual working environment. Teachers should pull in as many people as possible who are doing real work and get some questions answered. I occasionally talk to students, and I say I'll talk for about fifteen minutes. Then I'll ask if they have any questions. Nobody ever asks, "How do I get your job?" which is the basic question.

EL: Any other advice you would give to a young person pursuing this career?

JA: I see a lot of students who ask if they can come and talk to me, and the thing that continually upsets me is their lack of energy. I understand that they might be nervous or shy or whatever in an interview situation, but most of them have finished college and are in their twenties and what they haven't learned and don't seem to understand is that a lot of the job is going to be about presenting their ideas to a director and an actor. A person should be not only good at the project but have an energy, an interest and an involvement with the project in particular and life in general. There are a lot of brain-dead people. I get more energy from the guy at the MacDonald's hamburger counter. It's not as much of a problem in America. I don't think I'm the greatest designer in the world, but I'm very conscientious, and I work hard.

Robert Fletcher

·················

Robert Fletcher has been a designer for over fifty years. Following studies at both Harvard University and the University of Iowa, Mr. Fletcher served in World War II as a bombardier. He joined the board of directors of the Brattle Theatre in Cambridge, Massachusetts, designing costumes for over 87 productions, and continued on to design costumes for performing companies all over the U.S., including the New York City Ballet, the New York City Theatre, and the American Shakespeare Festival. He designed for numerous Broadway productions, including *How To Succeed in Business Without Really Trying*, and earned a Tony nomination for his costumes for *Hadrian VII*. Since 1969 he has been a member of the American Conservatory Theater. Mr. Fletcher served as NBC-TV staff designer from 1954–1960, designing for such personalities as Mary Martin, Dean Martin, and Jack Paar. His film credits include *Star Trek I, II,* and *III,* and *The Last Starfighter.*

EL: How did you come to film?

RF: Most of my career I had been a stage designer. I started as an actor and I got sick of that. I'd always been able to paint and draw, and I was interested in the history of design, costume, and architecture; I guess I'm self-taught. I had a long career in New York City doing things for Broadway and off-Broadway. I had no thought of actually working in films. I did a lot of television; I did costumes for the Bell Telephone Hour and Ford and General Motors specials. I did a number of things for the New York Opera like *Don Giovanni*, and *Turn of the Screw*.

EL: Did you go to television after theater and before film?

RF: Yes.

EL: How did that transition come about?

RF: It was in 1952 and television was just developing. We had closed our theater because everyone was exhausted. We never made enough money to give anybody a vacation. I decided that I didn't want to be an actor; I couldn't stand going to interviews. I started doing costumes and also set design when the guy we had hired at our theater quit during a production of *Henry VI* and somebody had to do it. I was able to do both costumes and sets. Over a period of four years I did a great many shows. Then I was given an opportunity with the New York City Ballet. I had to support myself and needed something to do, and I knew I could work in design so I went into NBC. This was at the time television had just blossomed in the early 50's. I walked into the supervisor's office at NBC with my portfolio, and he hired me that afternoon. At that time they had about eighty designers in both sets and costumes on staff at NBC because it was all live. Every show had to have somebody on it. You worked like a fiend. I was assigned to three or four shows: I did costumes, I did sets—back and forth.

EL: You did some opera at NBC, didn't you?

RF: Yes, that was a wonderful opportunity. We spent a lot of money which was unusual for those days.

EL: The film work came much later?

RF: Yes, I didn't come to California until 1968. I came out because Nick Vanoff asked me to do the costumes for *Hollywood Palace*. Bob Mackie went off with Carol Burnett, and Nick knew me from New York. I had worked for him there. I had been art director for Perry Como, so he asked me to come out to do it. Then I continued to work in television.

EL: How would you compare the differences between working in theater or opera and working for film?

RF: Working for film is not very satisfactory for a real designer because costume design is not particularly appreciated in modern filmmaking. It's the last thing thought of, and the costume designer is considered very expendable—the first person to be knocked off the film and the last person hired. On the stage you feel very much an integral part of the entire production. You contribute greatly to the mood, the style, the intention of the whole production. The audience cannot avoid seeing your work because it's sitting there in front and the actors walk around and all sides of them are visible. In film, it's up to the director and the editor as to what is seen and not seen. I've often done things that I was very proud of in films that were either cut out, not photographed, or photographed strangely or badly. I once prepared an entire scene and did a lot of work on it, and the director decided to shoot just the feet. You're at the mercy of all of that and I never felt very fulfilled working in film, although your work is a lot more permanent than it is in the theater. I was appalled when I first started to work in film in 1978 to learn that most designers didn't even do their own sketching. Most modern movies are done with purchased clothes; there's very little designing in film except in science fiction movies where it's required. In television I did some period work in "North and South Part II," and I worked on the moon landing sequence in the big series from Paramount called "Space." So I actually did some real designing.

EL: When you were designing films like the *Star Trek* films, who and how many were on your creative team?

RF: As for the actual designing, I was it. I have always done my own sketching. I couldn't have done the work without very good wardrobe and costumers' help. When we were actually shooting the films, there was a female and a male head of the department, and under them there were sometimes as many as ten people. It's one thing to design the clothes and another to have them made. I supervised all of that; I usually had two assistants in that area and all the workshop people who were essential. Once you're running the film, the number of people you bring in depends on how large the scenes are.

EL: When you did the *Star Trek* movies, at what point did you come on the production? I realize it was a series, so you had some continuity built in, although you did have different directors.

RF: I came in with Bob Wise on *Star Trek: The Motion Picture*.

EL: When did he bring you in? How much time did you have?

RF: I had quite a lot of time. I worked a long time on that film—everybody did. The script was changing as we went along. You usually get a script which you are able to break down and proceed, but in this case we didn't get a full script. Consequently, people stayed on it longer than they would otherwise.

EL: Some directors are very visual and, surprisingly, some others are not as visual. As someone whose work is creatively visual, how do you communicate with a director in order to really understand what is wanted and to communicate your ideas? Do you show them sketches?

RF: We talk a lot and I sometimes show reference material. I may say, "Is it like this? Is it like this painter or that painter? Do you like these preliminary sketches or should I make more?" I show them fabric sometimes. Some people are very quick to read and others are not. Some don't really understand what you're doing until they've seen a costume. Sometimes I try to make samples if we're doing many of them, such as the *Star Trek* uniforms.

EL: What kind of relationship do you have as costume designer with the film actors as opposed to opera singers? Is the relationship different?

RF: It differs greatly. I found opera singers to be the least visual people. They are more concerned with sound. A major part of your work is diplomatic. It would be wonderful if you could just make the clothes and send them out. The fact that I had been an actor for a number of years makes it easier for me because I tend to understand what is needed or wanted. I try to make everybody as comfortable as possible.

EL: Do you think it is advisable for a young person considering costume design to attend design school or film school?

RF: I would never advise anyone to become a costume designer—only if you can't do anything else or if it means a lot to you. You must enjoy it. I think there are many paths. Some people come out of the trade schools who are very good. I've seen some very good people come out of crafts courses in college: jewelry-making, pottery and sculpture. There isn't any fixed way; everyone has to find his own. I learned by doing it.

SEVEN

■■■■■■■■■

★ The Casting Director

The casting director is responsible for providing the director and producer with a preselected group of actors appropriate for each part in the film, and later negotiates contracts with actors' agents. Through actors' agents, the casting director schedules the actors to meet with the director and producer and often asks them to read a scene from the film. Casting begins with the leads, and follows in appropriate order. In most cases, the casting director reads the other parts in the scene. In certain circumstances, the audition may be videotaped. In a major motion picture, stars may be cast directly by the producer or director and not be called in by the casting director. Casting directors can work as freelancers or can be on staff at a studio, network, or production company

The salary of a casting director depends upon the production, the budget of the film, and the status of the casting director within the industry. Casting directors may belong to the Casting Society of America (213-463-1925) after satisfying several requirements: They must possess at least two years of on-line credits, must then be sponsored by two CSA members, and finally must be voted on by the entire membership.

Juliet Taylor

Juliet Taylor cast her first film, *Panic in Needle Park*, in 1971, and has since cast over fifty films. She has worked with directors Louis Malle, Paul Mazursky, Steven Spielberg, and Martin Scorsese. Her films as casting director include *Taxi Driver, Arthur, Terms of Endearment, Working Girl, Big,* and *Memphis Belle*, and she has cast every Woody Allen film since *Bananas* in 1971. In 1986 she won an Artio Award for Feature Film (comedy). On stage, Ms. Taylor has cast several plays, including *Hair* and *Doonesbury*. She is a member of the Board of Advisors for the Sundance Institute.

EL: Do you think that apprenticeship is still the way to enter the casting business?

JT: I sure do. It's the only way to learn, really. All of us who worked for Marion Dougherty got the most wonderful training. She has such high standards. She has such style and grace about everything she does. She tries to make actors very comfortable and gives them the most information that she possibly can, or is allowed to give about a project. At the same time, she does the same thing for a director—giving a director as much information as possible. Oftentimes directors are from other cities, other countries, and everyone they're seeing is out of context. They don't know the actors' work. Yes, I really believe in apprenticeships and in taking it slow and really learning how to do it properly. There are certain aspects to it that you can't jump into. Other than the actual casting, the more aesthetic part of it, casting directors negotiate all actors' contracts. That's a fairly sophisticated thing to do well.

I've also found that two out of the three people who have worked for me long term over the years are people who started out offering themselves as interns. Most casting offices are small. Many casting directors here and in Los Angeles freelance. They go from one office to another. Sometimes out in L.A. they really sit down at studios, but here they kind of go from one job to the next. They may have one assistant. A few people with offices have a couple of assistants. The offices are small and there is not a lot of turnover. It's not always that easy to get a job. The only way to learn casting is to work for a casting director. On two occasions I've had people who have offered themselves as interns for two or three months. In both cases they ended up staying for years as paid employees—someone else left, or maybe we added a third person.

EL: What kind of personal and professional skills suit a good casting director?

JT: You certainly have to like people. Friends of mine who have become psychiatrists and therapists and I feel that we have similar jobs. As a casting director you really put yourself and your own ego aside. You have to learn to appreciate people whom you may not like. There will be people who can be downright offensive, but you have to appreciate the actor. What's interesting? What's charismatic about them? You must be fairly judicious about judging them. I think it's a very intuitive job.

EL: Talk about that a little bit.

JT: You work very much from intuition. Someone walks in the door. Before they've opened their mouth, you have a feeling about them. Usually, the first impression holds. Of course, it's a great disappointment if that person doesn't have the talent to back up their original impact. Then of course, there are some people who grow on you and surprise you. Very often your sense of someone is based on a valid visceral response. There is a big pressure to be inventive and know more people than anyone else, to do the most original thing that you possibly can with a project. I think the most important thing about a casting person is someone who can really talk you through it, someone whose judgment you really trust. This is a huge part of the job.

EL: Do you talk with the director about the work you've seen the actor do?

JT: Say you set up a day for the director and they're going to see people they don't know. This is the kind of conversation you might have: "I called this person in because I felt that they had X qualities that would be right for this part." I usually say this before they come in. "I'm a little concerned that maybe their sense of comedy isn't strong enough. But I feel that this is what they could bring to the part. I've seen them do X number of plays. They did this in that one, and they were wonderful in that one." Whatever. Another thing that might be helpful would be to say, "This person is a much better performer than they are an auditioner." Or you might say, "This person will give a great audition, and that's all you're going to get. You're not going to get anything deeper than that." You warn them about all those little eccentricities too.

EL: Is there an average time period for casting a movie? I know it depends on the size of the cast and the difficulties.

JT: There really is. The new trend now is to hire casting directors ten weeks before a movie shoots. The big cry now is that casting directors want to get paid after ten weeks. They get a flat fee for ten weeks then want to be paid more after that. I've never worked on a movie where I wasn't involved from the moment I started casting to the moment the movie finished shooting. I don't know how people finish a movie before it shoots. You cast all the parts, or cast most of the parts, but then you lose people, things come up, dates change, you have to renegotiate contracts. That's the big one. You have to keep on top of dates all the time in order to save money. The production will end up spending a lot more money if you don't warn people and keep on top of the finances. You really have to follow it through. I like a lot more lead time. I don't do that many films and I like to start early. I usually work with directors whom I know very well. I work for Woody Allen a lot. I do one film a year for him. With Woody I usually get a lot of lead time.

EL: What is the most frustrating thing about your job?

JT: The things I like the least are the emergencies that take place during the shooting of a film. I hate having to recast because we've lost someone. You give it your best shot the first time around, and then when you have to do it under time pressure you always feel as if you're not getting what you set out to get. You're not making the decision with the leisure of putting the puzzle together. So you feel in some way that your original concept is thrown. I don't enjoy that.

EL: Can you describe what you try to do for the actors as they walk through the door? Although ultimately you're serving the film, how do you try to serve each individual?

JT: This is one thing that Marion always taught us, and it is great. Always have a friendly person greet them, and you must make them comfortable, make them feel like we're really rooting for them, really looking forward to their being there. Try not to schedule people for the same part together so that they don't see or hear someone else reading for the same role. You can't always do that, but try. Give them as much information as you can. If you can only give them a scene to look at, tell them as much as possible about the story. Maybe even give them a little bit of a hint as to what the director thinks about it. You're always a little nervous about doing that because you hate to cramp someone's style. You don't want to take away their artistic bent.

EL: Do you read with them?

JT: Yes.

EL: Your theater background must be helpful.

JT: I guess so. As a reader the point is to try to get some of the emotion of the part across but keep it fairly low key. You don't want to ever give so much that it overshadows the actor or takes the actor in a particular direction. You want to give them a little something to play off of without dominating.

EL: What kind of movies do you like to work on?

JT: I have to say I like to do good, meaningful movies. I guess everybody does. Movies that matter. It doesn't matter whether they're serious or funny. I like to have the sense of being part of something that is important. As a matter of fact, I've sort of gotten to the point now where I can't get myself to pump up for something that I don't care about. I have the luxury of not having to do it. That's a pretty spoiled attitude. Not everybody can do that. You have to pay the bills.

EL: What other advice would you give to a young man or woman who is going to pursue casting as a career?

JT: Go to theater and films as much as possible. That's extremely important. I go to something at least two nights a week. When I started out I used to go every night. Sometimes on Saturday nights my husband and I would go to two things a night. Off-Broadway and off-off-Broadway are not as active now, but there is still a lot to see. That is really the key. Particularly in New York, theater is a great resource. So, seeing as much as you possibly can is the thing. I have to say that I'm not a big film buff and I don't see everything.

EL: Let's say you've seen an actor on stage who is really remarkable and you bring him/her in for a film. How are you able to translate how well they will be able to do film work from their theater work?

JT: Anyone who's got a gift has a gift. Then some people are great types or have a certain quality. Marion always used to say even people who aren't actors have one quality they can bring—whoever they are. So you'll see people with great qualities that are useful. Most people can make the transition from theater to film very easily. Years ago when I first moved to New York people used to say Jason Robards was a theater actor. Ha ha! He went on to become a wonderful film actor. It really wasn't a problem. But twenty years ago they used to make that differentiation. I think most people can make the change.

EL: Any other advice?

JT: To apprentice and not be in too much of a hurry, to really take the time to learn to do it right. I don't think there's really anything else except do it. Be around someone who does it. Listen and watch and learn from as many people as you can. One of my assistants keeps books of notes on everybody who's here and she sees tons of films and plays. She's really very diligent, and she has gradually taken more responsibility as time has gone on. That's really all you can do.

Johanna Ray

■■■■■■■■■■■■■

Johanna Ray began her career in England as an actress. After moving to the United States and raising a family, she began working various odd jobs within the entertainment industry. She became a story editor at a small production company, eventually joining American International Pictures to work in story editing and development. Following freelance casting for small production companies and a stint as an agent, she was hired by director Bruce Cohn Curtis to cast the feature film *Hell Night*, their first of four pictures together. Since then, her film credits have included *Dreamscape, Firestarter, Blue Velvet* (CSA nomination), *Gaby: A True Story* (CSA nomination), and *Wild at Heart*. Ms. Ray won the CSA award for the casting of the television series "Twin Peaks."

EL: Can you describe the responsibilities of a casting director?

JR: I attempt to get the best actor for the part. Before I had confidence in what I was doing, I used to be torn between, "Is my responsibility to get the best actor for the part, or knowing what the director is looking for, is it my responsibility to get what he/she wants?" Sometimes the director and the producer want two totally different things. There are a lot of variables, and sometimes you are torn between wanting to do what you feel is best for the project because that's the goal. But on the other hand, there's this person paying your salary and saying, "This is what I want you to do," which may not be what's best for the project.

EL: How long have you been casting?

JR: About ten years now.

EL: Can you describe the process from the point at which you're hired by the director or the producer? Can you characterize your discussions with a director?

JR: I adapt to each situation. Each director is different, every producer is different, every film is different, each job is different. It's always a different experience, and you always learn something new, no matter what. That's what's great—it never gets dull or boring, and if it's not a good experience, at least it ends. I like to adapt to the director because it's his or her vision, and they have a right to want things done their way. If the director's not sure what he's doing, or it doesn't seem to be very practical or workable, than I'll make suggestions. Usually I've already read the script. You start with the leads.

EL: How many people do you generally bring in for leads on a feature?

JR: Usually you don't even bring them in, depending on how big the stars are and depending on the director. Some directors just don't need to meet them or know them already. Others want everyone to read no matter what. Sometimes I think the actor should be interviewing the director, because it's their career that's at risk, too. I always need to know how important it is that it has to be a major name. The first question is, "Are we going to get the best actor for the part, or does the studio need a major name?" It's amazing; often times they say, "Oh no, we want the best actor for the part." Then you go through every actor, and it ends up being someone who has name value who isn't so right for the part. It can be really frustrating.

EL: When you're in a situation like that, do you adjust the rest of the casting?

JR: Yes, you have to. Oftentimes that's what I have to bring to the producer's attention. I always cast the most important part first, because otherwise any actor who reads the script is going to want the lead.

EL: How do you anticipate the chemistry between potential leads when people aren't coming in?

JR: It's an instinctive thing, and hopefully it works more often then not.

EL: On average, how many people do you bring in for support characters?

JR: It depends on the director. For David (Lynch), sometimes it's only the first person, because if he likes the first person then it's done. For some directors, it's two or three people, for some it's six or seven. Some directors want to see every single hot actor in town who happens to be right for the part, and maybe see them over and over again before they make up their mind. It's always different.

EL: Describe the relationship you need to have with agents. How do you keep tabs on all of them?

JR: It's just something that's a matter of course, you're talking to them all every day, and they're calling and sending in submissions. In fact, my frame of reference for a particular actor is his or her agent.

EL: How much time does it take to cast a feature?

JR: That's often the first question that the producer or the director will ask when I go in for an interview. I say, "It takes as long as it takes you to make up your mind." I could do it in a week if I had to, and sometimes it goes on for three to four months. Sometimes when you have a time constraint it actually works for you because then everyone has to make a decision. Usually you bring in the best ones first. Even when you have to go through seeing everybody in town it is often someone who came in the first day who ends up getting the part.

EL: What kind of personal characteristics are advantageous for a casting director?

JR: The most important thing is to totally rely on your opinion and instinct. Once you start questioning that, you're in trouble. You have to like actors, have empathy with them, and be sensitive to the situation.

EL: Can you describe your audition process? What atmosphere do you create when the actor walks in?

JR: That's different, too. It depends on the project and the time that I have. When I started casting I didn't like to read actors on my first meeting with them. I met everyone and sat down and talked and chatted and tried to make it not seem like an interview. Sometimes the actor turns it into an interview; even though you're trying to make it casual and comfortable, the actor has certain expectations. A lot of it depends on my mood and the personality of the actor. I try to get a sense of who they are, how interesting they are, the look and the energy they possess, and whether there's some kind of charisma. Then I have them back to read for a specific part. That's my ideal way of casting. I remember them much better if I meet them that way. If actors come in and read for the first time, I don't remember them as well, but sometimes I have no choice.

EL: When you've set up an audition for a certain character, how do you choose the scene?

JR: Usually I pull the first scene that the character appears in because that's where the character has to make an impression and the audience decides if this person is interesting or not. Then I try to pick out the most difficult scene in the script, and next I'll pick one that shows just a whole different personality to the character. Sometimes I'll give the actor all the material and have them choose. For the first time I'll have them read just one scene. If they're totally not right for the part, then it's a waste of time to have them read further.

EL: In casting sessions, does the director give directions first and then the actors read?

JR: That's dependent on the director, too. Some directors will give direction first, or the actors will ask, "What do you want?" Sometimes the director will purposely not tell them anything because it's more important to him to see how well they can take direction. The director will then say, "How about trying it this way?" and we'll see how adaptable they are. Some directors don't give direction at all.

EL: What do you think is the motivation behind not giving any direction?

JR: I don't think there's any motivation at all, I think that their expertise may be in action, camera, and setting up a shot. I've worked with one director who is the first to admit, "I don't direct the actors because I don't know how." Then you have to be very careful about whom you bring in, because some directors just assume the actor can act.

EL: What's your relationship with the producer?

JR: Sometimes my relationship with the producer is closer than the director. For instance, if it's a first-time director, the producer sits in on the session and if there's a difference of opinion often the director has to defer to the producer. Sometimes my relationship with the producer is similar to what it would have been with a more experienced director, and sometimes it's just somebody to see when there's a question or when you need an approval. It's different every time. Sometimes the casting director's involvement helps the film get made. Often the producers will contact me for a list of actors or preliminary casting when financing for a film has not been greenlighted. The list of actors the casting director is able to provide often plays a major part in the producer's obtaining financing for the film to be made.

EL: Do you think casting is an open or closed field for young people? Are there opportunities?

JR: I think so. It's amazing because there are so many casting directors in the business. There are far more casting directors than there are jobs, yet for every casting director there's a job for at least one assistant. This is the best way of learning because you do everything, and everything comes through you. Most casting directors go through a lot of assistants because as much as you'd like to keep one, if you don't have a job you can't expect them to stay available for you. They have to go work for someone else. I don't know what the percentage is of how many assistants end up casting directors, but I know it's high. It seems once you're in the business, it would be fairly easy.

EL: You said there was a high burn-out rate among casting directors— what contributes to that?

JR: Just stress. However much you enjoy the job, you've got people coming at you from all directions. Everybody needs you, and everybody wants your attention—the producer, the director, the agents, the actors. If everybody had access to you, you'd never get anywhere. The job never ends—even when the film goes into production there are still agents calling and suggesting you cast people. Mail follows you all over town—the volume of mail is unbelievable. Aside from that there are all the actors who take it upon themselves to send you their pictures, those who have agents and those who don't.

EL: When you sit down and negotiate with an actor's agent, do you have financial parameters from the producer?

JR: Yes.

EL: Do you enjoy that part of your job?

JR: Not as much. When the agent is negotiating they only have your word that the actor's salary is indeed all that was allotted in the budget. An agent is in a very precarious position when closing a deal for the client. The agents have to be able to show the actors what a good job they can do because they can say, "This is what she offered, but I got you twice as much money." Sometimes you have to come in low just to help make the agent look good to their client.

EL: What advice would you give to a young person considering casting as a career?

JR: I don't know what advice I would give to someone who didn't have any existing connections except to apply as an intern. One of our current casting assistants started off as a receptionist in my office. She was always asking, "Is there anything I can help you do?," was very enthusiastic and helpful, and in the process, she learned about casting. She turned an entry-level position into something that was a really valuable experience.

EL: What's the up-side of the job?

JR: It's a very stimulating job. When I started casting, it wasn't like it was a job. It was fun. It was what I'd want to do even if I didn't have to earn a living. I would say the most enjoyable aspect is when someone who is really talented gets their first break. Working in casting also means that you're involved early on in the filmmaking process. You're in an excellent position to observe and learn about the many other aspects of filmmaking in both pre-production and production.

Marion Dougherty

Marion Dougherty graduated from Penn State with a degree in art. She moved to New York intending to pursue an acting career and was offered a job casting the new Kraft Television Theatre. Virtually unknown due to the lack of on-screen credits, she cast over 500 shows during the "Golden Age" of live television. She cast her first movie, *The World of Henry Orient*, while still working on the television series "Naked City" and "Route 66." She then started her own company and went on to cast such films as *Midnight Cowboy, The Sting, Reds, Lethal Weapon* and *Batman*. Most recently, she has cast *Lethal Weapon 3, The Last Boy Scout*, and the sequel to *Batman*. She is currently Vice President of Talent at Warner Brothers.

JF: What was the casting field like when you started out?

MD: When I was starting out I was like a kid in a candy store. I could pick from this great pool of New York. I gave Dustin Hoffman and Robert Redford their first jobs; this great pool of talent in New York had not been discovered yet.

JF: Is television a good place for some of these young people to start?

MD: Yes and no . . . if they have training first. When I go to New York and interview kids and they ask, "Should I go out to California?" I say, "It depends if you're really trained because you can train better here than you can in California. You have the theater here. You should be sure you really get your foundation." By and large, with most television you do not have the rehearsal time, you do not have the top directors, you can learn bad habits because it's so quick, particularly something like a sitcom.

173

JF: How do you find the people who are following your footsteps in casting? How do they find that eye, that sensibility?

MD: Well, I don't know. Of course I'm very prejudiced toward my gang. I think they're wonderful—Juliet Taylor and Wally Nicita who's now a producer. It's very important to give support and confidence to an actor who's reading for a director. Not all casting people do this, so they don't get the best out of the performers. I believe there are a handful of people that are good and who really have an eye and do good casting. I think there are others who are what I call "grocery list makers" or "telephone personnel." There are so many of them. You have to have a love for what you're doing, not only what you're doing but a respect for the performers. It's also important to find out what's in the director's mind. I'll fight a director if I think he's going the wrong way on a part, but eventually if I can't turn him around to thinking that this is right then I'll drop it. It's the director's view that is most important.

JF: Are more and more actors choosing not to read?

MD: If the kids really want a project they'll come in for it. The kids who are good and who are used to doing theater will try it out. Sometimes you know if somebody is really right for a part, but if you don't read them it's harder to see what their quality is so that you can match the other people to that quality.

JF: You have trained many of today's best casting directors.

MD: You know it's very funny, I never was conscious of training. Juliet (Taylor) was the first one, she was with me for about ten years. I've always told anybody that works for me that they can do whatever they want to do if they want to contribute. I always insisted that they read the script because you have to know what that is, even if you're sitting out at the secretary's desk, and if they had any ideas, fine. They'd hear me talking to people and they'd know whom I brought in for readings, so they just got it by osmosis. I never sat down and said "Now I'm going to train you." They were all very bright people and that was most important to me. Look at Nessa (Hyams) and Juliet (Taylor) and Gretchen (Rennell) and Wally (Nicita), all very bright and nice people.

They weren't people who were going to be mean to actors or try to abuse the power. That happens now, and I find that it's very distressing. There are a lot of good people that are casting, but by the numbers, I think it's a small percentage.

JF: When you've done projects with the same directors, are they consistent or do they bend with the material?

MD: I think if you work on a lot of pictures for one director, you develop a sort of shorthand, you get an ESP kind of thing and you know the thinking process. I've only worked with one director who wouldn't read people, and that's Mr. Eastwood. He said that he had such a terrible time when he was an actor, that he's too shy to read other actors. There are directors, though, who just want to tape people. I fortunately have not had to work on anything like that; I feel that reading the script is the most important part of casting.

JF: Do you think you lose something when you only see a video tape of an actor?

MD: Yes, I think you have to sit in the same room and read. That's very old-fashioned and the agents don't like it. When I first came out to Los Angeles, they really were aghast at that way of doing it. It's unfortunate that there are those few people who will not read. With the older people you've seen so much of their stuff and you've known them for so long that it's not always necessary to read; however, even then it's helpful to be able to match performances and make sure the chemistry is right between the players.

JF: Is your job the job to say no? Who tells the actor that they're not going to get it?

MD: Me.

JF: Is that hard?

MD: No, because I think if you tell the truth, it's not. Mostly you deal through the agent. For instance, if I read somebody today and I know we're not going to use them, I will not call the agent and say I'm not going to use them. I wait a few days because we're thinking it over. If it's a star, you just tell the truth and you just say, "No, it's just not right." I mean it's semantics, you can say, "It's just not right, they're wonderful, I love them, we'll use them again, but it doesn't work in this one." Not everybody is going to get every part that they're up for and they have to be realistic about it.

JF: Experience seems to me to be an incredible ingredient in what you do.

MD: I think what casting people have to do is to go to the theater. Now, of course they go to the movies. The theater is the best, and that's why I go back to New York every time I have an excuse and I see the theater. There's just something about it. You can tell more about people there, at least I can.

JF: How many staff do you have?

MD: I have one other casting director, and each of us has an assistant and a secretary, so there's six.

JF: Small number for a lot of projects.

MD: You see, there are a lot of things that Warner Brothers releases that are pick-ups, and the casting is done by independents. Also, if a director has always worked with a certain casting person, then Warner Brothers will hire that person for that film.

JF: Do the people who cast for television only cast for television?

MD: Basically yes, although there are some independents who do both TV and film.

JF: Do many actors make the transition from TV to film?

MD: Oh, yes. I just cast somebody who was in a good episodic show. I cast her in a wonderful part in *Guilty by Suspicion*. That was an independent film that we released. I asked to cast it because it was about the blacklist in the fifties. I lived through that period and I really wanted to work on it.

JF: You must have an amazing memory.

MD: It was better ten years ago than it is now, but you haven't forgotten people you've cast.

JF: Well, you see, there are some good things about preservation.

MD: I have people come up to me and say, "You gave me my first job," and I'll say "I did, what?" I don't remember. Directors say "Well, what has he done?" and I'll say "I'll get you the resume, all I know is he's good." That's a nice short cut.

JF: After the script and after the director, the next most important thing in a movie is the cast. Is that true?

MD: In that order.

JF: Do you watch movies and say, "If they had cast this another way, they would have had a movie?"

MD: Oh, it's terribly important, and for some pictures the cast is more important than in others—if it's a terribly complicated script or if it's one calling for real balance. For instance, *Memphis Belle* took a long time. Juliet saw people in New York, and I saw people out here. Since it was an ensemble, it was important to keep a balance in it. It was terribly hard. I'm very, very proud of that group of kids. With others, it's a fairly simple story; you don't have to balance as much. It's always wonderful to see fresh faces, and it's harder and harder to get them because television has combed the areas. Now people are beginning to pay attention to and are able to bring over the English and European actors, too. Unfortunately, you can't use them unless it's a starring role because immigration won't give them a green card.

JF: Do you have a favorite film or a film of which you're most proud?

MD: *Midnight Cowboy, The Sting, Slaughterhouse Five,* and a picture that was way ahead of its time that I did for Carl Reiner in New York called *Where's Poppa?.* I really liked *Lenny* because I fought with the producer and the director on that one. They wanted an actress who I knew was untalented and I begged for Valerie to do it and that was the best thing Valerie Perrine has ever done. She was so perfect for it. I liked *Lenny*, I thought it was an awfully good film.

JF: What was different during the time those films were made?

MD: You were allowed to cast actors who were not "hot" box-office. Do you know in *Slaughterhouse Five* there was not one single person, except for two English people, that had ever done a movie before? They had done television, but they hadn't done film. The kid who played the lead had had one week at a theater up in New England and had just come to study in New York. The character went from 14 or 15 to 80, and so we started in the middle like with Dustin. I got desperate and I called in this totally unknown kid just from a picture, his picture looked so silly. When he read for it (and this has only happened twice) the hair stood up on the back of my head. What I didn't realize was that the character Billy Pilgrim was naive his entire life; this kid was 21 and had never acted. His naivete *was* Billy Pilgrim and it worked. Same thing happened when I worked on *The Heart Is a Lonely Hunter* and I went down South and I looked all over the place for kids. I was in an Alabama reading, and this kid started to read and the same thing happened to me. That was Sondra Locke. She had just driven in from Tennessee or someplace like that; she had never acted and she was wonderful in the picture.

JF: You must have an intuitive sense about people.

MD: I don't know whether I'm so smart. I think I'm a workaholic. I think I would go crazy if I didn't work. I love to do it.

EIGHT

■■■■■■■■■

★ The Actor

For many filmgoers, the actors are the most memorable participants in a film. Film actors may come to a screen career with a broad background of stage work or with no previous dramatic work at all. Guided by the director, the actor must discover the characterization created by the writer and work collaboratively with his or her fellow actors.

It is extremely difficult to calculate salaries for actors. The categories that determine compensation include those of day performers, weekly performers, and term performers. An actor who sings may earn more for the additional talent. Television has different compensation rules from those of theatrical motion pictures; a major role on a series will be compensated differently from a guest spot. An actor also receives payment for extra events, including interviews. Actors are eligible for the Screen Actors Guild (213-465-4600) if they have been employed by a SAG signatory company in a speaking role, if they have been members of an affiliated performers' union for at least a year, or if they have worked as a SAG-covered extra player for a minimum of three work days.

Barbara Hershey

· · · · · · · · · · · · · · · · ·

Barbara Hershey was discovered by a talent agent in a student production at Hollywood High School. She debuted in the TV series "The Monroes" and made her film debut in the 1968 feature *With Six You Get Eggroll*. She has since explored a wide range of roles in such films as *The Right Stuff*, *The Natural*, and *Hannah and Her Sisters*, for which she won critical acclaim. Her most recent credits include *The Last Temptation of Christ*, *Beaches*, *Defenseless*, and *Tune In Tomorrow*. Ms. Hershey has also starred in several television movies, including CBS' "A Killing in a Small Town," for which she won both the Emmy and the Golden Globe Awards for Best Actress, and "Paris Trout" for Showtime. She is the only actress to garner the Best Actress Award at the Cannes Film Festival two years in a row, winning in 1987 for her performance in *Shy People* and in 1988 for *A World Apart*. Ms. Hershey starred in the film *Defenseless* and is also starring in the soon-to-be-released *The Public Eye*, with Joe Pesci.

EL: Why did you want to become an actress?

BH: I don't know why. I've always felt it's a little odd because there was nobody in my family in show business or even anyone who was artistically inclined. My earliest recollections are of going to my back-yard and playing, but I had an intensity about character that the other kids didn't have. I was very specific about how I looked. I remember falling asleep at night and making my face into photographs I had seen of people in newspapers and magazines. In my imagination I would just make my face into their faces. My nickname was "Sarah Bernhardt," and when anyone asked me what I wanted to do I said, "I am an actress"; I didn't say, "I want to be an actress." I feel very fortunate about the fact that I have always had a solid, core feeling of what I was put on earth for that other kids didn't have.

EL: How did you train to become an actress?

BH: I've been acting for twenty-five years professionally and I believe that my strongest and deepest training was in my backyard, in life itself. As a kid, when you're playing, it's joyful, it's an unselfconscious, cathartic experience. I noticed that when I took acting classes later they often approached the negative, the internal, and the narcissistic. If you read Stanislavsky, he talks about life being the greatest teacher, so I don't discount my backyard. I think you can go through any experience with an actor's eyes, or if you want to be a cinematographer, with a cinematographer's eyes. I went through life, from childhood on, with an actor's eyes. When I went through something, I always thought of it in terms of acting. When I'd cry, I'd look in the mirror and see what my face looked like. It sounds weird, but I consider that great training. Also, I was very fortunate to begin working at the early age of seventeen. Initially, the acting wasn't as hard for me (although it's gotten harder lately) as getting used to all of the eyes on me, and the crew and publicity and all the things that had nothing to do with acting. I had a hard time adjusting to all that. The acting itself was always a source of joy for me. The most difficult part is dealing with all the aspects of the profession—the rejection, the tension, the hours, the pressures—that have nothing to do with acting.

EL: When you were seventeen, starting out and learning on the job, were you learning by self discovery, trial and error, from fellow actors, your directors?

BH: I learned from life itself. I don't even believe there are mistakes, they're all lessons. Anytime you have a deeper life experience, it enriches you. When I became a mother I became a better actor. When my sister died, I became a better actor. Also, I have always aimed for variety in my acting and I always felt the way to attain that is to be varied as a person and have varied life experiences. This is not to negate teachers and schools, because I've experienced that also. I've put myself in various acting classes but I never found one specific

teacher. I found that the experience in the class wasn't always a positive one; it seemed to emphasize the angst part of it, which is fine because that's a big part of it, but it didn't seem to encourage a lot of the things I believe in as an actor. Most of the learning is through trial and error and, in terms of real training, my own conglomeration of experiences is more valuable.

EL: For a young woman, you have had a great variety of roles. Has that been part of a strategy?

BH: Yes. It's funny, over the years when anyone has asked, "What is it you want to do, is there any specific role you want to play?" I always said, "No, I want to do them all." I wanted to experience all kinds of films, low budget, big budget, adventure films, romantic films, little films. The emphasis with me so far has been serious films, and that's not so much of a choice, it's just where the juicy roles have been. Variety was always very important to me; it's stimulating to play parts that you've never played before. I admire the actors who do that instead of playing the same characters over and over—which is not easy either—but it's what I call "personality actors" versus a varied actor.

EL: Can you talk about your relationship with your agent? Do you develop a strategy with that person? How does he assist you?

BH: One of the most important things to do as an actor is to dream about what it really is you want and then express those dreams to your agent. You have to have good communication with your agent so your agent really knows what he or she is representing. My agent has an easy time of it because I keep saying, "Think about me for roles that aren't right for me. Think about me for roles that no one would ever think of me for, as well as the things they would." It's obviously a crucial relationship and a really hard one to find. It's a marriage of sorts, and like marriage you have to work at it. I think communication is the most important thing. I tell my agents to be very honest with me. I like to know what's really going on, where I stand when I go on an interview, who my competition is, what's in my favor and what's against me, and what they're worried about. I like to know as much as I can about the character and their conception of the character so that I can go in being the character as much as possible. An agent helps you find out all these things, as well as the rest of the obvious things they do.

EL: How do you go about conceiving a character like the one in *A Killing in a Small Town*, who might not be in your personal experience?

BH: I'm of the belief that if we look deep enough and hard enough inside of us, we'll find anyone. Me, with my body, mind, and soul, in an entirely different circumstance could do entirely different things. I work in many different ways according to what the part demands. Sometimes I just go and do it. Often, if it's a part that's far away from me, it will take a lot of research. I work from the outside in and the inside out. For *A Killing in a Small Town*, I talked to the real woman, I worked on an accent, I talked to people who knew her, I read everything I could, I read the transcripts from the trial and did all those kinds of things. I also worked from the inside out, which is finding the part of you that has some understanding of how such a thing can happen. I think this particular character's problem was one that we all share and see around us in the world, which is what I call the grey forces, denial, apathy, or nonfeeling. Woody Allen touched on it in *Crimes and Misdemeanors*, and there was a very interesting film called *River's Edge* that dealt with it. It's something that's very prevalent. Our society hasn't taught us to deal with our so-called "negative emotions," so they really become negative. You see inappropriate behavior on the streets, things that have nothing to do with the circumstance—it's pent-up rage. Once you understand where it's coming from, you understand how such a thing can happen.

The biggest challenge for an actor is not just to get some different look, or some different walk or accent or to be different in some way, but to truly find some reality in this person. That comes from very personal things. I once played the character of a woman in World War II who was tortured for ten months and finally killed; she was a spy, a very gentle half East Indian, half American woman. I had to ask myself, "Could I die for an ideal? How do I make this personal? Would I be able to do this?" and the answer was "I don't know." Then you think, "OK, how do I make this personal?," "What could I die for?" I could die for my son. You multiply that by other children, that she's dying for all the children, and then suddenly it's a personal thing. Hitler was like a madman with an axe in an orphanage, and suddenly you can do it. It's finding the personal, finding what's real, what you connect to.

EL: As an actor you must explore deep emotions, call upon personal experiences, and tie them to your characters. When you get on a set there are noises and people and lights, and you may have to do a scene ten, fifteen, or more times—how do you maintain concentration with all those distractions?

BH: It's really hard. People always say stage acting is so much harder than film acting, but they have the continuity and they only go through it once. In film, you're shooting wildly out of order. Including coverage, I counted the other day and I had done one scene fifty-four times. Sometimes you shoot an emotional scene over three days. It's a real push-pull in terms of energy because you have to maintain your energy and contain what's going on in between. You can't dissipate it in a lot of talk. If you let your energy go too much, rest too much, then you lose it also. That's hard.

EL: Can you characterize the kinds of conversations you like to have with the director and the cinematographer? Do you have conversations early on about the whole concept?

BH: I like to. Acting is odd because I think when it's really good, it's subjective, not objective. I'm objective, hopefully, when I'm reading the script for the first time and get a sense of it as a whole. Shooting out of order I usually have to keep some kind of graph for myself for the evolution of the character and refer to it because, otherwise, you're just lost if the character changes in the course of the movie, which hopefully she does. It's really important to have an overview.

I love the dialogue with the director, partially because I love an affirmative atmosphere, and I like the stimulation of being part of the team. I like knowing we have the same goal, or finding out if we do or if we don't, finding out how we can deal with that. When I'm on the set and in character, I like to get real subjective. I like to not think about the whole in a sense and let the director be the eyes, be the objective one, because in life I don't think we're watching ourselves. But everything that leads up to that moment is very objective; I'm looking at the whole and how the character serves the piece, what the point of the character is, what the movie would be like if you lifted out the character and it wasn't there.

It's the same thing with the cinematographer. I like talking to the cinematographer, although we don't usually have a long dialogue. I don't know anything technically. I don't know if I have a good side of my face or a bad side; I never wanted to be self-conscious about that. I have always felt very comfortable with the camera; I've always felt that the camera is my friend. The relationships with the cinematographer, the camera crew, those right near me are very important.

EL: What are the biggest challenges?

BH: I think the biggest challenge for any actor at whatever level is not getting bitter because of disappointment. I would say this to any young actor because I've been through a lot of very high times and very low times. I've been through people calling me incessantly to nobody returning my calls. I've been through all of that, and the thing that set me apart, helped me through and kept me on track was my love of acting. That is the priority. Deal with the other things; deal with publicity, be smart about that stuff, but concentrate on the love of acting and getting really good. If your love of acting isn't there I don't know what would sustain you during the lows. The tendency is to try to make yourself not care so much so you're not so vulnerable to the rejection when it happens. I think that hiding your true emotions when you're rejected is very dangerous—how do you turn that back on when it comes time to act? One of the things I really find true about acting is that you can only act what you are capable of feeling. If you start shutting out pain, or shutting out experiences because they hurt, or not feeling them, then I think it's going to affect you as an actor. I let myself feel everything and I get over it real fast.

EL: Since there are fewer roles for women, how does a woman sustain a career?

BH: It's tough. It means you don't work all the time, you don't work as much as men, you don't get as much pay. If you hold out for the really good parts it means you don't work very often. The terrible part about being an actress versus other art forms is that you have to be hired to do it, so sometimes I'll just work when I really just need to act. You try to hold out for the best of what's offered, that's what I've always done, to try, within what's offered, to have variety.

EL: Would you talk a little bit about the chance aspects of having a certain role and what that can do for you?

BH: I have an interesting career in that I have what I call a "stepping stone" career. I've never been in a mega-hit; I was not an overnight success. That happens to people, and I almost feel sorry for them when it does because what do they follow it with? How do they sustain this height? I feel I'm on bedrock, that I have a solid foundation. I wonder sometimes if I had done such and such a role, how different my life would have been. I know that ultimately, and I really do believe this, talent will come out; if you stick with it, you will get your chances. I read an essay on luck once that I thought was fascinating because I see a lot of actors who are really good actors who don't work and I wonder, "Why is it that I have this luck and they don't? Why is it that someone without talent has luck that I don't have sometimes?" This essay said you can turn bad luck into good luck—like Dostoevsky who was thrown into jail and turned it into art. The other thing the article pointed out was even more interesting to me. It said, "Luck is when the world says jump and you jump." I thought, "Well, then our half of that is being ready to jump." This is where that bitterness comes in. In the face of ten rejections you have to be ready and positive for the luck when it happens.

EL: Do you choose your film projects solely by the character you're offered, or have you ever chosen a project just because you felt strongly about the project?

BH: Sometimes if the project isn't so wonderful but the character is just so wonderful that I can't turn it down, I'll do it. Sometimes the part isn't so great but the film is something that I just adore, and I'll do that. That's happened a lot. Sometimes both happened, where it's a part that's fantastic and a project that's fantastic, and then you're in ecstasy. I do films for all three of these reasons. I'm always looking for films that I haven't seen before because everything is so repetitive; often by page 13 I'll know what's coming next.

EL: Is it critical to live in either Los Angeles or New York?

BH: I think if you're starting out it is because I don't know how else you would go on auditions. Not for training, though. If you want to study in school and do plays and theater and workshops, you can do that anywhere. In terms of auditions and getting out there and "selling yourself," you would have to be in one of those two cities.

EL: Could you talk about the audition process, and what you think is important when you go in for an audition?

BH: I do believe in reading for the director, but I wish there was another way of doing it. I like screen tests more, because in screen tests (which are hardly ever done anymore), you're in character, you're in wardrobe and make-up, you're directed by the director, you have two or three takes. It's a circumstance very similar to the filming circumstance. What I would say to the actor if he or she really wants a part is don't read—memorize. Don't come in with your face in a piece of paper, come in as close as you can to what you think the character might be. One of my big complaints about directors in reading circumstances is that they often have you read, especially when you're beginning, with a casting director. Often you read for a character with someone who may not even be the right gender. I don't know how they expect you to get to anything. It's really denying what acting is about; it's saying, "I don't believe in acting. Here do this love scene with another woman," and the part is written for a man.

People think acting is lying; I think good acting is telling the truth and as much truth as you can assemble. If they're not going to give it to you, give it to yourself. Go in as much as you can with your concept of the character. If you don't have a clear concept of the character, choose one so that you can be specific. Often directors in readings don't direct, they'll say, "Thank you very much" as if that's it. Sometimes I think they don't have a clear concept of what they want, and yet they want to get their socks knocked off.

EL: How much of your job is cerebral, and how much of it is intuitive?

BH: It's both. I'm glad you asked that because this is something I've discovered. I think there are many different actors with very valid methods. I don't have a "method," but I prepare a lot, and there comes a moment when you have to throw away the preparation. Preparation is intellectual, it's feeding ingredients into the computer. I believe in the subconscious, and all I'm doing in preparation is trying to stimulate my subconscious. I'll do a lot of research on all levels down to what the person eats, how she dresses, how she walks, what perfume she wears—all those things in addition to the deeper questions, the personal questions about the character and the history of the character, that's really important. Then I may work out a dialect, and use it in my everyday life until it becomes second nature and I get past what I call "the wall" (where it's an imposition) to the point where you're actually expressing yourself with it. Then you throw it all away—which is a scary time. If you don't throw it all away when you hit the set, the audience is going to see all that preparation, and you're going to see someone doing an accent or a walk. It's the difference between doing steps and dancing. When you hit the set and you're confronted by the other actors you must forget about the accent and the walk and everything you thought about and just trust your instincts so that you're really available for the other actors and for the circumstances. Then you can just be alive in the moment and trust that your subconscious will take care of the other stuff. It's very scary, especially if the character is very far away from you.

In answer to your question, it's both, it's intellectual and instinctual. I think the intellect feeds the instincts. There's a Hemingway quote that I love. He talks about writing, and I apply it to every art form. He said, "If you know something very well, you can leave it out and it will still be there, but if you don't know something well, you'll probably overdescribe it." I see that all the time, where actors are describing what they're feeling instead of just feeling it. You can leave it out, and it will be there if you've done your work.

EL: Is there any difference between television and film work?

BH: The effect is very different. In film, people can see you over a period of time, and in television it's over in one night, but you reach many more people. In the old days I think movies were much more adventurous than television, and lately you can tackle subjects on television that you can't tackle in film.

EL: Does speed ever work in your favor?

BH: Sometimes it might. I've worked on big-budget films where you have two hours between each set-up. Keeping your energy up during that period is really hard, and I think it loses some of the passion of the material. I also think sometimes certain projects do better with certain budgets. Two films I did, *A World Apart* and *The Last Temptation of Christ*, were extremely low-budget films and I thought for the subject matter, that was wonderful. They were humble films, humble subjects, and I think that's great. I also think if it's too low a budget and you don't have the time to make the film you want to make, it can be very damaging.

Clyde Kusatsu

■■■■■■■■■■■■■■

Clyde Kusatsu made his professional stage debut at the age of 17, playing the Crown Prince in a Honolulu summer stock production of "The King and I." He earned a degree in theater from Northwestern University, where he performed in numerous productions and played in summer stock. He moved to Los Angeles in 1971. His first television role was in an episode of "Kung Fu," and he has since performed in such television shows as "All In The Family" (recurring role), "Magnum, P.I." (recurring role), "L.A. Law," "Murder She Wrote," "Island Son" (recurring role), and "thirtysomething." Mr. Kusatsu has also appeared in several television movies, gaining recognition for his role in "Farewell to Manzanar." His feature films include *The Choirboys, Volunteers, Shanghai Surprise,* and most recently *Turner and Hooch.*

EL: How difficult was it to break into L.A. and how do you think it's changed for young actors today?

CK: I was like a fish out of water when I first came to Los Angeles. I got involved in a couple of showcase productions. I was never very motivated in the sense of "Got to hit the streets, make the rounds and knock on every agent's door." I still had a kind of personal fear to get over. In 1970, according to the IRS records, I think I grossed $1,250. But I got my Equity card because I worked in a theater called the Inter-City Cultural Center that was multi-ethnic. I wound up working in a drugstore because there was nothing else to do. Racially it was still kind of a closed shop; there wasn't much call for Asian actors. Also, the reputation of Asian actors wasn't great. They weren't trained, they got in during World War II making all the war movies. Even if they were lucky enough to get some lead roles, they weren't able to sustain

191

a career. In 1972 I joined the East-West Players, which was an Asian-American theater group. I was involved with them for eleven years, acting, producing, being the janitor, living in the back of the theater in one room. I finally got myself an agent and for two years could not break in. I kept on going to interviews but wasn't really prepared to go to interviews and meet directors. I had a chip on my shoulder; I assumed I wouldn't get cast because they prejudged. You learn not to do this; you get more with honey than you do with vinegar, as they say. In the meantime, those two years were well spent in acting classes, dance classes, children's theater, making $17.50 per performance.

People say "It's a racist society." I have to say, "It may be morally wrong to feel that you have to be ten times better as an actor than a white, but all it can do in the long run is make you better. It makes you become better prepared."

EL: You did a lot of stage work. How did that stage work help you or not help you when you began to work in movies and television?

CK: The stage work helps a great deal in the performance aspect of acting. You gain experience in front of some tough audiences. I remember one show at Northwestern that was just horrendous. It was called *The Duchess of Malfi* and it was a horrible experience. The show was so bad and so melodramatic that the tragedy was like a comedy. That's an example when you're laughed at and booed. But in good circumstances, you get to feel that you have an immediate connection with an audience. Then by doing it performance after performance, you get to hone it, you get a chance to work on your character. The experience of a long run on Broadway, two or three years, is one kind of experience. With summer stock, you have to rehearse one week and perform for two. While you're performing, you rehearse the next show. So you've got three or four shows in your head. You learn how to work fast and develop depth in characters quickly. What's good about doing theater and performing and training is that 1) you learn your craft, 2) you learn to hone and work your instrument, and 3) you learn how to perform, because not everything can be 100% from your soul like in method acting. Developing these techniques is the type of thing that will keep you going. I can remember the first time I auditioned and the casting

© 1989 Lorimar Television

director said "You're too loud." I was playing to thirty rows back. You have to do less with film and television; less is more because the camera is right in your face so that every little nuance can be read. When the film is shown in a theater, your face is eighty feet across, so if you're making weird faces, it shows. The thing I learned from film and television is the importance of being natural.

EL: The real test of being a good actor is to be able to do a scene well and then do it again and again. Is that where your technique layers into assisting your emotional approach?

CK: One great thing about film and television is that for the close up you can let it all out and then you can recreate for the other different set-ups, the medium shot, the master, etc., but you don't have to blow it all away and you're still able to capture something on film.

EL: Tell me about the audition process.

CK: I've developed a philosophy that the audition happens the moment you walk through the door. Even the mundane social thing of "Hi, how are you?" It's how you present yourself. They all know you're basically a good actor but they also want to have the secure feeling that they won't have to worry that you're going to screw up, or that they're going to have to hold your hand throughout the production—they don't have time for that. You can have a great audition but if you're sort of on the edge, they're going to say, "He's great, but not if we're looking at twelve weeks together." You also don't want a phoney-baloney type of behavior either because that's a big turn-off. I've also learned not to try and memorize the scene; if you get the material a day or two ahead, that's great. Don't try to memorize it. Carry the paper with you, it gives the illusion that you are doing a good reading but not looking down. You're familiar enough with the material so that your face is not buried in the paper, nor do you have the paper out of your hand and are wondering "Did I remember everything?" because then you're concentrating more on reciting the memorization than on giving the performance. You are giving a performance when you audition.

EL: How does one sustain a career?

CK: To sustain a career is to take a long view of what your goal is and how you're going to achieve it. I always use the analogy of football, albeit the players have short careers, but there are guys that have been 15, 16 years at the game. You have to always be prepared, you can't be a substance abuser, you have to work out, you may not have to take acting class, but work out your body, always be in good shape mentally, too. I know people who won't read for the director or the producer because they feel that their body of work should be known. I've learned to take the meeting, I'll take an audition, and I'm not going to be offended that they asked me to read. Also, by going to all these meetings and doing the readings and the auditioning process, it's a form of networking. They get to know who you are, they may not have known who you are but now they do. If you just blow them away at the auditions, they won't forget you. You have to be going out there constantly to challenge yourself to do it.

EL: How important is it to be in L.A. or New York, and which might be preferable?

CK: I think if you begin at a young age, get your theatrical training in New York. Try to get a reputation and then come to L.A. I believe in the philosophy that there will be a lot of tough breaks and good breaks, but you have to be able to deal with the rejection. If you can't deal with the rejection, then you can't be in this business. It's impossible to sustain 100% approval all the time. I try not to dwell on the "could have beens," just concentrate on what you've done and what you can do in the future.

EL: Any other advice for a young person thinking about pursuing an acting career?

CK: If you're going to college, it would be good to take a couple of sociology courses and psychology courses. I took one course in college called "Individual, Marriage, and Family." We were taught how to plan life insurance, health insurance, budgeting, all the practical knowledge one needs to get along in this world. As an actor, you're an independent contractor, so you've got to figure out, "I've got money for this, do I have money for that?" How much are you willing to have a limited lifestyle with the possibility that if you become successful those other rewards will come along later? Are you willing to suffer? That's the challenge.

EL: Is it easier now for Asian actors than it was because of what people like you have done?

CK: I think there are more casting opportunities for Asians because everybody wants to make it right to reflect society. There are many more opportunities now than in 1971 when I hit L.A., there's been a tremendous change in attitude. Every year there are going to be protests similar to the dispute about *Miss Saigon*, but the bottom line is twenty-five million dollars advanced sales says it all. I've learned to follow my own drummer and not be part of the group; if they say go right, I'll instinctively want to go left and make my own choices. I think one has to think of career moves as either lateral moves or moves that will move you up. Sometimes you take the lateral move to keep going, to provide cash flow, and then you pick some roles that will help advance your career. You always have to have hope, that dream. There's got to be something more than making money; you're in the business for more than just being a product endorsement for orange juice or tennis shoes. That's one thing I feel fortunate about; I'm doing work that I wanted to do since I was fourteen and I'm getting paid for this. I consider myself a very lucky person.

Danny Glover

■ ■ ■ ■ ■ ■ ■ ■ ■ ■ ■ ■ ■ ■

A native of San Francisco, Danny Glover attended San Francisco College and trained at the Black Actors' Workshop of the American Conservatory Theatre, where he appeared in numerous stage productions. His early film credits include *Escape From Alcatraz* and *Iceman*. In 1984 he received critical acclaim for his role in the Academy Award-winning *Places in the Heart*, and his roles in *Witness, Silverado,* and *The Color Purple* during the following year brought him increased attention. He gained international star status with his roles in *Lethal Weapon,* for which he received the NAACP Image Award, *Lethal Weapon II,* and *Lethal Weapon III*. He received his second Image Award, as well as an ACE Award, for his performance in HBO's 1987 presentation of "Mandela." Other television performances include PBS' "A Raisin in the Sun," "Dead Man Out," and "Lonesome Dove," for which he earned an Emmy nomination as Best Supporting Actor in a Miniseries or Special. His most recent films include *To Sleep with Anger, Predator 2, A Rage in Harlem,* and *Grand Canyon*.

EL: Can you briefly talk about your education? Did you study acting?

DG: Well, as you know, people are directed toward this field for various reasons. Some begin as writers, others begin as something else and end up doing this. I had been primarily moved at that time in my life by political circumstances and what was happening around me both politically and socially, including the civil rights movement, the anti-war movement, and the new emerging black consciousness movement. In fact, what I had intended to do with my new attitude and understanding of Africa was to major in economics and play some role in developing countries. Being able to play some role in changing the world was the main catalyst for whatever actions I took at that particular time. That's the whole premise. Initially as a kid I wanted to be a probation officer or have some job someplace where I could work with kids and young people.

EL: Did you find that you were attracted to acting and/or to the message of the work?

DG: I found that I was first attracted to the importance of art. That was essentially the first impression that I got. Such a strong impression. I'd never really considered art as anything other than a vehicle to move people. I never thought about that; I never gave any thought to it. But the fact that you could move people by this, that you could elicit some sort of reaction from them, was amazing to me. It was another kind of revelation. I became involved with this movement that involved purely community art—there was nothing commercial about it. The only thing that we did was to try to get people to come out and see it. It was not designed to be commercial art. It was total politicization. The plays I did generally had the same theme of racial exploitation, that we had been used and abused by the system. Most of the time, by the end of the play, we were made to look heroic. So it was an attempt to uplift the audience and make them heroic. We had no intention to develop a base that would eventually rival that of Hollywood or Broadway, or anything like that. We were doing very simple plays. We were providing what we felt was a particular need for the community.

EL: So did you ever study acting formally?

DG: For a year in 1975.

EL: What happened?

DG: Eventually I just stopped acting. I finished school and went to work. When I came back to acting, my approach was recreational. It wasn't until my thirtieth birthday that I made the decision that I wanted to try to make a living as an actor. That was thirteen years ago.

EL: Did you find that year of training helpful or not helpful?

DG: Oh, absolutely helpful. I think what training does more than anything is reaffirm your instincts. It has to do that initially; that's one of the objectives of training. Once your instincts are reaffirmed and you can begin to trust them, there are so many other places you can go. It provides a link or avenue for the other places you can go as an actor.

EL: With whom did you train?

DG: I trained with the American Conservatory Theater. I was in a special workshop. I worked in the daytime and went to the ACT at night. I did that for about a year and a half. I also did some training with several other scene study workshops. I did scene study with Wendell Phillips and Gene Shelton.

EL: When did you decide to try film?

DG: Film is not always a natural evolution because you always have a choice. In order to work on a different level you get an agent. My first avenue was theater. I was doing theater in places that were really well known for their theater. I was preparing myself on that level. There's a point where you can study and there's a point where you can work, but you begin to set your sights a little bit higher. The next sight was to actively look for work, to go out on film auditions rather than just theatrical auditions. So that's part of it. You begin to look for work and bigger challenges.

EL: Can you compare theater work to film work? Is there a difference?

DG: I don't dwell on the differences. Ultimately there is a real difference between approaching a piece that you're going to be doing for say forty or fifty performances. Quite frankly, it begins with the rehearsal period. In a rehearsal period you're looking at the script from the standpoint of having this enormous amount of time to associate yourself with and strongly develop the character motivation. It's a period of trial and error. The true difference is a major concern with film work—what it looks like, how it translates itself to the screen. Often the way a character translates onto the screen and the way it evolves on the stage are quite different. There are certain truths within both of those. But essentially they both employ an incredible amount of instinct. I think you rely on your instinct and your intuition. That's where the similarity begins with acting on both film and stage.

EL: Then it's the technique that changes?

DG: You act on both. I use the same process of evolution on film that I do on stage. I really do. Technique that is developed or does occur with film occurs from the standpoint that you're conscious of the camera. I really don't find the technique different. Perhaps I don't look for the difference. I try to use the same kind of process of exploration and understanding. In each story, whether it's on film or stage, the character has an arc of development, his own evolution. The story itself has an arc. For the story to work it has to have an arc. The character's arc itself is synonymous or part of that arc of the story itself. So you begin to try to find the character's truth and motivation. That's not general. You get down to specifics as you try to locate and discover them, but you try to find that within both those mediums.

EL: Do you ever talk with the screenwriter, or do you just deal with the screenplay as it is?

DG: Well, it depends. The film I'm working on now and the film I'll do after this one are films where I've had a great deal of contact and discussion with the director and the screenwriter. They're searching for something. I think that happens during the process of working on the film as well. When you're working on a play—and this is a major difference—you're able to construct everything right there for that moment in about four weeks. I mean right there. As you're working on the play you can make changes within it, during the four weeks' rehearsal, or whatever, until the play is up and mounted. You're able to make whatever decisions you're going to make before it opens. With film you may have only a quarter or a third of the film done within the fourth week of that process. Then you don't have it assembled. You have parts of it assembled. So what you're trying to do is tell the story cinematically by piecing it together. You're also informing what you're going to do subsequently as you continue the filming process and continue adding pieces to it. That's an entirely different process from theater. So your conversation with the director is different. With theater you're able to make the associations and the changes right there on the spot. But in a film you may shoot a scene, find out that the scene doesn't work (even though you've discussed it to death), discard it, and go shoot it again.

EL: It's much more complicated.

DG: But for the actor—the work I have to do in constructing the character remains the same. It's important that you don't get sidetracked by the fact that it's film versus the stage. My work is constructing and finding the character's truth. Finding it through the extension of my own honesty and vulnerability—all that remains the same process.

EL: Do you still study at all?

DG: I really don't. I remain a student by virtue of the fact that I still read the same books that I read fifteen years ago. They include *Respect for Acting* by Uta Hagen, *Presence of the Actor* by Joe Jonkins, and *Auditions*. In fact, I try to make a habit of doing that when I begin to work on a film—just to reorientate myself to what I think are those basic truths.

EL: You've had such a great career for a young man. Have you ever had any rough times in the early periods? Were there tough times, and how did you get through them if there were?

DG: I think tough times are relative in this business to each individual. I hear people tell stories about doing this and having to do that. I tend to be very pragmatic about a lot of things in life—the rent must be paid, my daughter must have shoes. Those are real things. I extend the energy to do the things that I have to do to meet those needs. Who is to say whether that's taking away from the time that I may be dwelling over this great acting book or this great scene study class or whatever? I was able to do the things I needed to do to develop as an actor and not have to go through this great period of deprivation. Ultimately, the place where I received the greatest opportunity to work, and consequently the greatest opportunity to grow, was in San Francisco. I think there's a point where, if it's really what you have a passion for doing, you move. But first you have to realize that you have the passion. You can move to the next level from anywhere. The lessons that I learned and the things that I did on the stage were no different than the things I did on the stage in San Francisco, or on the stage in L.A., or on the stage in New York. I didn't have to wait to get to New York to find the kind of truth that I tried to find; I had the opportunity to find them in San Francisco. I would have had the opportunity to find them wherever people were doing intensive work. If you surround yourself with good people you'll learn.

EL: What I find fascinating is that you have really structured your career on your own terms.

DG: Yes, I think so. You have to. The process of learning, the process of whatever we do in life, comes from everything we do. Every single thing I do. I'm the actor that I am because I'm the father that I am with the responsibilities that I take on. All those are important things. They inform everything that I do, and everything that I do informs my acting, as my life informs my work. You can't separate the two; it's impossible.

EL: What would you say to a young person who is pursuing acting?

DG: First you have to determine whether or not you have a passion for acting. I believe that persistence and passion can overcome anything. I tell this to young actors all the time. You start anywhere. You start by getting in front of a camera if you can, or on the stage. But realize that this is a process in life, that you're going on this incredible journey, and this journey is connected to your life. I think that's the first thing. You don't know where you're going to end up. You don't know if you'll end up as a Danny Glover, or a Kevin Costner, or whatever. But if you take this journey you're going to have to compromise along the way, but try to do it on your own terms; you have to do that. This is the process of learning. You build steps. You take one step, and that one step is the catalyst for another step and the opening of more doors, more challenges.

EL: It's a business in which a lot of people feel they have no control.

DG: There are a lot of things in life you don't have control over anyway. So it's basically defining yourself. As you define yourself in your life as a human being it leads you down that journey to defining yourself in terms of the work you do. Also remember that what you do is an act of giving, an act of love. It has to be an act of love. It must be.

NINE
∎∎∎∎∎∎∎

★ The Agent

The agent acts as representative for actors, directors, writers, cinematographers, and other creative members of the filmmaking team. The agent works with studios and producers and attempts to obtain employment for clients. Agents may represent only one kind of creative type—e.g., actors—or may represent a variety of creative professions. It is his/her job to strategize with their clients and develop a career plan, insofar as that can be achieved. Agents negotiate deals for their clients with the producing entity and may actually "package" a film, assembling several clients (director, writer, actor) on one film.

Agents may be paid on commission or on bonus. Some agents earn at least 10 percent of their clients' salaries. There is no union or guild for agents.

John Ptak

. . . .

John Ptak began his career in the entertainment industry in 1968. After graduating from the University of California at Los Angeles, he joined The American Film Institute, where he was a part of the team that established AFI's Center for Advanced Film Studies in Beverly Hills. In 1972 he became an agent with International Famous Agency, now International Creative Management (ICM). He served as vice president of the William Morris Agency from 1976 through 1990, where he was involved in the representation of numerous film and television producers, performers, and directors. In 1991 Mr. Ptak joined the Creative Artists Agency.

EL: Could you please summarize your formal education and how it did or didn't prepare you to become an agent?

JP: I received my Bachelor's Degree at UCLA. Then I transferred into the Film Department. It had more of an art school environment at the time, and there was very little professional training or drive towards learning about film as a business. We were "auteur-" and "filmmaker-" driven and foreign-film inspired, so when I graduated I barely knew where the studios were. It was, however, a good social environment, and the sixties was a wonderful period to be in college. I spent quite a bit of time just watching movies. For three or four years I must have averaged over 200 films a year. It became a valuable, lasting part of my education. I felt lucky to be working in a film environment while studying film at school. After graduation I ran a couple of movie theaters in town for the Walter Reade chain, and at the same time worked for the American Film Institute. I was part of a small group that helped set up the Center For Advanced Film Studies at Greystone, which was very exciting, but once out of the academic setting, things became complicated. It was the real world, and my professional focus was quite unclear.

EL: When you were studying film, did you have a goal in mind for yourself (directing, producing, etc.)?

JP: Not really, I think it was more making films than having any specific long-term goal in mind. To reflect, I think my own drive began more as a little kid who spent his Saturdays in the neighborhood theater watching double features, cartoons and newsreels, rather than as any formal business choice. Later, it was that Kurosawa/Truffaut/Bergman period that propelled me into film school. I really wanted to know what this was all about and to be a part of it. The professional focus came much later. I became an agent more by a series of coincidences, but if I had known what it was going to be like I would have planned it from day one. Generally, though, we had no idea; everybody wanted to be a "filmmaker," but you find out very soon that you're probably just not cut out for certain things and are perhaps better at others. You have to come to terms with yourself. The crafts involved with filmmaking are a lot more demanding than most people realize. Oddly enough, the thing that I enjoyed more than anything was editing. Editing is an absolutely wonderful exercise, but I didn't want to be an editor.

EL: How did you find your way into becoming an agent?

JP: I didn't have a job and I didn't have any money. I got the chance to be an agent and went for it. I had no idea what agents really did at the time, but it paid $125 a week. I figured I'd grab anything just to get into the business. I started working as an agent in 1972. I had tried producing for a while prior to that but couldn't last financially. I began to see that I was much better at organizing or speaking on other people's behalf rather than my own. As an agent I began to see certain similarities that this kind of advocacy could sometimes have to producing.

EL: So you started as an agent and you really didn't know what an agent did. Were you handed clients, or did you have to go out and find your own clients?

JP: The latter. I suppose if I was aware of how little I knew, I would have been quite intimidated by the situation. I was pretty self-assured and felt that I had seen every film ever made and had a bit of that sixties attitude. I knew a lot of people coming out of film schools such as UCLA, USC, and The American Film Institute. This came in handy as I became their professional contact and subsequently represented many of them. At AFI I worked directly with the grantees and first-year Fellows, although my role was largely administrative. I worked on various contracts, was a part of AFI policy discussions, and tried to arrange distribution for AFI films. During this period the Hollywood business was very established—an "old boy" business. A young writer, producer, or director was rare in those days. That alone created a certain sense of camaraderie and revolution among the Hollywood youth movement of the early seventies, just like the sixties. It was that way even in the agency business. The hands-on business experience at the AFI was a great help, practically speaking. The fellow that hired me as an agent, Mike Medavoy, was only a few years older than I was, which created a common spirit. We worked hard, but had fun doing it which allowed for a better learning environment. While most agents start out in a mailroom, I was an agent from day one, so I had to scramble as I learned.

EL: How would you characterize the role of an agent?

JP: In a word, advocacy, creatively and businesswise. Looking back, it's amusing how hard it was to explain to my relatives what I did as an agent. With no one even remotely connected with the entertainment business, they didn't understand how it worked. In fact, in the very beginning I had difficulty telling my friends that I was an agent because of the negative images it conjured up. That's since changed rather markedly. As to the process, the primary responsibility is to remember that it is a service business. You try to see that your clients are gainfully employed and that the business side of their lives is structured properly. You also try to ensure that there is a sense of career in mind, in other words, the long-term goal as well as the short-term goal. Thirdly, although it may be an employer/employee relationship, it's very much a partnership. Your obligation is to take care of business so that the client may properly attend to more creative matters. The advocacy element is important, as the agent is present on behalf of the client, so the manner in which the agent carries himself and characterizes his client is extremely important. It's a very careful, complicated business where personality, intent, and style are crucial. It's not just a numbers game.

EL: What kinds of skills besides business skills, such as understanding contracts and all that, are essential to the personality that can benefit an agent?

JP: I think that an agent has to be a people person as opposed to a numbers person. I think that the best training for someone aspiring to be an agent is to do whatever you can to be a generalist in your education. The numbers craft can be learned, even though it is becoming more and more complicated This is a business of people and ideas, movements, heroes, and storytelling. The worst thing you can do is simply take film classes. Don't limit your education to one source. Find out about drama and what moves people. I'm not discounting the business side by any means, only emphasizing that the business of film is very often a craft of intangibles, expectations, and surprises. It is crucial to understand the human element. Obviously if you don't understand numbers and contract language, you've got a problem, but I think that the emphasis should be film along with philosophy, art history, literature, history and sociology. A little time with law wouldn't hurt either, particularly contract and copyright.

EL: When a director walks in, how do you work with him to develop that long term goal?

JP: That depends on the director. There are directors and there are directors, as with producers, writers, or performers. A lot of directors, perhaps by personal metabolism alone, like to work a lot, in which case they are not necessarily dependent upon coming to a particular vision with regard to what they want to do. You look at certain directors' credits, and you wonder how they could possibly do so much. John Ford made five great films in 1939–40, including *Stagecoach, The Grapes of Wrath*, and *The Long Voyage Home*. Unbelievable, but then he didn't write or produce, and there was a supportive studio system. Ford had the classic studio employer/employee relationship at Fox with Zanuck. There are many directors that would love it if the business was still like that. There are many directors, however, who are driven by a different muse. Directors like Bernardo Bertolucci or Sydney Pollack only make a film every three or four years. As an agent, you must discern those differences. You have to be aware of different sets of circumstances, relationships, drives, and motivations at all times, whether they're directors, producers, writers, or performers. Above all, you have to be a believer. It's a business of emotions. Emotions turn tides.

EL: Is there any way that you can describe or characterize a typical day? How much time do you spend with your client; how much time do you spend soliciting work for them or working on deals? How does a day or a week break down?

JP: It doesn't. I would say every day is an aberration. There can be certain situations where most every client is working, and there are other cases where many clients are available. To answer in the most simplistic way, I would say that an agent's primary pressures, in order, would be to close deals, return calls and secure features.

EL: How many clients do you have?

JP: It can vary, and it's misleading to think in those terms. When you work in a larger agency, you interact with your associates and are often involved with their clients as well as your own. I'm also quite involved with the representation of films themselves via representation of the producer or production company, independent productions that involve banking transactions, foreign sales and distribution deals. *Dances with Wolves, Green Card, Until the End of the World*, and *Columbus* are examples. These productions can become quite complicated, often involving international co-productions between countries. It can easily turn your day into an eighteen-hour experience that can be pretty debilitating, but the reward is there as you can play an important role in actually getting the picture made.

EL: How do you acquire the expertise to deal with all these areas, particularly knowing how to work with banks, knowing how to work with other governments?

JP: You have to be aware of other modes of personal experience and business. If you're dealing with international situations, you must be aware of other cultures. This is the only country in the world that has an on-going corporate motion-picture business. The production of films elsewhere in the world is more on a picture-by-picture basis and is structured independently. My own growth in this area came about simply by servicing the needs of clients. The business is changing so rapidly that any agent must be sensitive to these changes so as to better service their clients. You have to stay on the cutting edge—eyes, ears, and mind open at all times.

EL: You're at a major international agency. What kind of back-up does the agency supply you with in terms of attorneys or contract people? Is there a team behind you?

JP: The support groups that exist at the larger agencies primarily involve an ability to access information. You are surrounded by associates who become your research sources. You find that you have access to information throughout the business very quickly. That may or may not be important to a client, but it is an asset that you can offer. The largest agencies all have business affairs departments, but they do not act on a legal basis on behalf of a client. The client, more often than not, will have an outside attorney for legal counsel, particularly clients that are involved in an independent production or with basic rights. Much of the basic work-for-hire situations in the business do not necessarily require much legal expertise, although it's usually good to build a relationship with an attorney as part of the team so that you are better equipped when the more complicated situations arise.

EL: What kind of changes have you seen over the time you've been an agent, and how do you foresee the business changing in the future?

JP: I've been in the business eighteen years, and I would say that when I first started it was truly a cottage industry, almost akin to a local

Rotary Club. There were six or seven places to go to get a film made and perhaps no more than twenty or so people who could make financial decisions. The success of *Easy Rider* obviously provided the genesis to a creative youth influx, but it wasn't until the mid seventies that the dam really burst. First it was the growth of the networks: As major motion pictures became more important to the networks, they would compete with each other for product. That caused inflation. It also encouraged the independent producer. As an independent, he knew that he could put together a director, a script, and, perhaps, a casting element and go directly to a network for a "presale" of limited broadcast rights. The producer would secure a financial advance for such rights to the film. This activity bypassed the one-stop studio "dependent" relationship. This way the producer gets the money solely for his picture, thus avoiding the studios' control of how the film would be sold. The studio has to look to its own priorities, stay competitive and deliver product to their distribution system. This agenda may differ from the producer's.

The next thing that happened was the astounding success of three films: *Close Encounters of the Third Kind*, *Jaws*, and *Star Wars*, which threw a blinding light on how much money there was out there. The minute that happened, all kinds of things began to pop; budgets began to soar; directors and stars became more marketable. A single film could change the course of a company. Each of those three films tremendously enhanced the studio that produced it. People began to see that this was no longer a little business, but an industry that could generate serious money all over the world. It was exciting being involved with two of these films. I agented the book sale of *Jaws* as well as the producers and initial writer of *Close Encounters*. The third event in the seventies was the advent of cable. HBO arrived and bought everything in its path to feed its subscribers an exclusive look at product without commercials, shortly after the theatrical run. This caused another inflationary spiral. After cable came video and yet another growth spiral through the eighties. Today a weakling dollar makes foreign revenues worth more than ever. Suddenly filmed entertainment is one of the most important exports in the country. What's interesting is that each of these events came along at a time when the business would otherwise have stalled.

Now Europe is expanding its home market. It's only been in the past couple of years that they had more than four or five basic television channels, and what was available was largely government run with no sense of competition for talent or product as we know it. The entrepreneurial spirit in television is still young in Europe. Imagine what will happen in the next five to ten years with twenty channels available in these countries. They will need new product and the domestic producers will not be able to supply it fully. There is one thing universal to the worldwide public, and that is the desire to see filmed entertainment from America. The same situation exists with video. In the U.S., I would say that the penetration level of VCRs on a household basis is somewhere around 70–75 percent. In Japan, maybe 70 percent if not more, France maybe 25 percent, the UK more then 50 percent and Germany about 40 percent. The next ten to fifteen years should bring incredible growth in this area. With an ever growing market in Europe, our films will be more responsive to European tastes as well. Remember that U.S. companies have the only firm grip on global distribution of filmed entertainment. Throughout the world one sees the logos of Warner Brothers, MGM, Paramount, Fox, Disney, Universal, and Columbia. These logos represent consistency and quality everywhere, yet the core of this business is still quite small. The studios will become even more international. They won't simply rely on the distribution of pictures that are shot within fifty miles of Burbank.

EL: Do you think the agency business is an open or closed business?

JP: It's definitely a growth business. The agency business will expand as markets become larger. The expertise will be increasingly specialized and more international. This is a business that must provide a continual stream of new product, and the need for youth and new ideas will grow as well.

Ronda Gómez-Quiñones

■■■■■■■■■■■■■■■■■■■■■■■■

Ronda Gómez-Quiñones received a B.A. degree in English Literature at UCLA and went on to receive an M.A. in Folklore and Mythology. She began her career in 1972 as the West Coast Story Editor at Paramount Pictures. In 1974 she became Director of Creative Affairs at Fox, and she joined the Freddie Fields Production Company as vice-president the following year. Ms. Gómez-Quiñones became an agent in 1978 when she joined Adams, Ray, and Rosenberg. When Triad Artists was formed in December, 1984, she became part of the merger. She is currently at Broder-Kurland-Webb-Uffner, representing numerous writers and directors.

EL: Can you briefly describe your formal education? How did it prepare you to do what you're doing now?

RGQ: I went to UCLA for undergraduate work in English literature, then I got a secondary teaching credential. I taught junior high school English for one year. I lived in Mexico when I was married and taught there for a few months at an elementary school. While I was there I took some courses in teaching English as a second language. I came back and went to graduate school at UCLA in the Folklore and Mythology department. When I was in graduate school I got interested in documentary film. I knew I didn't want to stay in academia. I had a cousin who was a casting director in New York. She came to California with her boss to shoot commercials in L.A. and introduced me to Howard Zieff. I ended up doing gofer work for them when they were out here. Howard then introduced me to a friend of his, Irv Kershner, who was going to direct a movie at Warners. He was looking for a secretary/ "girl Friday." I decided that was my opportunity. That was really the

beginning, that just opened the door. I started reading scripts for him—
doing everything. One thing led to another. From Kersh I went to work
for Terry Malick. In 1972 I started at Paramount and eventually became
the story editor there. There were no women V.P.'s at that time. There
were really just a few of us doing feature films. Then one thing led to
another. I was at Paramount for a couple of years until I got a better
job offer at Fox. I was at Fox for a year; I was fired. Then I went to
work for Freddie Fields in development. I got tired of being in development but never being able to really produce—just developing scripts
and then turning them over to somebody else. I knew all of the men at
what was then Adams, Ray, and Rosenberg, a small prestigious tiffany
literary agency. I worked with them through those years. They were
looking to bring in a woman. They offered me the job as an agent and
I decided I would take it.

EL: How did you get your first clients?

RGQ: Because I had been in the business at Paramount and Fox for
several years, I knew a lot of writers. Also, the way Adams, Ray, and
Rosenberg operated was like a family. It was wonderful. Ethically,
morally—they were just the best people. They didn't say, "You must
deliver clients or you're going to be out of here." I became an agent
and the first few months were spent just learning how to make a deal.
I was terrified. They would then turn over a territory to me once they
thought I knew what I was doing. Everybody represented all of the
clients. So if I had to call up the head of United Artists at the time
and he was interested in Alvin Sargent, he had to talk to me about
Alvin Sargent. That gave you a powerful position right away.

EL: What was the hardest thing about becoming an agent and not really
having gone through a "traditional" internship?

RGQ: Making the deals. I shouldn't say it's a male/female thing. I can
only relate it to myself, but I still think there is a basic difference. I
do think men enjoy the thrill of the dealmaking. That, in and of itself,
is what they love. I look upon it more as the means to the end, which
is getting the movie made, getting the client work, getting the client
recognized, and all of that. I think it was intimidating for me because

I'm terrible at math. I had a fear of making a mistake; I didn't understand the legal parts of it. But I was with this family, men of whom I knew I could ask anything; they were always there to back me up. I still remember Sam Adams telling me that what you have as an agent is your reputation. If you're not sure about something, just be straightforward and say you don't understand; you'll get back to the person. That was the biggest help knowing that I didn't have to worry about making a mistake, not having to bluff, and always being direct and above board. That's how I started out. That's the way it still is. That really did save me. I was able to say to a Business Affairs person, "Could you slow down on that point?" "What does that mean?" Everybody was great about it. You make a big mistake if you try to fake it and bluff your way through. Honesty is always the best policy.

EL: Can you characterize a typical day for an agent?

RGQ: One nightmare after another! Actually, there is no typical day. There are good days and bad days. The good days are when you get the client you wanted to sign with you; when the deal you wanted for somebody (a "go-movie" for a director, for example) closes. Those are the good days. The bad days are when a client leaves you for another agency; when you fail to get the job that you thought was coming the client's way; when a script that you've been waiting for from a client arrives and it's not good. Those are the bad days. In terms of the actual daily work—lots of meetings and phone calls.

EL: How long is an average day at work?

RGQ: Oh, endless. My day usually starts at 7:00 a.m. when I get up. I'm out of the house by 8:15 a.m. at the latest. I usually have an 8:30 a.m. breakfast or a staff meeting. Several mornings a week there are mid-morning meetings at the office. Of course, there's always a lunch meeting somewhere with a buyer, a client or a potential client. Yesterday's was with the head of a studio. Things like that. Sometimes there will be mid-afternoon meetings. I try to space it so I don't have meetings every single day of the week because then you never get to the phone calls. I like to go out to the studios and actually visit.

EL: You have a fair percentage of minority clients. Is that by design or by accident?

RGQ: Probably all of the above. First of all, I believe if somebody is talented they deserve representation. Nobody is really color-blind. I think that America is not really a melting pot. It's a stew, or whatever metaphor or analogy you want to use. As far as I'm concerned, there still is a lot to be done in terms of ethnic representation in Hollywood. The difficulty, everybody will tell you, is that this is show *business* not show *art*. The bottom line is, "Will it make money?" The Hudlins, whom I represent, are quite astute. They know that it could change tomorrow—that all of a sudden everybody won't be courting black filmmakers because they won't be making money at the box office. To me, that's criminal. But it is a reality that you have to deal with. I think both the Latino and the Asian community have not been included except peripherally. They should have a much more visible presence both behind and in front of the camera. But in terms of what clients I sign, I sign them on the basis of their work.

EL: How do you take someone who may not be well known and really get attention paid to them?

RGQ: You just pound on the table and you say, "Attention must be paid!" In reality, how do you get somebody started who is new and unknown? I think a lot of it does rest on my reputation. People know that I don't hype. If I say that somebody is good, they believe me. It's much easier to get an unknown writer started than an unknown director. Again, this is due to economics. A writer can sit down at the computer and write an original screenplay. If it's good, it will find a buyer somewhere, or people will get interested in the writing and eventually that person will get a job. But if somebody has only directed a short film, and that person is not a screenwriter, and you now want the studio to finance a ten to fifteen million dollar movie with this unknown person who has only done a twenty minute film, it's a lot harder. That's where it's tough. But if you read a script and fall in love with it and think, "OK, maybe I won't sell this one, but I think I can get this client work based on this script," then you get out there and you call people.

Again, I think if your reputation is good, you will get these people to read the screenplay. It's hard. You get cynical as you get older. I now understand why so many agents say, "I don't want to take on an unknown writer or director." It's too much work, and then when you finally get them established, they leave you. Somebody else more powerful comes along and plucks them away. There is no loyalty in this town. This is the cynical, negative side. I've seen it too often. It's very painful when it happens. You don't mind when a client leaves when, for whatever reason, it isn't working out. There are certain frustrations, and sometimes it doesn't work. But it's very tough when you've done everything right, the client is successful, and then somebody whispers in their ear and they just decide, "Oh yeah, maybe I do need a change," and they're gone.

EL: So if that's one of the downsides, what are the upsides?

RGQ: The upsides are that there are those few people who really are loyal and appreciative. You do feel that there is a partnership and you see their career progress, especially when you have found them when nobody knew who they were. You're there to also share in the rewards that come in. Everything in this business has its ups and downs and also has its craziness and fun. I think that's why we're all here. We're all gamblers and risk-takers to one extent or another. Within the parameters of this business the agency part of it is probably the most stable. Even though clients come and go, you get new clients if you're good at what you do. Studio executives get paid a lot more money, but that's a revolving door as we all know. Independent producers have a really rough time. And God knows, the writers, directors, the actors, and particularly the actresses, have the roughest road of all. They never know where the next job is going to be, whether there will be another job. It's a constant roller coaster ride.

EL: How did you develop a sensibility for good screenwriting? What is good screen directing? How much of your brain calculates the saleable and the "This is so good it just has to be made"?

RGQ: That is tough. When I first started reading scripts for Irv Kershner, I shared an office with Rick Richter (W.D. Richter), and I was intimidated by the job. Rick said, "What are you intimidated for? Here you are an English Lit major. You have an M.A. in Folklore and Mythology. Do you think any of these other people know anything that you don't know?" I realized he was absolutely right. First of all, I am an avid reader. I do think I have a brain. Once you start reading screenplays, you begin to know what the form is, and you talk to directors. It's a learning process in terms of what is on the page. Can you visualize what it's going to be on the screen? To me, good writing is good writing. Now, I do have certain blind spots. I'm not somebody who is good at picking certain action-adventure, *Robocop* kind of movies. I don't get them, and I don't really know how to judge them very well. So I usually turn that over to other people here. I don't need somebody to tell me whether I think anything else is good or not. As for the salability of the script, we work together as a team here. So if we have a script that a client has written, or maybe a potential client has sent us something, several of us will read it. Initially, at least two or three people, if not three or four. Because we really know what the studios are looking for at any time, we can take a fairly educated guess on whether we think it will sell.

EL: Do they tell you "We are looking for X, Y, or Z"?

RGQ: They do from time to time. A lot of it depends on what the latest big hit is. So right now any movie with kids in it—suddenly everybody's interested. Six months ago they were still into action films. You pick up on that.

EL: What personal and professional skills do you think a good agent needs?

RGQ: I think it's part psychologist, and depending on what age you are in relationship to the client, you're part mother, or part sister, or father, whatever. I also think that you do have to be tough, for lack of a better word. Tough and firm, and know in the negotiating process when to close the deal, and how far you can go with it. I do think you have to like to talk to people. I can't think of any agent who is shy. You're a salesperson—you just have to go out there and sell. Back in the Adams, Ray, and Rosenberg days, Rick Ray said to me, "Just remember that ninety percent of an agent's work ends in failure." It's true. You're always putting people up for jobs. You're always trying to get somebody work, or trying to sign someone. Most of the time you will not succeed. Somebody else will get the job. Eventually, you will get that person work. So there is a lot of frustration. You do have to be able to clearly communicate with people. I think everybody has their own style. You have to be true to what you do best. Again, that's why I like the way we work as a team. Everybody has his or her strengths or weaknesses, and we balance each other in that way.

EL: Is coming up through the mailroom still the only way?

RGQ: I actually think it's a terrific way. Looking back on a lot of the mistakes I made, I think that if I had had a better view of how the *business* works, I might have done better in other areas. I think the mailroom and coming up through an agency is an excellent way for somebody who wants to produce, or run a studio, or work with writers, directors, actors, and actresses. You learn both the business end of it, and you have access to scripts, to knowledge. Who are the players in this town and how does it work? It really is a wonderful training ground. At the same time, it depends on what they want to do. If the person wants to direct, then they should be trying to do short films, one way or another. If the person wants to write, they should be writing screenplays. Not just one script over and over again. If they have to write five or six, then that's what they should be doing. It's a hard business, with good days and bad days. Sometimes there's no justice. Nobody ever said this world was fair. I see people that I really think are mediocre talents and yet they're doing just fine. Somebody who is really good, for whatever reason, can't get that one break. You have to go in knowing that that's what happens—rejection. You have to be able to take rejection. You begin to understand why actors and actresses are psychotic by the time they become stars. At least with writers and directors, when they're rejected it's one step removed; it's not personal—the screenplay is rejected. Everyday actors are being rejected by the way they look, by their performance. You have to have the perseverance and that ability to take that rejection, go past it, and deal with failure. Did you ever read Tom Rickman's article, "The F Word"? Sooner or later everybody fails. I often think that every studio executive should have to do one year in the field. They should know what it's like to be an independent producer. To know what it's like to "pitch" ideas at those meetings. I've always believed that. Otherwise, they don't know how painful it is. Some of these people live for that one meeting. Many studio executives are former agents and know nothing about production. They've never been on a sound stage, have no idea what a gaffer is, and yet are in this position of power telling the director, who's had years and years of experience, what he or she should be doing. Also, as an agent, when you represent the people, you're their buffer to that world. You're the one who often has to break the bad news to them that their project isn't going forward, or that the writer is going to be replaced by another writer. I can never escape from it. What agents sometimes forget is that to the client you are their link to that outside world. You're the only one who is out there, supposedly, selling them.

EL: It's a big responsibility. I suppose you can't think about that.

RGQ: Well, I think you have to think about it from time to time. It's tough when somebody's career is not going well, and you have to try to figure out how to turn it around. It's not only the psychological devastation, but often the economic situation. Let's face it, in this business we are paid quite well. But what often happens is people live beyond their means. When there's a long strike or they hit hard times, boy, it's scary.

EL: Any differences between working for a small boutique agency and a big powerful agency? Advantages and disadvantages to either side?

RGQ: Everybody will be tooting his or her own horn in that respect. There is something to be said for a large agency. You represent all aspects of the business. You have more access to knowledge and power. You can put things together. For me, it's much more exciting to have access to the actors, to the whole music division. There's a lot of cross-pollination.

Rick Nicita

■ ■ ■ ■ ■ ■ ■ ■ ■ ■

Rick Nicita graduated from Wesleyan University in 1967. He began his career working in the mailroom of the William Morris Agency in New York in 1968. Two years later, he became an agent in the Motion Picture Department after spending two years as an assistant. In 1976 he transferred to the Beverly Hills office, and in January of 1980 he left William Morris to join Creative Artists Agency. He is currently head of the Talent Department and co-head of the Motion Picture Department at CAA.

EL: Would you tell me about your background?

RN: I attended high school in suburban New York. Then I went to Wesleyan University in Middletown, Connecticut. I was graduated with a B.A. in English, never a writer but always a reader. Then I had a great law school experience. I'd always wanted to be a lawyer, but I found that I didn't like it at all and I dropped out within a year. In this business the only time I ever say where I went to school is under a circumstance like this for biographical data. It has no weight, it's irrelevant except in the way I'm able to apply it. Your educational background is something that you never refer to.

EL: How did you find your way to becoming an agent?

RN: After I dropped out of law school I had to come to grips with the fact that I wasn't on an automatic path anymore. I had to decide what I really wanted to do. I had done summer work involving show business, particularly traveling with some rock and roll tours. There were a lot of forces compelling me one way or another. First was the pressure not to drop out of law school but to stay, slug it out and do something serious. I decided I wanted to go for what I really desired, regardless

223

of what ensued. I would wake up in the morning, have nowhere to go once I'd dropped out of law school, and I'd read the *New York Times* which was delivered to the door. I had a college friend who was working at the William Morris Agency, and I realized that though I wanted to be in show business, I didn't even know what an agency was, I didn't know anything. I called my friend and said, "I dropped out of law school, I want to work for the William Morris Agency; I want to get into show business." He said, "OK, but all I can do is get you an "in" with the personnel director. You'll be working in the mailroom for $35 dollars a week full-time." So I took the job and I started in May of '68 at William Morris in New York. It's now 22 years later, and I've worked for only two companies, William Morris and CAA. The only thing I've ever done is work at a theatrical agency.

EL: So how long were you in the mail room?

RN: On my first day David Geffen quit, so we had an overlapping William Morris career. It's a traditional place, the mailroom, like *The Famous Teddy Z*. It's a joke, but in truth it's the only way to learn. There is no textbook on how to do it; there's no way to study except first-hand, to study people who are doing it. It's hard to define what the work is, no amount of preparation or research will show you really how to do it, nothing even comes near it. You have to watch first-hand. Obviously, the cheapest way for a company or an agency to get you to observe things is to pay you something while you're standing around watching and having you do something for them. Traditionally you deliver mail and set up lunches in rooms for the agents and deliver scripts and then you become a secretary. It is an effective way of training. I can't think of a better way because it is almost as good theoretically as if you sat next to the agent and watched. But then you'd seem rather foolish. Through the hands-on experience you get a sense of the pace, and it's the pace that is so unusual about this business. That's the determining factor—whether you can be in this business. This business is about people and pace. You have to like a lot of things happening at once. If you have to do things in a slow and thorough manner, and you like to ponder, then you won't like it.

EL: Are there a variety of ways to do the work of an agent?

RN: At first all you see are the basics of the job: who the people are you're dealing with, what their function is, their relative importance in getting done the things you have to do, etc. As you get to the more experienced, sophisticated, higher levels you see that people have totally different styles—like pitchers in baseball. Some follow the basics, get it across on the plate, don't throw it too wide, get it in the strike zone, but then other pitchers are overpowering; some pitchers throw with more finesse. Whatever my style is, it is, and it's quite different from that of other agents.

EL: Can you identify basic characteristics that an agent must have?

RN: You have to love this business; you just have to love it without reservation; you have to be addicted to it. It has to be your idea of a great way to exist in this crazy, emotional, joyous, desperate world. It isn't an intellectual choice such as, "I've considered various theories and I believe that . . .", forget it. You're doing this because you couldn't possibly exist doing anything else. If you're into this, you don't have to be told what the payoff is. It's a business where you can make lots and lots of money, but I think the best way to go about this business is probably to ignore that aspect. Don't follow the money. Don't let your decisions have anything to do with money. You have to have a different goal; in this business the money will find you. If you're running your career well, know where the joy and the accomplishment are, know where your personal goals are, know what things you want and what the challenges are, you couldn't get out of the way of money! As long as I could pay the bills, I never schemed to make more money. I was too busy thinking of ways to do a better job.

EL: Do you think people feel negotiating skills are very important?

RN: Negotiation skills are acquired and somewhat overrated in many aspects of this business. There are always certain parameters you're working in. There are always some incredibly skilled negotiators, but I don't think that's the key. It is people skills. Actually it comes down to a question of style. I try to win without anybody knowing; I'm the only one that knows I won. Everyone should walk away not quite sure who won; then it's easier to come back next time. The people who advance in this business are those who speak with a certain amount of conviction, certainty, and authority, a quality nonquantifiable, as we were saying before. You can't measure how good an actor is by saying, "Why he's 48 feet and 6 inches, wonderful, better than the one who was 44 feet." It's not possible.

EL: How do you find and develop clients?

RN: We're not known for developing young talent even though we do. We tend to be a star-oriented agency.

EL: Is there any way to characterize an average day?

RN: An aerobic workout. This may sound weird but I try to work and think of just one thing, and it starts Monday morning and ends Friday night. I don't have a 9-hour, a 10-hour or even an 18-hour day; I have a 24-hour day. That's basically it.

EL: Is it a business open to young people?

RN: Yes, it's a business that's fluid, and the job can be created. There's always room for somebody bright, ambitious, with a touch. You can't be shut out because the slots are not that precise; there's room for somebody who's a pencil sharpener, a gopher, somebody to get a cup of coffee. Once you're in that door, the rest is up to you. With a generous amount of fate and luck, once you're in that door, you've got it made.

EL: How long does it take to really break in?

RN: I would say after about two years, you ought to be well on your way or you need a re-examination of your life.

EL: How would you characterize the kinds of clients that you like to work with?

RN: It always has to be someone that I feel that I can benefit, one that has more career opportunities to come, as opposed to somebody I might accompany as things sink. It's too emotional for me. I've great respect for those people but I can't do that. If the arrow is other than pointing up, I can't do it. I work so closely with clients that they must be people whom I enjoy because so much is asked. I feel so much is given by an agent that I have to be happy to hear that person's voice on the phone. If the phone rings at 3:00 a.m.—and it does—when I pick up and hear the voice, I have to be concerned.

EL: Do you prefer to work with writers or directors or actors?

RN: Actors. I like actors, actresses, directors. I enjoy working with directors, but my real love is actors and actresses. Every emotion is there, it's like a buffet of feeling working with them. As I said before, this business exaggerates or amplifies every emotion; if you're insecure you become more insecure; if you're happy, you become giddy; if you're sad, you become miserable during the course of the day, during the course of conversations sometimes. I admire them so, I enjoy them so, and I'll forgive them anything.

EL: Did you have a mentor, or was it an apprenticeship with many people?

RN: That's a good question. I did not have one mentor, but I think I'm not typical. Certainly I think it advisable and common to have a mentor or mentors in this business. Anyway, it's a natural evolution from apprenticeship to having someone to watch, someone whose style you gravitate to. It is really the way to learn in your own way. It's all guts; it's not a cerebral business, it's a business of instinct. You have to want it.

TEN

.....

⭐ The Attorney

The attorney acts as legal representative for actors, directors, writers, and other members of the filmmaking community. The attorney works with studios and producers, and negotiates the terms of a client's contract. Attorneys may be employed by large firms or by smaller specialized firms. Often the attorney is also involved in career strategies for their clients. Although the entertainment attorney's specialty is the field of film and/or television, the basis of their work is grounded in a strong legal foundation.

Starting salary for an attorney in the entertainment field can be approximately $75,000. There is no union or guild for this field.

Stephen Barnes

Stephen D. Barnes was born and raised in Los Angeles. He earned a Bachelor's Degree in English Literature from the University of Southern California, and received his J.D. from Harvard Law School. Upon graduation in 1981 he joined the firm of Covington & Burling in Washington, D.C., where he practiced corporate and entertainment law. In 1986 he moved to Beverly Hills to practice corporate and entertainment law for the firm of Weissman, Wolff. Feeling restless, he left the firm to join two other young lawyers in forming Nelson, Barnes & Sheehan, where he continued to practice entertainment law. In July, 1989, he accepted a partnership with Bloom, Dekom & Hergott, a prominent entertainment firm representing entertainers and companies active in the business. The firm's clients include Sylvester Stallone, Arnold Schwarzenegger, Bruce Willis, and George Lucas. Mr. Barnes currently practices entertainment law with an emphasis on music, motion pictures, and television. His clients include Keenan Ivory Wayans, Kool Moe Dee, Vanessa Williams, and Jennifer Holliday.

EL: Could you summarize your formal education?

SB: I went to Washington High School, an inner-city high school in Los Angeles, now known as Washington Prep. Then I went to a junior college, West L.A. Community College, for a year, and transferred to the University of Southern California, where I majored in English Literature and received a Bachelors degree. I went to Harvard Law School and received my J.D. degree.

EL: When you were entering law school did you know that you wanted to specialize in entertainment law?

SB: Yes, I did.

EL: What was attractive to you about being an attorney?

SB: Counseling people and negotiating were the most appealing aspects to me. Also, attorneys appeared to be among the few that really understood what was going on and were able to make a difference. They impacted deals, they got a measure of respect that I did not see others who were less trained get. They may not have been liked more, but they seemed to be the survivors of deals and the ones who really were pivotal in the process, and that was of great interest to me.

EL: What kind of clients do you represent?

SB: What I would call "cutting edge" clients; people I would consider to be somewhat innovative risk-takers who have a creative vision and perspective. Although they may not presently be in the mainstream, I feel that they ultimately will be. They're very talented, aggressive individualists.

EL: In both music and film?

SB: Yes, and television.

EL: Do you think that doors are opening for young people of color in this business? Is it any better than it was five, ten years ago?

SB: It's the best of times and the worst of times. I think it's better now because some people are getting opportunities, and through them, hopefully, there will be continued opportunities. It would be misleading, however, to suggest that because there is more visibility among some black entertainers that that translates immediately into opportunities. Those who make the decisions operate in a very narrow environment that is relationship-based. There are so few minority entertainment professionals, and we tend not to have or develop the relationships with the traditional entertainment community, and therefore it becomes more difficult to break through. I see it changing. There are people from more traditional backgrounds who will be more open, and as they are they will encourage others to act the same way. Those minority professionals most affected will be those with the more innovative, creative talent and perspective who will use their clout to bring about greater openness.

EL: How did you get positioned where you are today?

SB: A number of my clients specifically wanted to be represented by a black lawyer. A combination of being in the right place at the right time, having an educational background that provided me with competitive skills, and achieving success professionally has positioned me in a way that has made that possible. Ten years ago it was possible for a minority professional, but the circumstances have changed for the better, even though a number of the black professionals that were successful then are currently not working in the entertainment business. This causes me and many of my peers to pause and wonder if we'll be around in ten years. If we do not build businesses and make inroads into the more traditional structure, does that mean that our time is somewhat limited as well? Many of us really believe that you can't ignore the past.

EL: When you went to Harvard did you focus on entertainment law? Did they have that track at Harvard?

SB: No. Harvard has a more general curriculum. I took courses that I thought would be helpful to me in a business-oriented law practice. I took corporate and copyright law courses, but otherwise had a more general legal education.

EL: How do you build on that general legal education for the specifics and the the eccentricities of this business?

SB: A lot of it has to do with personal interest. If there is something you really want to do, you learn it. I did not join one of the entertainment law firms directly after law school, so I did not have—from day one—an institutional entertainment experience. Over time that has been a plus because I don't feel confined to the traditional approaches and people don't always know quite what to expect from me. My approach is usually sort of a combination of a variety of things.

EL: If a young person is fortunate enough to enter a prestigious firm right out of law school, what can they expect for the first year or two, and when do the heavy responsibilities come?

SB: Most of the large law firms say that they give you as much responsibility as you can handle, and in my case that was true. You define much of what happens. You do the low-level work initially, that is, a lot of research and writing, both of which I think are important skills to have. As soon as you can assume responsibility, they give it to you, in part because everyone is so busy. They like go-getters. There is great fear and concern among associates to maintain the quality of the work, so there's a lot of very meticulous work. The job entails long hours, hard work, yet it's usually fun to begin with. I have always enjoyed law practice, so I didn't complain that much. It did cause me to focus on what I really wanted to do with my life; because you spend so much time learning things you realize the impracticality of making a major career change. You become an expert in one area, can be very highly paid, and can receive a lot of other rewards—so to start all over again is risky and difficult.

EL: As an entertainment lawyer in Los Angeles, how do clients find you? Do they hear about Stephen Barnes, do they come into the firm, or is it a combination?

SB: Clients find me based on my reputation and through my existing clients. I have gotten some additional business since being at my present firm, partly based on the firm's reputation and partly because of the areas in which I practice and the visibility that has come from the success of my clients.

EL: Would you describe entertainment law as an open or closed field for a young person?

SB: I was recruited to work in an entertainment firm, but I was not recruited to do what I do today. Entertainment law practice is difficult to break into and required that I take an even greater risk. I went out on my own with several other people and formed a firm because I wasn't given the opportunity to be an associate in an established entertainment firm. It could be even harder for those who didn't have the benefits that I have, partly my family, my brother in particular who's involved in the entertainment business. That helped because I knew people who were in the music industry and was able to get a few clients in the beginning; it didn't open every door, but it certainly made it easier. Also, having gone to Harvard and having worked at Covington & Burling were helpful. I think it takes a burning desire to do it, and you cannot be easily discouraged. In that sense you're much like your clients who succeed, you must continue to persevere despite many obstacles. If you really want to do it, you can do it, but not everyone is good at getting clients. You have to look at what your skills are, focus on your strengths and try to round out the weaknesses.

EL: Why did you choose to be with a large, powerful firm rather than out on your own? What are the advantages and disadvantages to both?

SB: I've realized several things about working on your own as opposed to being with a large firm. When I was on my own, before I came here, I had a number of clients who are now very successful. They were just on the brink of becoming very successful. For example, the Hudlin Brothers' movie *House Party* opened a month before I came here, and Keenan Wayan's television show "In Living Color," which I had set up, debuted before I came here. I had confidence in my clients and I felt that they would succeed. When I took a look at the entertainment industry, I knew I wanted to become a partner in an established entertainment firm. I wanted a level of visibility and recognition and access to information and I felt that minority lawyers had been excluded from that environment. I hope to do as well economically here as I could do on my own, but that was not the paramount consideration. Part of it was that this reflected the fulfillment of a desire from years back. It came at a time that a partnership would have come to me had I gone immediately into a law firm and worked the required number of years. I felt that it put me back on a track that I had taken myself off of when I went out on my own. I also appreciated the significance of becoming a partner in an established law firm. With the success I was beginning to have, it seemed that there were other levels of achievement I could attain by associating. I also like the more collegial environment as well.

EL: What other skills besides a strong law background does an entertainment lawyer need?

SB: I think working with creative people requires a certain understanding of what a person goes through to be creative. There is a vulnerability that occurs in supplying creative work on a regular basis. I think a love and respect for the arts are important, and an understanding ear. I spend a lot of time just listening to my clients. I think a protective instinct is necessary as well. I find that no matter how good a job I do for my clients, the relationship is most fully secured when they feel vulnerable and I come in and help them. I am the person up front who takes the heat and is the aggressor for them. I've often thought about it because there are times when I feel I've done an incredible job for my clients and they take it in stride. When a problem comes up, and they realize they can call me anytime and rely on me, I think that is the point at which they realize that I am their lawyer. I can see the nature of the relationship change. It occurs at different times for different people. Those are the skills that are the most important as you relate to clients. There are certain client-recruiting skills that are also important, some of which are developed and some of which are more natural. I'm very loyal to my clients and I feel that we're on a mission together. I have an eclectic group of people whom I truly care about, so I could never lightly give up my practice.

EL: Can you characterize that mission at all?

SB: The mission is to, in some way, change the status quo and provide opportunities on a level that have not been provided before. I try to establish a firm foundation for what my clients do, one that is not so dependent on others to determine their destiny. This dependency on others was a contributing factor to why people who were very successful ten or fifteen years ago are not as successful now. Times have changed, and maybe at that time it wasn't possible to establish the kind of foundation that we can now. I think we're witnessing such transition in the world in the way we operate that I believe it is now possible. I think many people take it for granted that you cannot succeed on the highest level in this business, but that is certainly not my perspective. I think there's an equity that can be reached, but it requires making sacrifices and approaching things from a totally different perspective.

EL: What other advice would you give to young people who are considering entering this field?

SB: The first thing would be to concentrate on school. I am constantly approached by people who want to be entertainment lawyers. Many of them are in school already, either college or law school. I tell them that the opportunities are still going to be there, but you've got to get the skills. Verbal skills are crucial and one must learn to express oneself effectively and forcefully, and that comes through study and training. I always encourage people to focus on their studies, which is the last thing they want to do. I hope that people realize that it takes years and years of hard work. The other thing would be to learn about the entertainment business. Entertainment law can be attractive because it looks exciting and glamorous, but you've got to figure out where you fit in. If what you envision is hanging out on the set with Arnold Schwarzenegger, you're unlikely to make it in this profession because your priorities are wrong. If you want to become the best lawyer you can be and understand the business to such a degree that people want you to represent them, then you're heading in the right direction. The celebrities may like you as a person, but when they want their business handled, they're going to go to a person who has been successful for other people. I make an effort to encourage minorities to pursue college and graduate school, but not exclusively law school because I don't think it's for everyone, and there are certainly many great opportunities in the entertainment industry for educated people.

Melanie Cook

....

Melanie Cook was born in Salt Lake City, Utah. She attended the University of California, Los Angeles, and graduated magna cum laude in 1974. She continued her studies at UCLA, winning the UCLA Nathan Burkan Memorial Copyright Competition in 1977 and earning her J.D. degree in 1978. She was admitted to the bar a year later. Ms. Cook is a Phi Beta Kappa and a member of the Beverly Hills, Los Angeles County, and American Bar Associations as well as the State Bar of California. She is currently an attorney with the firm Bloom, Dekom and Hergott, where her clients include Tim Burton, Laura Dern, Holly Hunter, James Spader, and Tom Stoppard.

EL: How would you characterize the role of the attorney in film production?

MC: I think the role of the attorney in the film business has changed since I first became a lawyer twelve years ago. Lawyers now play a much more prominent role in the business which has become much more sophisticated. Years ago lawyers played a more passive role; they were involved in formalizing the agreements and documenting them in written form. Now there's a much more active role for the lawyer in terms of being part of the negotiation process. Lawyers are involved in the negotiation and the assemblage of financing for motion pictures. I think that many lawyers today have taken it a step further and, while they're not creative forces, they certainly help put various artists together, various clients together with producers, perhaps even with studios.

    I view my job to be that of an advisor; I don't think lawyers are necessarily limited to just giving legal opinions. In the entertainment business, a client faces many difficult issues concerning their representation, the type of material they choose, their career development. I have found that I've been asked my opinion in all these areas. As a lawyer we have a fiduciary duty; we keep the confidences of our clients; and people appreciate knowing that there is one person that they can talk to with complete confidentiality. In a town that thrives on gossip and information, people need a safe party to share their thoughts with.

EL: Can you characterize an average day?

MC: I don't start with breakfast. A lot of people start with a breakfast meeting but because I have a two-and-a-half-year-old daughter, I organize my day differently. I usually start at my home very early in the morning before the phone starts ringing when I still have some peace and quiet, and I do several hours of paperwork. When I get in the office, I spend the majority of my day on the telephone. I will be negotiating agreements, conferring with clients and agents on various projects—basic troubleshooting. I will usually have a business lunch with an agent, a studio executive, a manager, a business manager, or a client. The purpose of the lunch is to get to know someone, to talk about a specific project, or just to stay in touch with the people that I do business with every day. I usually work quite late, until 7:30 or 8:00 p.m. Sometimes I have dinners or screenings in the evenings, and it makes for a very long day. I do a lot of paperwork because, unfortunately, as much as the lawyer's role has increased in terms of being more active in the negotiation process, it has not decreased in the paperwork area. I need several hours a day just to do my paperwork. Then on the telephone, I will be negotiating specific deals.

EL: What kind of clients do you represent?

MC: I represent mostly individuals. Most of the individuals have corporations that loan out their services, but I primarily have an individual practice. I represent directors, writers, producers, actors, actresses, production designers, cinematographers, animators, novelists, and a very few companies.

EL: How much did you need to know about the filmmaking process when you started out in entertainment law in order to serve all those different creative people?

MC: The more you know, the better off you are. When I started out, I did not know much. In time, and as you work with various artists on specific projects, you learn an enormous amount about what your clients do. I firmly believe that the only way you can be an effective representative is by knowing your individual client and knowing what their particular goals and needs are. I don't believe there is one straight road to take in terms of commenting on an agreement or making a deal unless you really know the concerns of each specific client. Some people are more concerned with an amount of money. Frankly, most of the clients I work with are most concerned about creative control.

EL: When you're negotiating for them, with whom are you generally negotiating?

MC: Depending on the level of the deal you usually start with conversations with a creative executive, then you will negotiate with the head of the studio's business affairs.

EL: Are those people generally attorneys also?

MC: Yes, generally, particularly in features; sometimes in television they are not attorneys. You negotiate with business affairs to really establish the deal. Then the business affairs executive at the studio will send a memo, and they'll have one of the lawyers in the legal department at the studio prepare an agreement, and the next round of negotiations will usually be with a lawyer in the studio legal department. Sometimes I will negotiate with other lawyers in private. For instance, I may represent a producer who wants to acquire rights from a writer who's represented by another law firm.

EL: Is entertainment an open field for young people?

MC: I think it really depends on a person's personality and dedication, like any field where there is a lot of competition. If someone is very passionate about what they're doing and is talented, they will succeed.

There is plenty of entertainment work. There is no shortage of people needing entertainment attorney services, so once someone has the knowledge and is associated with a good firm, I think that there's endless opportunity.

EL: Is mentorship part of entertainment law?

MC: I think that it is, very much. Most people starting out, most associates, will work with a specific partner and will learn from that person. They will learn not only about the law, but also how to deal with clients, how to handle difficult situations, how to counsel people, and the ethics of the business.

EL: What is attractive about entertainment law? Why did you go into entertainment law rather than regular litigation or patent law?

MC: I like artists, I love movies, and I like creativity. It was an opportunity to practice my particular legal skills in an area that interested me and also in an area where I felt I could be constructive. So many lawyers are in situations where no one is happy; people are being sued, getting divorced, the foundation on their house is falling apart, etc. No matter how terrific a job you do in one of those negative situations, no one is going to be terrifically happy. In the entertainment field, you have the opportunity to work on something from the beginning—to contribute to a project coming together and succeeding. It's fulfilling because it's constructive. You have the opportunity to start with a client who acquires a script and see it through to the completed film on the screen.

EL: What is most frustrating about your field?

MC: The thing that's most frustrating to me personally is that I never feel like I have enough time. There's so much work to do, and in addition to doing all the legal work, I make an effort to try to stay current with movies and screenplays, so I never feel that I have enough time to do everything. It's also frustrating to work very hard on a project that doesn't get made, that doesn't succeed, that doesn't go into production after a lot of effort.

EL: What is the most satisfying thing?

MC: Knowing that you've contributed to someone's success. To be part of an ongoing process that results in movies that you're proud of, and also in careers that you can be proud of.

EL: What personal skills should someone have in order to succeed (taking it for granted that the person has good professional skills)?

MC: It helps to be a good listener, to really understand and be able to empathize with clients. The movie business is a very tough business. Even the most successful artists and creators are constantly faced with adversity, whether it's in the form of rejection for an actor or actress, or for a director from a studio. It's a very difficult business, and it's a very high profile business, so everyone's successes and failures are usually very public. If you fail in a corporate job, it's not something that's usually broadcast in critical reviews on television and in print. To appreciate the amount of strength that a client has to have just to make it through the day, and to understand the pressures that they have is really key to being a good advisor. Also, you have to have good sense and a knowledge of the business. It's not just a business of contracts, it's a business of relationships. You must really understand how the industry functions and be able to share that knowledge with a client, and offering insight is another valuable tool.

EL: Is it a good field for women?

MC: I think it is. I think there is probably less resistance to a woman in the theatrical feature area than in many areas of law.

EL: What advice would you give to somebody who is considering this as a career?

MC: Study hard, get good grades, and learn as much as you can about the entertainment business. That can be learned through seminars, summer programs, internships. I often wish that I had spent a summer at the mailroom of a major talent agency. I think it would really be an important experience. I truly love my job. It is not a job for wimps— there are some very tough times and as a lawyer and advisor, you are sometimes put in difficult positions. The more important you are to your client—which I think is a good thing and a satisfying thing—the more responsibility you will have, which is a weighty thing. It's not a job for somebody who wants to tidy things up at the end of the day and go home with a clear desk and a clear mind.

Don Tringali

■ ■ ■ ■ ■ ■ ■ ■ ■ ■ ■ ■ ■

Mr. Tringali is a partner in the Entertainment Department of Rosenfeld, Meyer & Susman, a Beverly Hills California law firm that practices primarily in the entertainment and related fields. His clients include major motion picture studios, film and television producers, writers and directors, several individuals, and independent companies involved in various aspects of the entertainment business. Since 1987 Mr. Tringali has served as general counsel for the American Film Institute. Mr. Tringali graduated Summa Cum Laude and Phi Beta Kappa with a degree in economics from UCLA and received his J.D. from Harvard Law School in 1982.

EL: How would you characterize the nature of what you do?

DT: It really depends on the client, how much involvement you have with a particular client. For individuals in film such as directors or writers or actors, you are generally a support to the agent. The agent's job is to find the work; in the case of stars it's usually fielding phone calls and deciding which offer to take. A lawyer will support the agent. Often it's the agent's job to be the salesman and do the broadstrokes. Attorneys often have to come in and get more detailed, more specific, clarify things that weren't defined. Often we can improve upon things that may have been just generally discussed by the agent. When you're talking about high-end people, where there might be a lot of money involved or the transaction may not be typical, there is a lot of opportunity to be creative. You may structure something differently, say for tax reasons. When you're dealing with production companies, finance entities, or individual producers who don't have agents, you tend to be the point man of negotiation and really take a lead in establishing the deal.

Again, the amount of latitude you have in the deal depends on your client and how much they want to give you.

EL: Was your background in tax and corporate law a good way to enter entertainment law?

DT: It was for me; you have to have some experience in other disciplines to do entertainment law. That almost begs the question because entertainment law in a funny way is not really a discipline, it's a combination of so many things. As a transactional entertainment lawyer, I think you have to know corporate and business structure, that's a must. If your only perspective is dealing with an entertainment contract, you don't have a sound foundation for certain simple things. You can't pick up an old agreement for actor "A" and say, "Oh, it was done this way this way last time, let me change the names and have the same contract." You need another discipline to give you perspective. Tax and corporate are very good; I happen to be more business oriented. Even people who have come from litigation are a step ahead of people who have just done entertainment law because they'll look at a contract differently. You can probably take a provision in a contract and have three entertainment lawyers—one who was a litigator, one who was a tax or corporate lawyer, and one who was always an entertainment lawyer—and you will get it negotiated three different ways. The corporate lawyer would probably focus on the deal points and trying to get as much out of it right now. The litigator would position his client for litigation. And the entertainment lawyer, who knows? I reserve judgement because some of my colleagues would not like what I have to say.

EL: What are the creative aspects of your job?

DT: They come into play mostly with clients who are smaller and growing, often producers or production companies. There's only so much you can do for an individual who has an agent. We get to be most creative with a client who recognizes that you have more experience in a particular thing than he or she does and lets you be the architect. It often arises in acquisitions or business combinations where a lot of money is involved and tax is a major consideration.

EL: You deal in the areas of film and television and music?

DT: I am more company-oriented; I am not a talent specialist who works solely with TV actors or film writers. I have some individual clients in all those areas, but I tend to represent more producers or companies, such as record companies, film and television producers, and film and television production companies. What's becoming particularly interesting is that we're starting to put them together. We recently did a joint venture with Michael Douglas' film company at Columbia. We got him into the music publishing business, and we're working on similar ventures with some of our other clients.

EL: Are some law schools better than others for young people considering going into entertainment law? How would a young person choose a law school?

DT: Having gone through the recruiting process from both sides, that's a very easy question. You should go to the best law school you can, unless you get into two law schools that are so close in stature that you can let other factors affect your choice. We're talking about the top ten or fifteen law schools. It's very tough, and it's going to get tougher for lawyers to get jobs.

EL: Why? Is it an open or a closed field?

DT: It's a closed field. As long as I've been in the business, entertainment law has been very closed and it's staying closed. The law market really boomed in the eighties while everything else was booming. Some local firms recently had big layoffs and it's going to get even tougher. I imagine it will slow down for people just out of law school. Graduates used to come out of the top law schools and have their pick of jobs anywhere. That may still happen with the top five, maybe even top ten law schools, but once you get below that I think it's going to get tougher. Entertainment law is a closed shop, and potential employers are going to be as selective as they can; they'll only choose the best, unless you have the proper family lineage—which is certainly the second, if not the number-one criterion. The whole business is built on relationships. Some people get into it based upon their performance, and some people get into it for other reasons.

EL: What kind of inherent skills does a good entertainment attorney need?

DT: You need a lot of common sense. The issues you deal with cut across all areas—tax, corporate, general contract principles. You're looking at contracts, and even though you're not a litigator, you have to think about litigation. You can't possibly have trained as a specialist in all these areas. You need to have good common sense and good general analytical skills. In some ways we are a breed of generalists; you have to be able to analyze and spot issues even if they are not right within your area of expertise. The other thing that is critical is that you have to be organized because you deal with several things at once. This is like no other practice that I have seen and like very few professions I have seen, except maybe real estate brokers with a hundred listings. You have fifty to one hundred things going at once, and you have to know where they are at all times. A typical day for me is spending no more than half an hour on any one thing and probably between a quarter and a half an hour on twenty things. That is something that some people can do and others can't. It's not like litigation where you can have a big case and you can drop everything and focus. You have to be patient, you have to be willing to give your home phone number to clients whether you like it or not. If you're taking a long vacation, you're going to have to expect to call in.

EL: Are the days long?

DT: The days are long. The days don't get started until 10:00 a.m. and they generally go to about 6:30 or 7:00 p.m., and it's nonstop. If you're a busy entertainment lawyer, if you have a full practice, it is literally nonstop. It is one phone call after another. The good thing is, unless you're on a particularly big deal, most office activity basically stops by around 6:30. Then you have some quiet time, you can do some paperwork after that. Also, unless you're going to come in and clean things up on the weekend, you're generally not going to work too much on weekends because there's nobody to talk to.

EL: What's the most frustrating thing about the job?

DT: You're basically as powerful as your client; that is, unless you are of a certain stature that you create your own power and leverage, but this is very rare. For the most part, a lawyer is a facilitator and not a principal. As long as you accept that role (and there are exceptions, particularly some lawyers who are very active in companies, on boards of directors, or have a piece of the company, you are a hired gun. You have a lot of people leaving this profession to go to the "front line" to be producers. It's a very common thing; they want to be the principal. In law we call it the agent and principal relationship. We are not agents in the Hollywood sense, but we are just representatives. And you deal with a lot of people making exorbitant amounts of money. Sometimes you may create something or negotiate a transaction and do such a wonderful job but still all you get is your fee; whether it's a percentage fee or not, you aren't the principal. People who become lawyers tend to be more risk-averse and aren't entrepreneurial. You find a lot of lawyers thinking that it looks easy, whether or not it is (and it probably isn't very easy) to move out and become a principal and do their own thing. It happens daily. You may have the success story like Tom Pollock, who went from being a lawyer to being head of the motion picture group at Universal, or Ken Kleinberg, who went to run Weintraub Entertainment, which is now bankrupt.

EL: What are the best things, the most exciting and fun parts?

DT: For me it's where you have a lot of people working together, where it's a big deal and you close it and you've worked very, very hard to do it. You have a sense of accomplishment, you have a closed deal, you sign the papers, and then you go out to a celebratory dinner afterwards. That's not a typical entertainment law scenario. When I'm negotiating a writer's agreement or a big actor's agreement, I just don't get the sense that you celebrate. I'm bringing my corporate experience into it when I suggest more of a team effort. You have two or three or four parties involved, and everybody wants it to happen, you negotiate real hard and you close. That's the most fun for me. It's not going to screenings, it's not going to the Academy Awards. The other thing—I don't know if you'd call it "fun"—but the biggest reward is doing a good job and having it recognized by your client, having it appreciated. It's frustrating enough to be a representative and not be the principal, but if you are unappreciated when you do a good job, that just compounds the frustration. The other side of that is, if you are appreciated, it validates you, makes it worthwhile. You're going to get paid either way but I don't think you can validate work by just making more money.

You validate it by someone saying, "Hey, thanks, you did a really good job."

EL: What other advice would you give to some young person who wanted to enter this field?

DT: I would say to be successful you have to be bright. They should do as well as they can in college in order to get into the best law school, whether you're going to be an entertainment lawyer or a divorce lawyer, it doesn't matter. I think if you really are serious about entertainment law, you have to make a decision to make it your world. It's a very closed shop, not just entertainment law but the entertainment business in general. Relationships are probably as important as anything in getting a first shot in this business. I'm not saying that people continue to get work or continue to have projects funded just because of relationships. Ultimately you have to have the ability and be good. You're not going to survive forever just because you have the right genes or the right relationship. But by the same token, you do have to be tied into the community, and lawyers, just like agents and producers and directors, spend a lot of time just getting to know people. You go to lunch with people you deal with just so you see their face. I don't know how many hundreds of people I talk to, there may be a few hundred. If you want to be successful, you break the barrier after several phone calls and you meet that person for lunch. It changes the dynamic of the relationship once you see their face. I think young people would be kidding themselves if they thought they could be an entertainment lawyer without socializing with the people in this business. You have to like the business and you have to like the people. I suppose at some point you could become successful enough where you could pick and choose. Also, I would not recommend people getting into it just because they love going to the movies. It's not about that. You are a lawyer. Maybe the most sobering thing to realize is that you are ultimately responsible. Whether you call yourself an insurer or whatever, that's what you are. If things go wrong, you will be blamed, so you'd better be good. You better be a lawyer first and a socializer second.

ELEVEN

......

⬛ The Film Editor

The film editor generally begins work on a film as soon as the crew begins principal photography. Occasionally, depending on the editor's relationship with the director, he or she may begin discussions in pre-production. Seeing the film the day after it is shot and processed by the film lab (viewing "dailies"), the editor is charged with taking hundreds of shots, which are out of sequence and of varying length, and crafting the film into the linear vision and style desired by the director. The editor works very closely with the director to achieve the director's style throughout. It is essential that the editor have a good sense of narrative structure and dramatic form.

According to the Motion Picture & Videotape Editors Guild, IATSE Local #776 (213-876-4770), apprentice film editors receive $703.00 per week. Some professional editors receive between $6,000 and $8,000 a week, but salary always varies. The guild does not release information regarding the number of members or openings per year, but initiation fees range from $1,000 to $3,000.

Carol Littleton

....

While studying for a Master's Degree in French Literature, Carol Littleton spent two years in Paris with the goal of becoming a teacher. Upon her return to the United States, she entered the doctoral program at UCLA, taught for one year, and then decided to change her career plans. In 1972 she began working as a script supervisor for low-budget films and commercials, which then led to a position with a small film company specializing in sound transfers, commercials, and documentaries. The owner of this company, an editor, employed Ms. Littleton as his assistant, and she spent several years developing her editing skills on various projects. She left the company to work freelance as a commercial editor, venturing into features by editing films produced by students at the American Film Institute. After joining the union in 1977, she edited *French Postcards*, her first mainstream feature. Since then Ms. Littleton has edited numerous films, including *Body Heat, The Big Chill, The Accidental Tourist*, and *Swimming to Cambodia*. She was nominated for an Academy Award for her work on *E.T. The Extraterrestrial*. Ms. Littleton has edited the upcoming film *China Moon*, directed by her husband, John Bailey. She is in her second term as President of the Editors Guild and is a member of A.C.E.

EL: Would you summarize your formal education and how it prepared you to become a film editor?

CL: I suppose it prepared me indirectly, although I was not aware of it at the time. My undergraduate education was a bit peripatetic. I spent two years at a small women's college in Missouri as a liberal arts major. I had a scholarship to study in Paris for a year during junior year. Then I returned to the University of Oklahoma, which is in my home state and finally declared a major, graduated, and received a liberal arts degree with a major in French Literature. During that entire time, I studied music as well. I played in an orchestra throughout college and studied oboe, piano, and cello, which were my passions. I think I had the good sense to know: 1) that I wasn't going to be a professional musician, didn't really have the patience for spending hours upon hours practicing, and 2) that earning a living as a musician would be very difficult. Music was not my major, although that's clearly what I enjoyed most in college. I tried a number of years in graduate school.

I was in Mexico for a year on a scholarship, teaching and going to school at the University of Mexico in Mexico City. When I finished my year in Mexico I decided to continue studying language. In order to pass language exams and be accepted into graduate school, I took the opportunity to study and work in Germany. I returned to the University of Oklahoma for two more years getting my graduate degree in French Literature. Then I got a Fulbright to write my thesis in Paris. After I finished that, I moved to Los Angeles in 1970 and took a number of odd jobs. I enrolled at UCLA to continue graduate studies and had a part-time job teaching English as a second language, which was the only job I could get. I discovered that I really did not like teaching and was not cut out for it. I thought I should reconsider my career options at that point before doing any more graduate work at UCLA. John Bailey, my boyfriend then and now my husband, had a similar situation as a cinematographer. He had gone to undergraduate school as an English major at Loyola (before it was Loyola Marymount). He too had a junior year abroad, in Austria, and he came back to L.A., finished his undergraduate degree, and then went to film school for two years at USC in its graduate program. Hanging around with all of those kids, I caught the film bug. I started getting odd jobs in film. I worked as a script supervisor, then I got a job in sound transfer in a small company that made documentary films. It was there on the job I discovered that I really liked putting the story together on film. The fellow who owned the business was a well-known editor. He did documentaries and feature-length films. I started assisting him, and shortly thereafter, I started cutting sound and picture on the minor projects, so I got my training on the job. I think that the one thing my education afforded me was a very thorough background in literature. The skills that you learn in studying literature, the sense of analysis of story and character, are two very important aspects of film editing. On the other hand, I feel that while I didn't realize it, another large influence was my study of music; I think much of editing is musical, the sense of the musicality of the language and the sense of the rhythm of the images, an inner clock of cadence and pace. I'm very aware of all those aspects in music and more so in film. The skills and the discipline that you learn in a practice room are precisely the same things that you have in a cutting room—working in the tiny little rooms for hours and hours until you get not only the subtleties the way you like them but the overall sweep of whatever you're working on. In some respects I think my musical background has been more of a plus then I would have ever thought. I cut with temporary music, not because I think it's something the composer needs as a guide, but because I need it as a guide.

EL: What were your first few solo shots as an editor?

CL: They were at the AFI. I did my first feature film with Karen Arthur, an AFI Fellow, in '72–'73 called *Legacy*, and I also did Lee Grant's directorial debut, *The Stronger*, in 1974 in the AFI Directing Workshop For Women. I worked on another film with Karen called *The Mafu Cage*, which was partly under her auspices and those of AFI.

EL: Was it a somewhat more supportive situation to be working on those initial films with other women, or didn't it make any difference?

CL: Looking back I suppose it did, because that was the era of the encounter groups and the consciousness-raising aspects of the women's movement. It gave me a real sense of solidarity. It's not easy for any woman to work in the business, and it certainly is helpful to work with other women. I find it particularly helpful, so I always hire at least one woman on my editing crew. I feel very strongly that women should give chances to other women to work. We must support each other.

EL: Can you describe who are the members of your creative team, your crew?

CL: Initially, it is the picture-editing crew. I'm sort of the nonofficial head of post-production.

EL: How many folks do you generally work with?

CL: I work on a flatbed, which means that you need to have two qualified assistants until we turn over for sound. At that point, or at about a month or so before you turn over for sound, the supervising sound editor starts. He or she then brings on his/her crew, a supervising sound editor, the dialogue editor, sound effects editor, ADR editor, and Foley editor, and usually there's one assistant for those three or four editors. There could be as many as five or six people, depending on the complexity of the film and demands of the schedule. Obviously the shorter the schedule, the more people you have to have.

EL: When do you generally come on to a film, and/or when do you prefer to come onto a film, and is there an average length to the commitment?

CL: I've worked with directors who have long pre-production and rehearsal periods. I like to be involved with the rehearsal for at least a week before principal photography starts, primarily because it allows me to observe the film in total, to see the emotional arc of the film, although I have nothing to contribute in many respects during that period. It gives me a very strong sense of the story the director wants to tell and of the particular problems that may arise in the interpretation of characters by the actors. I get to be an insider for a week, and that serves as a tremendous advantage to me in editing. I don't have to bother the director during shooting with a lot of questions that have been answered during the rehearsal period. If I'm not able to do that, I start the first day of principal photography, and I'm cutting simultaneously with shooting. It's very important, while on location, to be with the film unit, because you learn so much by being at dailies every day with the director and occasionally going to the set. I'm there to cut sequences as quickly as possible first, to see if there are any problems and if we need additional footage. I can also give the director a sense of how the film is playing so that he can make adjustments in his direction, can deal with subtleties that are revealed in the cut footage, and make adjustments either in performances or camera, art direction, lighting, or any number of things.

EL: When you talk with your directors, what kind of vocabulary do you use? Do you make musical or literary references, or is it film vocabulary?

CL: It's probably a vocabulary that is more closely related to the theater because we're talking about the overall life of the scene. Since these are moving pictures and have a life on film, you use film vocabulary. It's a technical as well as an artistic vocabulary.

EL: What is the difference between editing a larger-scale epic film and a smaller, more personal film? Do you go in with a different mindset?

CL: If you accept the idea that the best epic films work on a human level, you're making the same film, only the scope is different. The best epic films—*Lawrence of Arabia*, for example—tell the human story. You're really concentrating on the truth of life, for lack of a better way of putting it.

EL: What do you look for when you're choosing a project?

CL: I look for a story that's worth telling, one that seems to have certain emotional truths. I have great difficulty working on films that are exploitative to the degree that many films are today, either of womens' positions in society or pictures with a very high body count and no sense of moral restraint. I would rather work on a film that has a human connection than the exploitative, blockbuster-type movie that is largely based on hardware, special effects, high body counts, or explicit sexual, gratuitous material. It could be on epic scale, it could be a Western, it could be a musical, within any of the genre, but what I prefer is a truthful story of the human connection.

EL: Do you think of yourself as having a particular style?

CL: No, I don't. But, hopefully, I conserve the style of the filmmakers, meaning the director, the art director, the cinematographer, the actors. I am more instructed by the film than by imposing my own style upon it—I hope.

EL: Do you believe that in the nineties attendance in film school is important, critical, or not important for someone who wishes to pursue a career as a film editor?

CL: I don't want to say that film schools are not important, but I think the important part of film school for film editing is story analysis and the development of a strong sense of film criticism. Technique is, frankly, better learned on a job. I've interviewed a number of kids who have graduated from film school, and the technique learned is usually out-of-date by the time they use it on the job. Parents send their kids to a university primarily for job training rather than for a liberal arts education. It makes the $60–70,000 they spent on higher education seem more worthwhile. I'm working with an apprentice right now who's a biologist by formal education, but she's a wonderful film-editing assistant. In my estimation, the most important quality is a very sharp, critical sense of story analysis and a heart for material. Also, there's a sense of responsibility and discipline that can be learned anywhere. On a more practical side, we have long hours and deadlines to meet, and it takes someone who's in very good health with a very positive attitude to be able to get the work done. The physical and psychological aspects of editing are important. In fact, I don't see much drug abuse in film editing. You can't afford it—there's too much work to be done. A lot of people ask me, "What do you want to do when you grow up? What do you want to do when you finish this editing thing?," the notion of editing somehow not being sufficient, as if one were asking, "What do you want to be ultimately?" I'm asked that question a lot, and it's strange when it's addressed to a middle-aged woman. I'm not interested in directing because I don't have the personality for it. I really work best in the environment of a cutting room where there's less chaos than on the set. In fact, what I'm doing, in a sense, is ordering the chaos.

EL: Do you think editing is an open or closed field? Are there opportunities still available?

CL: Yes, of course. If young people who are interested in film think that they would have a love affair with editing, by all means they should do it. There's nothing more exciting.

EL: Is there any other advice you would give to a young person?

CL: I think it is worthwhile to remember that making a film is an on-going process. My advice is to think of the process. Obviously, we all have to think of long-range goals, but before you reach your goals, as a student, before you become an editor, while working all the odd jobs, doing all the things that precede, sitting down in front of the KEM— everything that precedes that moment is just as important as sitting down to cut. It's the sum total of one's experience that's very important. Don't forget that on the way to that moment you are accumulating the raw material from which you will be drawing when you edit. It never stops. A short story may not have much bearing on your present circumstances, but it may ultimately give you an idea, may provide a shortcut in storytelling that is brilliant, so wonderful that you store the idea in the back of your mind. You may read a novel and may see four or five films that are not at all like the one you're working on, but there may be something that lodges in your mind and is useful later. Everything we do is derivative. Be aware of what you're watching, what you're reading, what you're listening to, because it's going to become what you use to express yourself in the actual editing. I want to encourage young students to enter the profession, especially if they feel drawn towards the life and the kind of exploration of the mind and emotion that is found in a cutting room. If they enjoy that, are really nurtured by it, and fed by it, then they should do it. Hollywood filmmaking is a business. The pure sense of art we might nurture is not necessarily compromised, but one has to weigh the business and the artistic aspects on the same scale. You can chose to interpret your work as "selling out," or you can interpret it as a challenge. I would rather think of it as the latter.

Dede Allen

. . . .

Dede Allen began her career as a film editor in the sixties. She has worked with such directors as Elia Kazan, Arthur Penn, Sidney Lumet, and George Roy Hill. Her work on *The Hustler* and *Bonnie and Clyde* earned her American Cinema Editor Award nominations, and she was nominated for Academy Awards for *Reds* and *Dog Day Afternoon*, winning a British Academy award for the latter. Her numerous film credits also include *The Breakfast Club*, *The Milagro Beanfield War*, and *Henry and June*. She is affiliated with Motion Picture Film Editors, American Cinema Editors, the Academy of Motion Picture Arts and Sciences, and Women In Film, from whom she received a Crystal Award.

JF: Could you please characterize the role of the editor?

DA: A film is shot scene by scene with many different photographic angles. The editor's job is to put the picture together so that it flows and tells the story effectively. It's not a matter of cutting things out but rather selecting just the right pieces to put in. It's a matter of taste, a knowledge of acting, and of scene structure. You have to know story, you have to know performance, pacing, and you have to be totally proficient in the mechanics. The technical aspects (the Moviola, the splicers, the synchronizers) have to be extensions of your hands; their use—automatic, second nature.

JF: How do you approach a film?

DA: You do it scene by scene, sequence by sequence, then act by act, if you're speaking in theater terms. Your first consideration is the director or producer you are working for. You are trying to make the film that they envision. Editing is an interpretive art. You fulfill the concept

Ken Regan/Camera 5

of the director as a violinist fulfills the concept of the composer. How much freedom you get to contribute to the interpretation depends on the person you're working for. I've been lucky. I've worked for a number of wonderfully confident people who give you a lot of freedom, and that makes you grow. Bob Wise was the director on the first major picture that I edited, and the confidence he gave me has lasted to this day. He didn't feel that he was taking any chances with me. He was a hard taskmaster and challenging, and he was just so excited if you did something in the editing that surprised him. He didn't care how many ways you tried something. He knew if you did something he didn't like he could always put the film back together the way he wanted it. Film is very plastic. Nothing is ever set in concrete. In the beginning, I was terrified Bob would see all my indecision, but all he ever said was, "Just make it play." Once I got into a bit of trouble doing a complicated scene. Bob gave me extensive notes on how he wanted it cut. I cut it exactly the way he had requested it, and when he saw it, he told me it wasn't playing. I said, "But, Mr. Wise, this is how you told me to do it!" and he said, "Dede, let me tell you something, I don't care what I said. If it doesn't play, don't show it to me. You make it play, then show it to me." I never forgot that lesson. He is a man of great confidence, and therefore everyone around him just gives the most they can. Bob had never worked with a woman editor before. After working with me for a while, he said, "Women think differently than men." Bob loved the fact that I didn't always ask him, that I went ahead and tried things, that I wasn't afraid to have outtakes printed up if I thought I wasn't getting what the scene needed in the printed takes. It was a very exciting experience.

JF: How did your experience in sound help you?

DA: Sound adds a very important dimension to a film. In editing, a thorough knowledge of what sound can do gives you the ability to be very loose and free with it. You can manipulate the picture and sound in creative ways. If you have total technical fluidity in dealing with picture and sound, you can take all the bits and pieces of what you have in a film and not be frightened about how you're going to work it. That's what editing is all about. You have to become as involved in the scene as the actor. Every film is a life experience. You learn about the people. Actors say they have to become the part. The editor has to become part of the part. You live in the world of what the story is. In working with picture and sound, you have to know the rules before you can break them and, for years when I was learning, one of my great insecurities was that I didn't feel that I knew all those rules, and those I knew I didn't particularly like. But after you learn them, you go for the next step. I've broken many rules in my time.

JF: Do you think the increased speed of production hurts a film?

DA: Some pictures come out of it okay. Some pictures don't. A certain kind of pressure is not a bad thing because everybody's adrenaline is up. But mayhem is another matter. As long as you can think and still see what you're looking at with an objective eye, pressure is okay.

JF: Let's talk about the environment in which an editor and a director collaborate while making their film.

DA: Collaboration involves competing in a positive way. It involves trust and respect. It takes a director who has a lot of confidence and a lot of patience—with me. Because I ask a lot of questions. I want to know what they have in mind so sometimes I get a little rambunctious trying to find out. Sometimes I push them into thinking about something they haven't thought through. And they don't necessarily want to. That can get you into a bit of trouble. But most directors I've worked with don't feel threatened, and when you have a confident human being it's a great experience. That was the kind of thing I formed with John Hughes. I spend a lot of time with my director trying to get a total feeling of what he feels about the characters and the story. The editor is definitely a sounding board for the director. One thing I learned from Arthur Penn was not to ever leave anything out in the first cut. Even if a scene doesn't work, a director always wants to see what he's shot. You may be a step or many steps ahead of the director at the time he or she sees the first cut because you've been living with the footage in the cutting room much longer. I've been lucky to have worked mainly in autonomous situations where a director has some clout. If you don't have that, it can be mayhem. There's an arrogance now in the studios, people who don't really know what you do, people afraid of their jobs, thinking they know how to do it, trying to get their little digs in. That doesn't work. It's unpleasant, and it degrades the pictures.

JF: How do you pick the films you work on? Do you choose a project because of your schedule or because you want to work with somebody?

DA: All of the above—or I get panicked and think I'll never work again. I'm scared every time I start a picture that I'll never measure up to it. But I have much less fear now than I did in the past. There are always certain tensions that accompany wanting to make whatever you're doing as good as it can be.

JF: Would making *Bonnie and Clyde* ten or twenty years later have produced a different film?

DA: *Bonnie and Clyde* was a Depression picture. About the thirties, not the sixties. Arthur Penn and Warren Beatty had originally wanted to make it in black and white. It was made in color because at that point nobody would make pictures in black and white. Jack Warner said, "I couldn't tell the good guys from the bad guys." He never liked the picture. I remember Jack Warner, looking at the streamers (you mark the film with a grease pencil to indicate a fade or a dissolve) asking Arthur Penn, "You mean you're going to fade out and cut in?" Arthur said, "That's what we're going to do." It shocked a lot of people at the time. Today it wouldn't make a ripple. Arthur wanted a certain kind of tempo, and in that case the more rules I broke the better we were able to achieve that effect. The mismatches made in order to speed the tempo did not necessarily make the cuts look great. In fact, they sometimes looked ridiculously bad. Many aficionados thought that was the worst cut picture they ever saw. It created a lot of controversy. Later, they imitated it. That was also the time when pictures like *Last Year at Marienbad* and *Hiroshima Mon Amour* were made.

JF: Do you think this is a good profession to enter?

DA: I think there are going to be a lot of changes. Technology is having a tremendous effect. Editors will no longer handle film. They will be dealing with time code instead of frames. More and more editing will be done on videotape and video disk. It's happening now. The tools and the techniques will change, but the fundamental concepts of editing will be pretty much the same. There will always be a need for someone who knows where and how to make the cuts. The methods of training people will change as well.

JF: Do you train young people?

DA: I like to very much. I like to work with assistants on a continuing basis. We learn each others' language, and the work goes faster. The whole process becomes enriched.

JF: How long does an assistant or apprentice usually stay with you?

DA: It depends on how much work there is. Being an apprentice is not necessarily the most glamorous job in the world. It's difficult to learn technical proficiency. But with faith and patience, the answers will start coming. Some find that editing isn't as glamorous as they expected, and they have trouble getting over the assumption that it is.

JF: Is it hard to get into the field?

DA: It's always hard but it's always possible.

Thelma Schoonmaker

■■■■■■■■■■■■■■■■■■■■■■■

Thelma Schoonmaker Powell was born in Algiers, Algeria, where her father worked for the Standard Oil Company. She grew up on the island
of Aruba and attended Cornell University, where she studied political
science and Russian. While doing graduate work in primitive art at Columbia University, she saw an ad that offered on-the-job training as an
assistant film editor. Although it involved editing movies for late-night
television shows, it provided the start for Ms. Schoonmaker's career as
an editor. During a six-week summer course at New York University's film
school she met Martin Scorsese and Michael Wadleigh. Within a few
years she was editing Scorsese's first feature, *Who's That Knocking*. She
edited a series of films and commercials before editing Michael Wadleigh's 1971 film *Woodstock*, for which she was nominated for an Academy Award. In 1981 she won both the British and American Academy
Awards for her editing of Scorsese's *Raging Bull*. She has served as
editor for Scorsese on numerous films, including *King of Comedy, Last
Temptation of Christ*, his segment of *New York Stories, Goodfellas*, which
earned her another Academy Award nomination, and *Cape Fear*.

EL: Can you briefly describe how you got started as an editor?

TS: I saw an ad for an assistant film editor in the *New York Times* placed
by a terrible old hack who was butchering the great foreign films of
Antonioni, Truffaut, and Godard for late night television. He was advertising in the *New York Times* which rarely ever happens because people
usually get jobs in the film business through knowing someone and
getting a foot in the door. I was attracted to it because I was uncertain
what to do at the time. I had always loved watching old films on television but had no idea how they were made or how one got a career in

movies, but I was interested enough to answer the ad. Because he would teach me a few technical things (how to cut negative, how to put subtitles on a film), I decided to follow it up.

At that time there was a six-week summer course at N.Y.U. where they put ten people together to make a short film. I applied and was accepted and there I met everyone who became the dominant influences in my life. I met Martin Scorsese and Michael Wadleigh, with whom I made *Woodstock*. There were a lot of good filmmakers there at that time—John Binder, Jim McBride, and Lewis Teague. My seeing that ad now seems predestined.

EL: Was that summer session the only formal film school training that you had?

TS: Yes, and as a matter of fact, I don't even think it taught me very much. I learned from other filmmakers; I learned how to make films by doing them. After that summer session, I helped Martin Scorsese save a film of his which had been butchered in the negative cutting because no one in the film school really knew too much about how to cut negative. I had learned enough technically from this other job to cut negative, so I helped Scorsese salvage his film from the mistakes that had been made. Then we all began making films together for television. Merv Griffin would sometimes commission small fifteen minute films on, for example, John Wayne on location for *The Green Berets*, or an Aretha Franklin concert. We were also making documentaries against the war and in Harlem—things like that. I never learned from books or being taught in a classroom; I really learned from my fellow filmmakers.

We all did everything (except shoot and direct) in the wonderful, sort of idealistic crews that we put together mainly of friends. We all ran the sound, loaded magazines, drove the cars and held the microphones. I ended up in the editing room because I have a good organizational ability. A lot of the men found editing physically and mentally disturbing, the organizational part of it, and also the physical manipulation of the film—with the exception of Martin Scorsese, who has always been a great editor, and who taught me everything I know about editing. He always had a passion for editing; he loved to get hold of a movieola and rip film to shreds. But he wanted someone to work with him. We all volunteered our services to complete the shooting of his first feature film, which was made for very little money. Scorsese's parents, who were not well off, believed in him so much that they invested their life savings in the film. He shot the first part of it in 16mm which was later blown up to 35 mm. Then I edited it with him and learned a tremendous amount.

EL: How would you characterize what an editor does?

TS: The editor's job is to try to create rhythm, mood, and the best possible performances from the dailies. You take the raw footage and shape it and give it speed and rhythm so that the actors' performances work well together. The overall pace of a film and making sure the dramatic structure works are also an editor's responsibility. That often means dropping scenes or parts of scenes. As I have said, Scorsese is a very gifted editor and thinks a great deal about the editing when he writes and directs. In this situation, I'm a collaborator and try to carry out his vision, try to give it proper rhythm and speed. But he does a lot of the work already for me because he plans how the editing will go. A lot of editors find themselves in the position of having to save the director's footage. I get to work with something that is already very well thought out and just help to get it on the road.

EL: Scorsese is such a master director. What kinds of conversations do you have when you're sitting there together and what kind of language do you use to communicate what you want or what he wants?

TS: We're very old friends, so we talk a great deal about everything while we're working, but one of the most important times for me is when I'm with him in dailies. Every night after he comes back from shooting, we look at the footage that he shot the day before. Scorsese has a tremendous gift for reacting very directly to the screen in a way a lot of filmmakers have forgotten. He's never lost that freshness and the ability to really be part of the audience. When he's looking at his footage, he gives me his reactions to it all the time and I take very elaborate notes of everything he says. He tells me what he likes or doesn't like, or explains how he is gradually shaping the scene, and how the actors' performances are, and how he envisions the editing of the scene. Sometimes he is working with the actor to develop a character a certain way and he will say, "I like it much better at the end of the performance," or "The beginning is the best." The next thing I do is carve out all the things that he likes, and I like, and then I put them into an elaborate structure of what we like, in descending order of preference. When I go into the editing room with him after he's through shooting, we have a very elaborate assembly which still leaves him many options in terms of the acting. As we're in the room together, we both talk about what we think is best—if that is the best performance on that line, or not. We gradually begin to cut the scene into a real first cut. We do that by constantly communicating with each other: "What do you think? Do you think that's the best way to go?" It's really nuts and bolts in some ways: "Let's start with that shot and then go to this shot." That kind of thing is being discussed between us all the time, along with discussions of what is happening in our own lives or in the world at the time.

EL: Do you think that your editing ability is intuitive, is there something in your background that gave you a strong affinity for editing?

TS: I don't think so; I think I learned it almost entirely from Scorsese. Of course, experience teaches you a great deal. Every year you're learning something new, you're becoming more confident and certain things get easier. I do think in my particular case I *learned* it. Scorsese had it probably from the day he was born. My contribution to him is that I am someone he trusts. I am an old friend and a collaborator. I'm not the type of person who is going to fight over every cut (which never happens with us anyway because Scorsese is very quick to see if something he dreamed of didn't work out exactly the way he wanted it to and we have to figure out a way to make it work). He's very honest and very quick to see those things. Occasionally we'll get stuck on something, but our battles are always big joke battles; I mean we pretend to fight with each other because we agree so much. We'll delay the decision and have a screening in which we show it his way and see that it was wrong or right, or we'll screen it my way and then we'll see that it is wrong or right. We never get into the difficult situations that some editors do get into with directors where they fundamentally disagree entirely with the director on how to cut the film. I've been in that very difficult situation with other directors and it's hard—every cut is a battle. It's agonizing. I just happen to be quite lucky that it's not that way for me. Editing is an art and one of the things that many people don't understand is that it should be part of the initial conception of the film. It can't just be done in the editing room. The editor can help, can refine and perhaps make something that was terrible a bit better, but you will never be able to make it great if it was not originally conceived properly by the director.

EL: When do you first get involved in a film?

TS: I'm not needed until Scorsese starts to shoot. He's so good at editing himself that I don't have to be around initially, although some editors are, particularly these days, because a lot of directors are directing for the first time and they rely very heavily on editors to help them. Scorsese already has a very clear idea in his mind of a certain editing style for each different film. I wish more directors did. Sometimes I see a film where the editor is desperately trying to make something out of nothing. When you've been in the business long enough, you can see when an editor is struggling to make the footage "sell." It's not that that doesn't happen to us sometimes, particularly in a very difficult scene where there's so much complicated material that something may not work and we have to struggle, or in heavily improvised scenes because we don't have the coverage. Something wonderful may have happened and we only had one camera on it, maybe we don't have the other actor's reaction, which happened a lot in *Raging Bull*. Now when Scorsese shoots a scene like that and he knows that's going to happen, he shoots double camera so we have much better coverage. Having been a documentary film editor originally, I love working with improvised material.

EL: What did your documentary filmmaking teach you about narrative filmmaking? Do you edit differently or basically the same in feature films and documentaries?

TS: I think the experience in documentaries probably affected Scorsese and me very much. Being passionate about cinema verité in the early days gave us a liking for the accidental, spontaneous, non-cliched approach to acting and cutting. A lot of that came from documentaries. The fact that I enjoy a scene where it's going to be difficult to pull out the improvisation comes from my love for working in documentaries; it's fun to try to figure out a way to make it work. Scorsese's greatest joy is seeing if his initial version worked or not, so he loves the first carving-out. It's much more fascinating for him to see whether something he dreamed of really worked well. Then when it gets down to the fine-cutting and the more slogging work, I think he loses some interest. That's the part where I come more into the fore to get the final thing in shape. It can also be a lot of very long, hard work; but I love it and I'm not complaining.

EL: Is there something about editing that lends itself to the female sensibility?

TS: I really don't know about that. I have no idea what the ratio of men to women editors is. Editing requires a great deal of patience, which I think is something women possess more than men. Filmmaking at its best is collaboration, and women are very good collaborators. When the editing of *Raging Bull* won an Academy Award, the Academy sent me a list of all the people who had won Academy Awards in the past, and the interesting thing was that they were mostly women in the beginning. Later, the list included more men and then many more women came back on the list. I don't know what that means. There are so many great male editors that I don't think one can make a statement that the profession belongs to one or the other.

EL: How do you come to a project? Is it the story that attracts, or is it just working with Scorsese?

TS: It's just working with Scorsese because he's always got another film in the works. I was married for ten years to Michael Powell, the great British film director. He died last year, unfortunately. He was a great influence on Scorsese and, in turn, Scorsese really saved him from total obscurity. During my marriage I was desperate to get as much time as I could with Michael, so I was very happy to take the three or four months off in between Scorsese's films. I was lucky enough to know there was always another Scorsese film coming up, except when *The Last Temptation of Christ* got cancelled. So I don't choose the projects. When Scorsese is debating about what his next film is going to be, he sometimes talks to me about it, expressing his anxieties, his desires, or his difficulties getting it funded. He decides what he wants to do from feeling in his gut. Sometimes he has to do certain things to prove something to the industry—that he can make a box-office film, for example.

EL: Are editors characterized by the kinds of films they make?

TS: Yes, I think certain editors become very skilled in particular kinds of films. Comedy takes a real skill. That was something I had to learn about when making a comedy like *After Hours*. To learn how to make a laugh work right is a real skill. Comics themselves use actual counts to refine their timing. I remember hearing Jerry Lewis saying to one of the actors in *King of Comedy*, "No, no, you count to three before you answer me." I was stunned by that, but I had heard from my husband, who knew a lot about silent film comics, that it was true. They actually count to perfect their timing. I had to learn how to make laughs work.

EL: Was it trial and error learning? Did you watch other comedies?

TS: To a certain extent. Of course, previews are always agonizing for us because we have to show the film before we're ready but in the case of a comedy, they're very helpful. You can hear whether a laugh is working or not, whether you should delay a bit or tighten up. There are editors who are much more gifted in certain areas, for example, in music, or a horror film cutting, or comedy—the art film editor vs. the Hollywood, slam bang, *Raiders of the Lost Ark* kind of movie. There are very different colors to all those styles.

EL: What is the most frustrating thing about being an editor?

TS: I love it, so I don't have a lot of the frustrations that other editors do. I think it would be fair to say that many editors feel that they are being called upon to save other people's work and don't get enough credit for it. I would never say that; I'm in the opposite situation. I have no frustrations at all. The only thing that is very hard is the demand on your personal life. I don't have a family now so it's a bit easier for me, but for anyone who is a mother, father, husband, or wife it is absolutely awful what a family has to put up with. The hours are very, very long and the pressure towards the end of a film is horrendous. You often end up being awake three days in a row and working your assistants terribly hard. That's the only negative aspect of this job, and, of course, the uncertainty of where your next job is coming from is a real agony suffered by most filmmakers.

EL: Do you think that film school is essential, important, or not important at all for a young person?

TS: Being self taught and having learned from fellow filmmakers, I really can't say. Certainly any school that will teach you the history of filmmaking is very important; one of the most important things anyone could do is see as many films as you can and learn about them. That's why I think Scorsese is such a great director, because he has incessantly watched other movies. Every night he watches one or two films. I wish more filmmakers did; I don't think there's enough studying of the aesthetics of filmmaking. I think too many people get attracted by the money and the glory and not enough people are in it for the right reasons, which should be to make art. They certainly are not aware of what's gone before, which is tragic.

EL: Do you think this is an open or a closed field for young people?

TS: It's difficult to get your foot in the door, then it's all a matter of luck—not all a matter of luck; obviously your ability has a great deal to do with it. Whom you happen to work with the first time and how word of mouth then spreads about you are very important and difficult. Once you get your foot in the door, if you've done well and you're a good person, you can usually get a crack at it. There are not that many jobs and it's hard. When I'm advising young people I worry most about the uncertainty of where the next job is coming from. It can be awful waiting six months for another job to come along—and that does happen.

TWELVE

▦ The Sound Editor

The contribution of sound in a film is often overlooked. Film is more than a visual art—it is an aural art as well. The development of the Lucas THX system and the audience's increasing awareness of the subtleties of sound testify to its critical role in the filmmaking process. The sound team is responsible for the creation of the film's soundtrack, which includes dialogue, sound effects, and music. The soundtrack must support, complement, and enhance the storytelling without becoming a separate entity.

Union minimum for apprentice sound editors, according to the Motion Picture & Videotape Editors Guild: IATSE Local #776 (213-876-4770), is $703.00 per week. Professional sound editors usually make no more than $4,000 per week. The guild does not release information regarding the number of members or openings per year.

Tom Holman

▪▪▪▪▪▪▪▪▪▪▪▪▪▪

Tomlinson Holman graduated from the University of Illinois in 1968 with a Communications degree, emphasizing engineering, theater, broadcasting, and film. He worked for a time as chief electrical engineer for Advent Corporation before helping to found Apt Corporation in 1977, where he designed their chief products, a preamplifier and an amplifier. In 1980 he joined Sprocket Systems, a division of Lucasfilm Ltd, where he worked on technical motion picture production/post-production and designed and built new technical facilities. During that same year, he designed the THX Sound System, which brought higher fidelity sound to theaters and dubbing stages throughout the world. Currently the corporate technical director for Lucasfilm, he provides overall technical direction and sets technical standards for the company. He also teaches film sound at the University of Southern California School of Cinema-Television.

EL: As a young man you were interested in both sound and lighting. Did you understand then that the progression of technology in sound offered more than the technology in lighting?

TH: Not at all. In fact, film sound was a rather bad field to enter at the time because it was definitely in its ebb. In the fifties film sound had to get better because it had to compete with this newfangled thing called television. Stereo sound was a 1931 invention, cinemascope was a 1917 invention, but neither was widely applied until 1952 or '53 when television competition forced the need to do something to remain competitive. Because of the cost of printing, the difficulties encountered in *Ben Hur* and other pictures, very few pictures came out in stereo and wide screen, and they remained a kind of specialty format. When I was growing up, the number of theater screens was shrinking and only the

© Lucasfilm Ltd.

occasional special movie like *Lawrence of Arabia* would use stereo. So, at the end of five years of school at Illinois, during which friends of mine had graduated, gotten jobs in Chicago, or come here and shot pictures, I too came to L.A. and was boom operator on a picture called *Cool Breeze*. Los Angeles didn't turn me on very much at the time. I decided to bend my career in another way and went to work for Henry Kloss at Advent in hi-fidelity equipment design. Advent made better loudspeakers than theatrical ones in terms of frequency range and smoothness. So I became a design engineer by experience. That was very much a watershed, because it had a wonderful group of people in sales and marketing that had been attracted to Henry and his inventions. Henry was very involved in large-screen projection television at the time, and more or less handed me the audio company in terms of product design. Though I had to report to him, I had an awful lot of freedom considering this was at the time a fifteen-million-dollar or more company. I was young, worked very hard, built a bunch of loudspeakers and various products, including the Advent 400 radio.

1977 was a watershed year in film sound because Dolby had applied their noise-reduction technology to film, and *Star Wars* came out. The two, the hardware and the software together, had a tremendous impact on raising quality. Another person took Advent over and changed the whole corporate style so that it wasn't a very fun place to work anymore. I decided to leave and started a company called Apt Corporation that made preamps and power amps for the consumer marketplace, and it did very well from 1977 to 1980. In 1980 Lucasfilm was looking around for someone who could look past the front panel, understand the inner workings of the equipment, but who had some film background. I hadn't very much, but I did have a 16-mm documentary background. That, combined with the engineering, was enough for them to hire me.

EL: How would you characterize what you do now?

TH: Well, I'm a generalist. I am a bit of a circuit designer, a bit of a loudspeaker designer, and a bit of an acoustician. I'm not fully fledged in any one of these areas. I serve on many standards committees; I go to the SMPTE convention, and I'm the only guy I know who tries to attend projection practices, lab practices, HDTV electronic production, sound, and many others. I have this catholic interest in trying to pull many technologies together—which shows up in something like the THX sound system. It represents a compendium of a lot of people's work over many years coming together in one form. There is a U.S. patent on it and some patentable ingredients, but the fact is that it's built on the building blocks of others that I consolidated. THX is not a pure invention like the telephone, but more a further refinement of principles already in use.

EL: Was there a need for the THX system, or was it rather that you recognized all the components and saw the possibility of an enhanced technology?

TH: I think George Lucas set the mandate. He wanted to look at the whole process with a new vision and no constraints. There was no point in working on every part of the film sound chain. What I did was find the stages that were the most backward and work on those; I left alone the more advanced technologies, and slightly improved others. So I was looking up and down this whole system. What I'm currently working on is production-sound-monitoring, to make what one hears in the head-phones as much like what is heard at dailies and in the final auditorium. I don't know how successful I'll be or how long it will take. It's not a commercial problem at all because there's no money to be made, you might sell only a few dozen of these things. It's something that's needed because now the finger is pointing back at production sound as being the biggest limitation. So that's the sort of thing I do.

I've also been working for several years on Home THX, which is just coming out on the market. The point is to make a home sound system that sounds more like a good theatrical system. I'm also looking to video, which doesn't look like film. I've taken engineers who have spent their lives in video and shown them a piece of film and a video made from that film, and they get tears in their eyes. They realize what they are missing. Film isn't a perfect medium, and it's probably not a permanent one since it's subject to scratches and dirt and all. However, it has some possible features that video has not yet recognized or incorporated.

EL: I remember the first time I was in a theater when the THX trailer came on—there was an audible gasp. Did you anticipate that?

TH: No. No.

EL: Have you heard similar stories?

TH: Oh yes, I've heard it applauded. I was sitting in a restaurant and a bunch of fraternity boys sitting at the next table were talking about THX. That's great fun.

EL: That brings me to the psychology of sound. It's an area that has a strong impact on the way one perceives a film, and most people seem unaware of this.

TH: I know. There's no question about it. I teach that. The kids I'm teaching are the *Star Wars* generation. I show them the first reel of *Star*

Wars and then I repeat it with the production sound. (This is their first class in sound). Their jaws drop because they realize the extent to which they have been manipulated. Not everyone can tell you what method a certain Tie fighter flying through is—an optical element, or a bluescreen element, or whatever, but they can all identify it as an object. In sound, most people can't even identify the elements. Criticism in this area is very bad, and there is a dearth of decent critical studies in sound. Little work is being done, and most of it is completely uninformed by the technology. None of it has addressed the issue of the specialization of sound, and how, for example, in *Raiders of the Lost Ark* you are brought into the cave by the ambiance track being in the surrounds so as to make you a part of the action. This level of awareness is a missing ingredient in the whole area of history and criticism. Some historians and critics even think film is ruined by the sound. What is the meaning of the ambiance track being in the surrounds? What is the meaning of the ghosts at the end of Raiders? I remember the effect when the ark is opened, and the ghosts fly through the surround channel past you—again you're put into the action. The process is being used to involve you with the action in a way that I've never seen addressed in print.

EL: How important is an engineering or technical background for a young person entering this field?

TH: It depends on what you want to do. As an editor, a sound editor or sound collector like a Ben Burtt, one probably only needs a smattering of skill to be a good competent operator. Ben's genius lies in the fact that he remembers from the third grade the sound of the ruler twanging on the desk, and when the arrow shoots out of the side of the tunnel in the cave scene into the big piece of wood, he uses that sound. He has this aural memory and genius for doing things, but he's not an engineer. Engineering, however, is a way to break in because there are so few people trained in it in the industry, but it also means that you may be pegged. You're not going to be asked to write scripts, and you have to recognize that limitation. We have a lot of people send in resumés claiming they will do anything, but, of course, what they want is to direct movies.

EL: Have computers impacted greatly on sound technology?

TH: Computers have had a large impact on the short form, and they will enter the industry by way of the shortest form that can afford the most money, namely, the television commercial. They will work their way up from the television commercial to episodic television, to movies of the week, to low-budget feature films, and ultimately to high-budget feature films. However, not all the technology may climb that pyramid because the quantity of sales as you move up becomes more and more rarefied to the point where there's no point in the manufacturer making the equipment for you. So at Lucasfilm, just as at Warner's, Fox, and other studios around town, there are engineering staffs that are building equipment. Lucasfilm sound library has over 1,000 hours of program material. Transferring that is an enormous job, and it could possibly cost as much as $2,500,000 to do it digitally. Everyone would love a transparent sound library where one could sit at a workstation and listen to any of that thousand hours instantly, randomly, and be able to synchronize that with a picture. Such things are doable, but the computer power needed to do them lies somewhere between the Bank of America and the IRS. Film post-production just isn't going to do it for some time. It will eventually, everybody in sound looks forward to the day when there's less grunt work.

EL: Can you characterize what kind of careers are available in film sound for a young person?

TH: There are probably three or four in the production area. First, there's production sound, which divides into two camps. I call them the wind and sunburned camp, and the totally pale camp, because they're either in production or post-production. In production they're always out in the sun and run the risk of skin cancer, and the other guys never get any such vitamin D—so you choose your health risks. That's the way it is. The guys out in the field, of course, are production recordists. The best do very well, but there are very few of them as it's a tough union to crack. However, an advantage for young people today is that we now have some forty TV channels. Somebody has to record all of that. They're not paid very well, but there is a lot of entry-level work. I guess the next area would involve those few people, very few people, who make a living recording sound effects and producing sound effects libraries. Some will go to the ends of the earth to get unique sounds—spend five months in Australia living in a tent to get something. The biggest career category is probably that of sound editor, and the most available work is here in L.A. We've had students leave here and get jobs as sound editors. After one year out of school they can be chief Foley person. There are opportunities because the amount of production is very high, the kids are good, really specialists who know what they're doing. Sound is probably easier to break into than some other areas, certainly easier than writing or directing, but still hard. There are also the re-recording mixers. In music, the biggest trend today is the home studio that is "engineerless." So jobs are shrinking because the big studios are under a lot of pressure, and a lot of work is going to the home studios. However, nobody would think of post-production sound dubbing on dubbers at home. That's not going to happen. Still, there are only so many places to work in film post-production sound. Martin Polon of Polon Research has done a survey of all audio engineers and found that those engaged in film post-production are the highest paid of any audio engineers. Audio engineers are not very well paid.

EL: Is film school important for somebody who wants to go into this field?

TH: I don't honestly know. In engineering it's not. The question is where is the regular engineer to get the training in film today? There is no curriculum. I had to essentially invent my own curriculum twenty years ago, and we don't teach it here at USC, though we would like to. The engineering school, like all engineering schools, is largely digitally based, and the industry isn't yet. The technology is ahead of the industry. The entertainment industry seems to wait for manufacturers to come up with something, and these innovations are driven by the demands of the largest markets, which are frequently television advertising.

EL: What books would you recommend to a young person?

TH: There are some very dated books of technique of the sound studio. There's nothing modern. The books about it are lightweight. There is some stuff to be found in journals mostly. With the information explosion you have to be selective, and it's fairly easy for me to keep up. I'm not an expert in any single area, and I don't have to read every journal that comes out.

EL: Is there any other advice you would give to young people pursuing this field?

TH: Read widely! The whole point of undergraduate or graduate education is to become a critical thinker and to accumulate an opinion of your own that is based reasonably in fact. In audio there are an awful lot of theories out there that have no basis in fact and don't wash, though they may enjoy some commercial success, or even succeed. The *Journal of the Acoustical Society* is very difficult to read, very tough, but they are the people who are working on real problems. I'm a member of the Society, and I'm not very good at synthesizing what it is they're saying or accumulating wisdom there, but I do see that from the understanding of human psychology, physiology, brain structure, and everything else, that perception of sound is so important. Every engineering decision is psychometrically weighted, weighted for human perception. So, you need to make informed tradeoffs. There's a wonderful quote from Harvey Fletcher, a Ph.D at Bell Labs who invented or discovered some very important factors in human hearing back in the '30's. He said "Engineering is a series of informed tradeoffs. The person who has the best information to make the best tradeoff—that's the best engineer." Engineering is putting together the right elements and weighing them correctly and coming up with the best systems. That's a perfect definition of engineering.

Walter Murch

Born in Manhattan, Walter Murch earned a degree in Art History and Romance Languages from Johns Hopkins University. After further study in France and Italy, he returned to the U.S. to earn a Master's Degree from the University of Southern California's Department of Cinema. He began his career in sound montage and re-recording with Francis Ford Coppola's *The Rain People*, which was soon followed by George Lucas' *THX-1138* and Coppola's *The Godfather*. He began editing with *The Conversation*, for which he won a double British Academy Award for his film editing and sound mixing. He was nominated by both the British and American Academies for best film editing for *Julia*, and earned an Academy Award for Sound on *Apocalypse Now*. His credits include *The Right Stuff* and *The Unbearable Lightness of Being*. Mr. Murch's most recent films, *Ghost* and *The Godfather Part III*, each earned him a 1990 Academy Award nomination for Best Editing.

EL: Where did you go to school?

WM: Johns Hopkins in Baltimore. I had spent my junior year in France studying the history of art and French language and literature. This was in 1962 right at the crest of the New Wave in film. I don't think you could be twenty years old in France at that time and not find yourself interested in film; it was all over the place. It still is a very good city for exhibition, although the French say it's gone way downhill since the old days. At that time it was like a year-long festival in film from any country of any period. You could say, "I want to see a Bulgarian film from 1936," and you could find it somewhere, or American film from 1972 or 1962—you could find that.

I had this wild idea, "Well, maybe I could study film." I had heard that there was actually such a thing as film school—which sounded strange and very exotic. So I applied to three schools and got accepted at USC with a scholarship, and that sealed it. I thought, "Well, if they're going to pay me to go there, of course, I'll go." I wound up at USC and within a couple of weeks, somebody happened to say, "Well, we'll have to record sound for that." Until that moment I had never thought consciously about films having sound at all. I volunteered, and everyone was very happy to let me do it because it was definitely not where the glamour was. My interest in film sound began from that moment. If someone wanted somebody to mix a film, he would try to find me to see if I could do it in my off-hours. I wound up doing that in addition to all the other things; sound was kind of my sideline. There was something called a Warner Brothers scholarship and if you won you were allowed to go to Warner Brothers. They paid you $200 a month or so and you could hang out at the studio for six months. It didn't lead anywhere but it was an apprenticeship.

There were two of us who had qualified for the finals, me and George Lucas. We were waiting for the final interviews, pacing up and down outside the room, and we said, "Well, one of us is going to get it. Let's make a pact that whoever gets it will help the other one if something comes of it." George got it and he went to Warner Brothers. The only person actually making a film there was Francis Coppola and they got together. About a year later I got a call from George saying "Do you want to do the sound on *Rain People*?" I agreed and he said, "Well, it's in San Francisco. We're going to move to San Francisco. Do you want to move to San Francisco? I don't know what's going to happen; we may be back here in six months, but it will be interesting, whatever happens."

Living in San Francisco sounded great and so did working on a feature rather than short films and commercials, which was what I had been able to scrounge together after leaving school. We moved up here in 1969, and I did the sound for that picture and then worked with George on the script of *THX-1138* which we had also collaborated on as students in school. Then I did the sound for that. I did the sound for *The Godfather* and *American Graffiti*, and I just kept doing sound. I was really in the same position that I had been in film school; I was

the guy who did the sound! After *The Godfather*, Francis was planning a film called *The Conversation* which is about a sound man. He looked at me and I was a sound man who had also edited films although not features, and he said, "Why don't you edit *The Conversation*? You're a sound man who can edit so why don't you do both?" and so I did.

EL: It's rare to find somebody who has done so many of those things, because people do tend to specialize so early.

WM: That's one of the benefits (for me anyway) of going to film school. I think anyone who goes to film school should adopt this attitude that you should try to do it all. You'll be more talented in certain areas than others but anti-specialization is a positive thing.

EL: Do you have a philosophy of sound editing or of editing that you stick to in every film?

WM: Well, it changes the way different languages change. What you are trying to say with the language may remain the same, but the words that you use are different. To that extent you are trying to learn the foreign language spoken by that film. Nobody really knows what that language is until the film is done. Yet you're trying to learn and present it in a way so that the audience looking at the film can understand that language. You have to teach them to enjoy it at the same time. I'm talking about very subtle things, but the subtlety is very important. It's what distinguishes one film from another.

EL: Is your primary relationship with the director or the producer, and is there a vocabulary that you use to communicate with them?

WM: I've always worked with the director. I've never had a relationship with the producer alone and I don't think that really happens in features often, unless the director is the producer. It happens more in television. In the old studio days the director and the editor were seen as two different places on the assembly line, and the producer was the one who oversaw everything. Basically, the director was somebody who did the painful process of shooting the film and when he finished, it was handed over to the editor. The director did not work with the editor except to give him a few notes about understanding what was being tried here or there. What has emerged in the last thirty or forty years is a much closer relationship between the director and the editor than existed in the 30s and the 40s.

I usually sit next to the director during dailies and if the director says anything, I'll write it down, but the directors I've worked with have not been talkative at that stage. By and large, with a few exceptions, I'm alone with the script, the dailies, and the mood that somehow has been set by the director or by the tone of the production as a whole. I make a best guess in terms of the initial assembly on my own and then show that to the director. It is the way I prefer, and I also recommend it. You also have to be on the same wavelength; that's really a question of whether you were correctly cast as the editor of this film; it's like casting an actor. The editor brings something to the scene, and then the director reacts to that. I have certain techniques that I think help the direction. If I am beginning a film from scratch, I select representative frames from each set-up, and I make 35-mm blow-ups—still snapshots from those frames. When I'm editing a scene, I hang these pictures up on the wall. Being as fast as possible in that selection process, nonetheless, I try to find a single frame that distills not only the technical question but the emotional essence of what that set-up is about. It's a version of the decisive moment in Cartier Bresson, snapping the still photograph at just the right moment that captures the whole field of action in one instant. I think you can do the same thing for a set-up, maybe not with only one photograph if it was a complex camera move but with two or three or four. I hang these up on the wall and the director can look at them as well. The problem is that frequently the English language can fail you when discussing certain emotional states because there are emotional states for which there is not a specific word. Yet you look for a facial expression or a gesture of a body that can—in a hieroglyphic way—capture the essence of that emotion. So we're looking at kinds of emotional hieroglyphics and the director can say, "I want more of that feeling." and what you're really looking at is somebody whose face expresses an ironic mistrust with an underlay of humor. There's no word for that, and yet that expression is one we're all familiar with—someone amused by you but not quite knowing how to take you, and they're mistrustful. It's there in that photograph. It's something that gets you further down the road than you would be if the director simply said, "I want him to be mistrustful." What he means and what you mean by mistrustful may be two different things. Maybe he didn't really mean mistrustful but he didn't know how to say anything else.

EL: Do you think that a great editor can be trained or that it's an instinctive talent since it involves the sense of rhythm, understanding of psychology, visual construction, those elements?

WM: You have to be able to sit in a room for a long time. If you're the type of person who likes to be out there in the elements, it's not for you, so on that level, people are born liking those things, so you're right in that sense. Definitely there are psychological types that are better suited for editing, but there is a certain amount of training that can go very far to help. You mentioned rhythm, and I think that's very hard to teach. You can dance or you can't; you can get kind of good at dancing, but to be a dancer it has to be something beyond that.

Certainly the top professional level of editing is the equivalent of being a great dancer. You have to have it in you. Training can go so far, but at the higher levels there is that element of intuitively under-standing things. There is a mystery buried in there, but there's a great deal of what I would call "murality" in editing. It's one thing to paint a small painting, but it's another thing to paint a mural because a mural is beyond human scale to put together. You have to step away from the mural. When you're working on it, you're very, very close, and what you're looking at is nothing like what it will be seen from a quarter of a mile away. There are tricks that muralists use to compensate for that problem. If you said, "I'm going to paint a mural without any training," you'd be much worse off then if you said, "I'm going to paint a smaller painting without any training." There's a rapid feedback in painting, you try to correct yourself, and you stand back and say, "No, not that." Unless you've had certain training on how to break the thing into grids and how to use certain juxtapositions of color that look totally wrong when you're doing them but you know that from a distance the combina-tion of that distance and the atmosphere of the human eye will merge into something that snaps into place, you will have difficulty with a mural.

Obviously we're not dealing with something that's physically as big as a mural except on the big screen ultimately when it gets shown, but it is something that's muralistic in the sense that it goes over such a long period of time, and you have to sustain an emotional intensity and know what's correct for something that will be consumed in two hours in real time in a totally fragmented situation. You're editing half of a scene that will occur in the middle, and you somehow have to figure out methods so that it will all fit together and snap into place. You're not alone, of course, because the screenwriter is facing the same prob-lem, and the actors are facing the same problem. They, too, have to have their own tricks. How do actors prepare for an emotional scene when they've just done an insert of a shot where they were not emotional at all? Then they may have to do a scene that comes an hour later in the film and ten years later in time and they're in a totally different emotional state. That's the craft of film acting. There are methods and tricks that you use as you cut things up and analyze the parts, yet maintain a sense of the whole. If you wander too much, if you cut things up into tiny little bits but lose the sense of the whole, you're in trouble. If you have a wonderful sense of the whole but you don't know how to get at the little bits, you're also in trouble. You have to find a way to do both at the same time. That's training; there are tricks just as there are tricks in painting a 150-foot advertisement on the side of a wall.

EL: As directorial styles have changed, have the styles of editing changed over your career?

WM: I probably came in at the time when there was the biggest shift. Except for some technical things, I think that we're still pretty much the same; I may be wrong.

EL: How would you characterize that period?

WM: It was the simultaneous advent of the New Wave and cutting for commercials on television. The pace is much more rapid, and images are juxtaposed on commercials that were unacceptable in a feature film. You could do the "wrong thing" in a commercial, and it would work, whereas if you tried that in a normal film of the fifties people would say, "What?" People's eyes were trained to accept certain things by commercials and by the New Wave, and I believe we're still in that world. By the same token, you look at some of the cuts in feature films from the late thirties, and we see things that would be unacceptable today; for example, cutting from a master shot to a slightly tighter master and the actor's feet are cut off. Today that looks like a jump; at that time, I believe they thought it was an invisible cut—that the audience didn't see that. It doesn't ruin our enjoyment of films from the thirties. I was just looking at *His Girl Friday* which is full of that kind of cutting. Everyone was laughing and responding to it as if it had been just made. However, if you made a film today in that style, people would have a hard time understanding what you were up to. I'm glossing over a whole range of different directors and styles; Jim Jarmusch has a style that's not like Francis Coppola. Francis Coppola has a style that's not like Marty Scorsese. There are styles of cutting. Even from one Scorsese film to another, there's a slightly different style. I just finished cutting *Ghost,* and now I'm cutting *Godfather III*. I have to be careful that I don't apply the lessons or the language of *Ghost* to *Godfather*. I have to find the language of *Godfather* and cut accordingly. They're shot very differently using very different approaches.

EL: What's most rewarding about your job?

WM: The most fun is putting something together that goes beyond what you thought it was. Finding a juxtaposition, sometimes by accident, that you wouldn't have thought of consciously but you recognize as being an intriguing way to go. Putting a scene together according to a new concept and finding out that it works. Looking at it and recognizing in some mysterious way that this doesn't have anything to do with me. None of the decisions seem to come out of my consciousness; they came out of somewhere else. The way you really sense this thing that's running through the picturehead, alive, wriggling in front of you. It's more than the result of a number of deliberate decisions that you made. I think if you asked the same thing of most directors, they would probably say the same thing, and so would writers. We are most bored when what we do simply reflects us back to ourselves. We see ourselves everyday in the mirror and we're bored with that. What we want is to be magically lifted beyond ourselves into something else because then you feel some sort of miracle taking place. That's the strange and wonderful thing about editing! It applies to a certain extent to the writer too. It's a solitary moment; you're alone at two in the morning and this thing suddenly is happening in front of you, and it's just you and this thing. It gives you the shivers in a wonderful way. During the shooting of the film there's another kind of wonderfulness which is a communal wonderfulness. That's the sense that a team feels when they did something incredible. Somehow everyone knew exactly what the other person was going to do. That's wonderful too; it just has a different flavor because there are other people involved in it. The aloneness of editing has another quality to it.

EL: Is it an open field for young people?

WM: It's certainly more open now then when I started. The Editors Union just did away with a roster system that for many years was a union within a union. It's more open now in the sense that there is a much broader array of ways of editing and things to edit. You can buy a video editor for $500–$1000 and edit. I couldn't do that back in the early sixties. Videotape just didn't exist. You had to edit in film, and film meant more money. The getting-started aspect, the hump that you had to pass over, was much bigger. It's like sitting on a three-legged stool, trying to keep all three legs on the ground at the same time, but life is tossing us around and we're tipping back and forth. One of those legs is luck; another leg is talent, and the third leg is persistence. If you can get all three legs on the ground at the same time, if you are simultaneously lucky, talented, and hard-working, nothing can stop you, and you can walk through walls. 99.9 percent of the time all three legs are not down on the ground. You might have two down at any one time and hope that you occasionally get three.

If you're talented and lucky, you can get by without working hard. If you're persistent and talented, you can get by without being lucky. Whatever the third combination of that is, two of them will compensate for the absence of a third to get you along. If you have only one down, you'll be gone like the morning dew; it just won't last. By the same token, if you're talented, that will get you in, but if you don't work hard and you're not lucky, talent alone can't get you through.

There's a strange, unwitting wisdom, I think, to the fact that the film industry presents such a blank wall to the outside world—a wall that says "You can't get in; there's no way to get in." If the sight of that blank wall makes you dispirited and causes you to walk away, it's better in the long run that that happened. On the other hand, if you look at the blank wall and say, "I have an idea; I'll climb over the top; I'll bring a bulldozer and I'll blast my way through; I'll dig a hole underneath it; or I'll make my molecules go apart so that I can just walk right through it"—by virtue of that very fact, you have shown an aptitude for situations that will confront you every step of the way once you are "in the industry." It really should be called the "outdustry." There is no "in" in the industry. Even the people who seem most secure are battling this same thing. In fact, security sometimes is a liability because it freezes one to thinking only in a certain way. There's always a risk that nothing does come, and then you have to be patient. Something that rises spontaneously is better than something that you've superimposed on it. The blankness of that wall is something that you will become very familiar with, and you have to cope with it because it looks like an opponent, but really it's an ally as well. If there were a little train that took you from outside into the industry it would be a disservice, the same kind of disservice as a train that took you into the jungle and then left you, and you found yourself in the middle of the Amazon jungle with no machete and no idea of how you got here. You'd die. The only way to get into the jungle is to survive the trip in, and then you know you can get out.

EL: Any other advice for young people pursuing this field?

WM: It's changed a lot, but I think that's nothing compared to what's going to happen in the next twenty-five years. In other words, the system will be very different in the future because of two things: the world market, this unity of the world that is going to reach some kind of critical mass soon and technology—the merging of miniaturization, satellites, and high-definition television, and things we don't even know about. This world unity will shift things in ways that are hard to predict. Words of consolation—it's good that you're getting in at this point because you will be moving up and out with a certain growth that's starting now. There will be opportunities no one can foresee.

Richard Anderson

■■■■■■■■■■■■■■■■■■■

Richard Anderson moved to California from Missouri to earn a B.A. in Cinema from the University of Southern California. Upon graduation he worked on low budget films as an assistant picture editor and quickly became employed as a sound effects editor. In 1976 he became the head of sound editorial for Gomillon Sound, an independent post-production company specializing in low budget features and television movies. He left in 1978 to work on *More American Graffiti* for Lucasfilm, and was then hired by Paramount as the supervising sound editor on *Star Trek: The Motion Picture.* His film credits include *The Color Purple, Beetlejuice,* the restoration of *Lawrence of Arabia,* and *Raiders of the Lost Ark,* for which he won an Academy Award. He garnered an Emmy award for "Amazing Stories," an Academy Award nomination for *Poltergeist,* and three Golden Reel Awards from the Motion Picture Sound Editors. Mr. Anderson is currently working on the feature film *Noises Off.* He is the co-founder of Weddington Productions, Inc., which has developed one of the best sound libraries in Hollywood.

EL: Could you describe the nature of your job?

RA: As a supervising sound editor and even as the sound editor who cuts an individual reel, essentially what you're doing is creating a sound symphony or a sound concerto, much in the way a composer designs all the elements of an orchestra to work together. Sometimes it's a sound effects symphony, and sometimes it's very sparse—like a guy out alone in the Mojave desert with no one around so you might just have a very light little deserty wind, and maybe at one point a bird flies overhead and you hear the "caw, caw." At another time you could be working on something like *Total Recall,* on one of those big scenes where everybody's shooting, and things are exploding. My partner Steve Flick did that film, and I know they had 150 or more units on one reel by the time he put it all together. There's no way you can listen to it all at once before it's mixed, so you've got to keep all this information up in your head and imagine what it's going to be like. Usually we work against impossible deadlines in order to deal technically as well as creatively with the sound track of a motion picture. I don't deal with recording the dialogue or whatever else happens while they're shooting the motion picture on the set or in a studio. I don't deal with music, that's done by the composer and the music editor. Our main areas are two: dialogue editing and sound effects editing.

EL: Can you elaborate?

RA: The dialogue editing is the less creative of the two, in the sense that dialogue editing is like working with one of those plastic model kits you buy and glue together; you have a limited number of pieces you're given. You can do certain things to it, paint it, sand it, and so on. There's a certain amount of variation, but in the end it's limited to the pieces that are supplied. Of course, the alternative is to do looping, but in fact most directors and actors start off by saying, "I hate looping, I hate looping, it's awful!" There's a certain quality to production tracks, the ambience, the echo of the room, and the actor's actually being there and being in character, all that is harder to duplicate when you go in the mixing stage with loops.

EL: So dialogue editing is pretty functional. Why is sound effects more creative?

RA: You're starting with a clean palette. Though we do often have a certain amount of sound effects that are in the production track, we can control them better artificially. Often we can clean something out of the production dialogue by finding an alternate tape, looping it, and then putting a sound effect in that we can mix against the dialogue level.

EL: Can you briefly explain Foley?

RA: Foley is named after Jack Foley; he invented the process. In a nutshell, Foley is the sound effects equivalent of looping—you go in a studio and you record sound effects while watching the movie and attempt to synch to it. Originally it was done by the sound effects editors themselves—it still is sometimes—but over the years it's become an adjunct to our craft. There are people for whom this is a specialty. I find two reasons for hiring them; first, their synch is incredibly good; it's worth it because they do it faster and better. The other reason for hiring them is that since they do it all the time, they learn to use objects that are not necessarily the real thing but get the desired sound. Foley artists usually—though there's a certain amount of props at the Foley stage—bring suitcases and dufflebags. They show up with this real eclectic mix of things like plates, knives and forks, broken appliances, chains—you name it. They've learned over the years that you can take a fork and a chain, wrap it around whatever and make a sound of something completely unlike a chain and a fork. Foley artists work in semi-darkness because they need to see the picture projected. If I'm in the little control booth and I say, "We need a sound for that," or "Play it back," or "I don't know if I quite like that sound," they'll say, "OK, how about this?" and I'll say, "That's interesting; what is it?" and they say "It doesn't matter what it is, do you like it?" If they told you it was a chain on a fork, you'll listen to it as a chain on a fork; but if you see it with the picture, the sound works!

EL: How did you choose sound, and how did you break into it?

RA: I fell into it. Maybe it's a little better today, it's hard to say, but when I got started, sound editing was the dorky little brother of picture editing. They really didn't teach us too much about sound editing at USC. I took a class in sound, but it had more to do with recording techniques, signal-to-noise ratios and technical stuff like that. I understood editing, picture editing, and we cut the sound, but the attitude was, "Well, you just go out, get a bunch of sound, put it in your picture, and it will help."

EL: How did you learn?

RA: Just trial and error. I was interested in picture editing; I always liked editing. I was interested in directing too, but most people don't step out of film school and say, "Here I am, I'm the next Orson Welles.

I'm ready to direct your $50,000,000 feature." I figured editorial was the way for me to get in the business; what's more I liked it. My first job was as an assistant—assistant to the producer, assistant to the editor, assistant to everybody on looping a Chinese Kung-Fu film into English.

EL: What is your union?

RA: It's the I.A.T.S.E., but it's the Motion Picture and Video Tape Editors Guild, Local 776 here in Hollywood. I am in the Editors Guild which is lumped together with picture editors and music editors and assistant editors and apprentices. I also work with the production mixers and the re-recording mixers. They are in a different local, Sound Local 695. I don't know the full name of their union. There's been this rivalry between the unions as to who can do what. Officially, we're not supposed to record anything or touch a tape recorder, and they're not supposed to cut things or deal with tracks. The problem is that the business is changing technically and rapidly now, and we're getting these new systems in, particularly in television, whereby the editing process—sound editorial work—is done on a system that is essentially a multitrack tape recorder or a computer digital storage device. Essentially, you select a piece of sound from a master roll and re-record it onto something else. It's still editorial, but it's more like computer cut-and-paste in a word processing program. There's a big controversy because the Sound Locals claim that constitutes re-recording and is therefore under their jurisdiction, and the Editors' Union say it's still editing. What we do, even though it's very creative, is not an end unto itself. In the end we prepare the tracks so they are mixed, and the production tracks we get are recorded by somebody else. So I see the mixers and sound editors as working together. I'll be the first person to admit I record things, I'll go out and record effects, I know how to run a Nagra (a brand name of a professional reel-to-reel tape recorder) and other tape recorders. Maybe in the early thirties you needed a five- or six-man specialized crew, an optical film recorder, a truck full of equipment, but now it's simpler. I wish that we could all work together. Eventually there will be a room that looks like a re-recording studio today where you'll lay up the sound effects, dialogue, or whatever on some sort of system, either tape or in a computer memory, and then you will be able to mix them all in the same facility. More and more, these two crafts are merging.

EL: What are the advantages and disadvantages of being a professional sound editor and a businessman?

RA: The disadvantage, of course, is the responsibility and having to do extra, dumb company things that aren't creative. I'm the first person to admit I don't like that. The reason we established the business is that, through various tax reasons, it was a way for us to get more tools or toys to do our craft better. That's the part of the business I enjoy; the least enjoyable is the financial.

EL: Can you judge fairly well how much time you will need?

RA: It depends on the film. Anywhere from about six to seven months (the longest I was ever on a film) to maybe a couple of weeks. I remember years ago in television, I worked with a post-production house and supervised all the sound editorial work there. In one month we did four TV movies, so we were averaging a ten-reel TV movie every week.

EL: So the size of your team depends on the time you're given.

RA: You have to look at it as man-hours or man-weeks. A project is so many man-hours and man-weeks. You can have more people and less time, or fewer people and more time, and do an equally good job. The biggest problem is that as everybody gets behind on the front end of the project, we get further and further behind. Today so many films have this brick wall of absolutely, positively having to have a film called *X-Men From the Moon* released on December 7 because they have contracts for its opening in 2,000 theaters nationwide, and there are incredible penalties if they don't make it. When I first started off in low-budget pictures, they would cut the film and then they would give it to you. Unless there was a disaster, like a piece of negative got destroyed or an optical came in at the last minute, it pretty much stayed the way it was. You cut on its sound for that footage, and then you went to the dub. The problem I see more and more now is that films are never completed! All the while you're doing your sound editing work, the filmmakers are re-editing the picture. They'll look at the film and decide to use the other take, maybe the close-up or feel the need of a beat on the end of a scene. I'm not saying that these are or aren't improvements to the film, but we spend huge amounts of time re-cutting as opposed to cutting. The worst for us are additions, taking film out is easier, but additions mean we have *holes* in many layers of soundtrack we've prepared. When they're doing picture editing, it's real easy for them to add six frames onto the end of a cut. They add six frames in the picture and track, and then they send us a change note that says they've added six frames. We may have anywhere from 50 to 100 units or more for that reel that are in synch with that picture. It means that at that point we now have to add six frames to every one of those units. On some projects we'll get these change notes throughout the whole project and in the end we have a book the size of a large dictionary of change notes. It's very frustrating for sound editors; instead of spending your time creating something new and making something better, you're spending all your time just switching everything around. Also studios seem to do more and more test screenings, which means we always have to do temporary dubs, that is, quickly prepare the film for a mix so they can take the film out and screen it for somebody. After looking at that screening, they re-edit the film, and we have to re-edit everything, re-mix it, go out and screen the film again. We often end up doing the film five, six, seven, eight times. That's why on modern films you'll sometimes see this huge team of sound editors for what seems like a simple film.

EL: When you're working on a project, can you characterize the amount of contact you have with the producer, the editor, or the director?

RA: We talk at least weekly. It depends on the person. With a lot of big directors (Steven Spielberg for one), we sit down and have what you call a "spotting session" where we discuss the film. After that it's pretty much, "See you later at the dub." I like that, actually. If there's a question we can call and say, "What about this?" Other directors feel they have to be involved in every little thing; they have to put their thumbprint on everything. In a way that's annoying. You spend a lot of time auditioning effects and screening things with tracks and all. But that's fine, after all it's their movie.

EL: What title do you like to be known by?

RA: I usually use Supervising Sound Editor; I don't say Sound Effects Editor because I deal with the dialogue, too. It is very controversial now because some of the newer people use the term Sound Designer. I'm not that old, but some of us who have been in the craft for a while and have come out of an editorial background tend to think of this as a bit pretentious. It's somewhat nebulous because sometimes other people take that credit, people who didn't supervise the project but who had a bank of synthesizers in their garage and created sound effects for the sound editors to work with.

EL: What do you look for in young people in your business; what skills or what characteristics do you look for?

RA: I look for eagerness, the go-getting, stick-to-it, it's-got-to-be-done-no-matter-what-attitude. What I hate is, "It's 5:00, time to go home." People should realize that regardless of the craft or area, filmmaking means long hours, which is sometimes very hard on personal relationships. The tradeoff is that in between projects you'll have some time off and can spend it with your loved ones.

EL: What kind of background can a young person come from other than film school?

RA: Engineering. We also have people with backgrounds in broadcasting, theater, and art. College is helpful, but enthusiasm is a big thing. When Ben Burtt (of Lucasfilm, Ltd.) started off, he knew every studio's gun shot and could watch a film and say, "Oh, that's the Paramount gun shot." It's true because in the classic days of Hollywood, everything was done within the studio. MGM was a complete plant. They had their own library, their own recording department, and so there was a certain sound to each of the studios. Since the break-up of the studios, it's now become many independent people and sound houses.

EL: Is that good or bad?

RA: Well, in a way it's good because it gives the filmmaker more choices. In the old days if you were doing an MGM picture, you had to use the MGM Sound Department even if you hated it and thought they were awful. I'm not saying that they were awful; but you were stuck with them because it was an MGM film.

EL: How would a young person get started?

RA: An awful lot of people get started in the nonunion film business doing whatever they can get. Often you work for practically nothing. There are basically two roads. When I got out of USC, I had a friend who got a job as an apprentice at a studio; that's the traditional start through the union system. First, an apprentice, then an assistant, and then possibly as an editor. He became an apprentice about the time I started working at places such as New World Pictures. I became a sound editor much faster then he did; in fact I was also cutting a picture at New World. So he slowly worked his way up and became a music editor. At about the same time, the Union opened up, and I got in as a sound effects editor. In a way we both reached the same place at the same time. I felt as though I had a much better background because I had done more things. You can make pretty good money in this job. I think currently the Union scale for a sound effects editor, (meaning the minimum) is $1,100–1,200 a week, something like that. But people have to realize that motion picture jobs are not based on being employed fifty weeks out of the year with a two-week vacation. A lot of people think it's wonderful pay, but the reality is that many people work maybe six months or less, particularly in television which is very seasonal.

EL: Is the field of sound an open field for young people?

RA: I don't see it as particularly closed, but there's only so much product being done. The general problem with making motion pictures is that it's a somewhat glamorous business; it pays fairly well *when* you're employed. In general, there are more people than there are jobs. I think that our Union is getting better.

EL: Do you think today's audiences are more aurally sophisticated?

RA: Yes, definitely. I think home stereos, CDs, and all the hardware that people have at home now are far more sophisticated than the stuff than you had in the theaters in the fifties and certainly better than that in the forties when you had monaural, optical tracks. In general, as in any other technology, there's always something new on the forefront. I remember when it was Dolby, and now there's this new digital track system. These new systems are technically better, but until enough theaters have these installed, the producers and the studios don't want to use them because what's the point of spending so much money if it can only show in four or five theaters worldwide?

EL: The technology that affects your profession changes daily, weekly. How do you keep up when you are so busy?

RA: Well, that's a big problem. The whole concept of it is changing. From the beginning of sound movies in the late twenties through about the seventies, the process was essentially the same. You did your editing on optical film. In the late forties or fifties magnetic film came in. Other than that you listened to it on a different kind of machine, it was still the same process. It was still edited on a movieola, and you cut it with a splicer. Now we're getting into new systems based on working in a place that's more like a sound studio, punching in, recording levels, transferring, and using the new machines where you sample something, put it into a memory, alter it, and later cause it to play back. It used to be if you wanted to make a bird sound effect run for a three-minute scene, you'd get a bird recording and very seldom would the bird sound run that long, so you'd find a good section of it, cut out the bad stuff, and make a loop—a physical loop on film. You would then put that loop on a machine, run it continuously and that would be your bird background for the scene. Now there are machines that can electronically make a loop, and they can keep running infinitely. Every day somebody announces that there's a new machine or a better system. One of the problems is that there's no standardization. A certain number of these systems are designed by engineers as opposed to editors.

EL: What advice would you give to young people considering this profession?

RA: People think motion pictures are exciting and glamorous. When I go back to St. Louis where I grew up, a lot of people think, "Oh, it must be wonderful to be in Hollywood." They have this vision that you get up at 11:00 a.m. and then you go on the set. The reality of motion picture making involves long, long hours and a lot of pressure. If you don't love it, stay out of this business. I can't tell you how many times I've worked all night, and I still work all night on projects to meet deadlines. No matter how much you love the film, the project, or the craft, at 3:30 in the morning it's just not fun! At that point it's every bit as much of a grind as working a drill press at the shop stamping out widgets. It's very creative, but it's also very much of a grind. The industry's changing and I don't really know where it's going in terms of technology. In a way, it's a scary time to be entering because what you learn now may be obsolete in five or ten years. At the same time, periods of transition have traditionally been good times to get in. When sound motion pictures came in, the whole industry changed. All of a sudden so-called sound experts came out of radio, and actors who had been stage actors came in and took over the business, so everything changed. Maybe it's a time for people who traditionally have done other things to get in.

THIRTEEN

· · · · · · · · · · · · · · · ·

★ The Composer

Some of the most memorable popular music of the twentieth century has come from the movies. The film composer must meet the challenge of translating, enhancing, and/or contrasting the screen's image with original music. This career necessitates extraordinary musical abilities coupled with a unique capacity to translate the director's vision into musical terms. The film composer is generally not brought onto the film until post-production. The composer writes the music, often orchestrates the score, and occasionally conducts the orchestra during the recording session.

The highest paid composer may make $175,000 per film. The lowest salary usually involves a package deal in which the composer must hire the musicians out of his or her own pocket. On average, a composer earns a few thousand per film. There is no union or guild specifically for composers. Most composers belong to the Society of Composers and Lyricists (213-669-5444), which has a membership of 300+, but is not a union or guild. The only musician's union is the American Federation of Musicians (IATSE #47, 213-462-2161), but people are only admitted to that union in an orchestrator or conductor capacity. ASCAP (the American Society for Composers, Authors, and Publishers) is *not* a union—it merely handles performance rights where music is performed or broadcast.

Elmer Bernstein

■■■■■■■■■■■■■■■■

Elmer Bernstein has composed scores for film and television for almost forty years. He scored his first film, *Sudden Fear*, in 1952, and went on to write the soundtracks for *The Magnificent Seven, To Kill a Mockingbird, Thoroughly Modern Millie, An American Werewolf in London, Ghostbusters,* and *Rambling Rose.* He has composed and conducted for numerous television movies and specials, including "D-Day: The Making of the President," for which he earned an Emmy Award. Television series to his credit include "The Rookies," "Serpico," and "Ellery Queen." He has earned a Golden Globe Award for his score for *To Kill a Mockingbird* and an Academy Award for Best Original Score for *Thoroughly Modern Millie.*

EL: Can you summarize your formal education?

EB: I started studying piano at the age of nine in the public schools in Brooklyn, and apparently showed talent right away because at the end of the year I won the prize. I don't think any of us took it seriously. I went on studying piano like a good little kid, and we moved to Paris for a time when I was about eleven; I continued studying the piano there. When I was in Paris we met a lady whose relative was a famous piano teacher by the name of Henriette Michelson. She taught at Juilliard in New York. When I was about twelve I was taken to play the piano for Henriette Michelson. She liked me enough to teach me as a scholarship student until after I came out of the Army, until I was about twenty-eight. She also took me to play something I had composed for Aaron Copland when I was about twelve. Aaron was about thirty-one I think, and he had just returned from Paris. She asked, "Has this kid got any talent?" He said, "Let's give him some instruction and find

301

out." So he sent me to study with a student of his in New York City, and from the time I was twelve I was studying harmony, theory, and composition. Subsequently, I studied with a composer by the name of Ivan Langstroth and then studied with Roger Sessions. Finally, I would give the most credit as a teacher to Stefan Wolpe who is an avant-garde German composer. I think the greatest musical influence was certainly Aaron Copland. But from a learning point of view, I would credit Stefan Wolpe.

EL: With that kind of illustrious training and beginning at a very young age, why didn't you pursue strict composition and a performance career? How did you get involved with film?

EB: I gave my first piano concert when I was fifteen in New York. I was headed for a career as a concert pianist. What changed everything, of course, was World War II. Just about the time under normal circumstances I would have been pursuing my concert career, I went into the Army. That would have been in 1943 when I was twenty-one. By the time I got out I was twenty-four, and I picked up my concert career and concertized extensively for about four years on the East coast, giving concerts in Town Hall in New York and then in Chicago and Philadelphia. While I was in the Army, I was studying composition. Because I knew something about music I was sent to a unit that was doing propaganda shows for what was then the Army Air Force—Glenn Miller and all that sort of thing. Each of these shows contained a dramatic section that had underscoring. I was called to this section because I knew something about American folk music which was a pretty exotic subject in those days.

The music director, a man by the name of Harry Bluestone (who still plays violin in Los Angeles), called me into his office and said, "Do you think you could compose the score for a dramatic show?" I had never done that, but I had all this composition training, and I was young enough to say yes. It had to be written overnight. I really fell for that; I really loved doing it. That gave me a real taste for doing this kind of work. When I got out of the Army and went back to concertizing, I always thought that this would be a nice thing to do.

In 1948 one of the people I had been in the Army with, a novelist by the name of Millard Lampell, was doing a radio show for the United Nations. It was a show called "Sometime Before Morning" and I wrote the music for that show. It attracted enough attention so that when Millard Lampell got a chance to have his novel, *The Hero*, made into a movie (it was made into a movie called *Saturday's Hero*), Millard was able to twist the producer's arm and get me the job doing the music for the film. I didn't attract any attention until I did a film by the director of the first movie I did, David Miller. David got a chance to direct a film called *Sudden Fear* with Joan Crawford and Jack Palance, which was a thriller. He engaged me to do the music.

This was 1952, and I was able to do some of what then seemed to be unusual things in the score. There was tremendous use of solo woodwind instruments like the bass flute, not a commonly used instrument. The chase at the end of the film was almost a concerto piece for two pianos and orchestra. Using the piano in that kind of bare way at that time was fairly unusual; that score attracted attention. But in 1953 I became a victim of the witch hunts that were going on and I sort of went into eclipse as a result of that. By 1953 I was only employable for movies like *Robot Monster* and *Cat Women on the Moon*. I was a rehearsal pianist in 1954 for Agnes De Mille on the film *Oklahoma*. That got me a chance to do the ballet music for "Peter Pan" with Mary Martin and allowed me to work with Jerome Robbins, which was a great thrill.

EL: Have you ever regretted leaving a formal music career?

EB: Well, let me put it this way. I wouldn't say regret. Sometimes I regret that I didn't run my two careers congruently. Certainly André Previn did for a very long time. And certainly Miklos Rozsa did. I have no serious regrets. I had ascertained that I did not enjoy concertizing, playing the piano. I found that playing the same works over and over again was basically boring. I looked at myself (I was in my twenties) and thought, "I can look forward to playing the same pieces when I'm seventy—forty-five years hence." I think if I have any regrets that I didn't pursue something I really enjoy, it would be conducting.

EL: Have you conducted the symphonic repertoire?

EB: For ten years, I was music director of The San Fernando Valley Symphony. It was fun; I learned and conducted all the repertoire. Some of the greatest music thrills of my life were conducting things like the Brahms Symphony and the Nelson Mass by Haydn. Those were great thrills, and I'm sorry that I didn't persevere a little bit more with that, but I've always been busy writing music.

EL: Music has its own language. How did you come to learn the language of film and integrate the two?

EB: Well, I suppose it sort of crept up on me. I've always had a flair for the dramatic. When I do lectures at universities the question most often asked is "What is the single most important attribute that one should have in order to be a composer for cinema?" I will invariably answer, "Assuming that you can compose, I would say the most important characteristic is that you have skill as a dramatist." I have always been interested in drama. In fact, after I got out of the service in 1946, I wrote music for theater. I was one of the regular composers of what was called in those days the New Dance Group in New York. I had a feeling for associating music with drama.

EL: At what point do you come on the film? Can you describe how the length of your term may vary, and describe your relationship with the director during that period of time?

EB: That is a very complex question. No two projects are exactly the same. Usually the composer, any composer, myself included, doesn't come on to the project until all the principal shooting has been completed and they're editing and trying to assemble the film. There are exceptions to this. In my association with certain people, for example with Alan Pakula and Robert Mulligan on *To Kill a Mockingbird*, I was involved in the project before a camera even turned. We talked about what the project was going to be like. By the time the film was shot, I had been living with it for at least a half a year, so it was completely familiar. That is the exception to the rule. The same was true of my relationship with John Sturges in a film like *The Great Escape*. I must say that it's no coincidence that some of my best work was when I was involved in the project.

The general rule is that you don't become involved until the picture has been shot. Unfortunately, at that point, if the director and/or producer are sort of conversant with film music, they may have concretized their ideas to the point where you are presented with a sort of creative *fait accompli*. You may not like what they have already decided they want, and try to change their minds, if you think their minds need changing. If you can't, you may have to walk away from it.

EL: How do you guide a director who may not have any sense of a musical vocabulary through which to communicate to you what he or she wants?

EB: The director that scares me most is the director that starts the conversation by saying, "Now I want you to know I don't know a thing about music." That's the director that's going to give me the most trouble, and it's the same director who will ultimately tell you whether to use an oboe or a clarinet. Generally speaking, if the director is a nonmusical person (and most of them are), I will ask them to communicate to me in the English language, provided they can speak it. I like them to just tell me how they feel and what they think.

EL: Rather than using other musical examples?

EB: Absolutely. There's a tremendous tendency on the part of directors to use musical prototypes. And, if they want to use a musical prototype, my attitude certainly is, "Go and get the composer who wrote that." One of the great evils that has befallen composers lately is what is called the "temp score," meaning temporary score, or a score that's put into the film by the director and the film editor. Now, no intelligent director that I've ever worked for has done that or agreed to do that. Or if they want to do that, on one or two occasions I've done the temp score. It is inevitable, unless you're very sensitive to music, that if you put music in a film and listen to it twenty or thirty times you're going to think that's exactly the way it ought to be, and thus the new piece of music is a stranger. Albeit, it may be an elegant stranger, but it's a stranger, and therefore very suspect. It's a very horrible situation. I think the demise of the so-called creative producer in this business has been a disaster. Because the creative producer, that producer who became the center of all the elements of the film, provided a much healthier situation than the auteur director who has absolutely no reins on him at all.

EL: How would you characterize what the score should do for the film?

EB: I think it's very hard to make a general statement about what a score should do for a film. It depends a great deal upon the nature of the film. If I had to make a general statement, I would say the score should heighten implicit emotional elements of the film. It should inform emotion. That's what it should do. Now obviously, that would not be true of a picture like *Dirty Dancing* because the function of the music there is to be an entertainment in itself. But I think that the heightening of that which is implicit is its best function. It is most often called upon to heighten that which is weak in the film. In other words, let's say a scene that is supposed to be frightening is not frightening enough, so we do it with music. For a scene that is supposed to be passionate, but for some reason or another isn't passionate enough, music is used to fix it. There's a tendency for people to want the music to simply mirror the film; that's not the best use of the music either, because you shouldn't have to repeat with music what is already apparent in the film. It's only when it's fuzzy that the music can help clarify. Take a film that everybody knows, say *To Kill a Mockingbird*. What was the function of the music there? We were clearly living in a child's world. There are elements in a child's world that you can't express through dialogue. Children are magical, and they can create magical worlds. You can't say that in dialogue, but the music can do that, and that's what the music was there for. That kind of use of music in a film makes a contribution. It becomes a character, another voice. Examine the art of music. The best description I've ever heard of music as an art is that music is art that begins where words and pictures end. Now if you take that as a description of the art itself, it is very clear that the best use of music in a film should be to express what neither pictures nor words can.

EL: Do you think that being an American, with the eclectic musical heritage that we have, uniquely prepares you to be so genre-versatile?

EB: I must tell you, that's a brilliant question. I had never thought of that before. I think you're absolutely right. We are a sort of melting pot here. I was brought up in New York before the Puerto Ricans came, but we were very aware of Jewish music, of jazz, of the Italians and their music, of the Germans and their music. You know, you're absolutely right. We do not have a parochial music background. I have personally always been interested in folk music. That's why I wanted to do *The Magnificent Seven*, because I loved Mexican border music. You're absolutely right, I think Americans are exposed by the nature of the country to these various ethnic influences.

EL: Do you think that film composition is an open or closed field for a young person? I understand your son is pursuing it also.

EB: Yes. My son has been working primarily in television so far. He does the music for "21 Jump Street." Is it an open or closed field? I think it's a very open field that's very hard to get into. That sounds like a contradiction in terms. It's open because of television. Television absolutely devours music. There are so many shows on the air, and so much music necessary, that this makes that area a reasonably open field. But it's always open to somebody with an original or different idea because producers are always looking for a "new sound." But of course, what's killed the whole concept of a new sound is synthesizers. Where can you go from synthesizers for a new sound? Hitting a hammer on stones, I suppose. It reminds me of the famous Einstein story about World War III, when he was asked, "What kind of weapons will World War III be fought with?" He said, "Well I don't know about what kind of weapons World War III will be fought with, but I can tell you about World War IV. World War IV will be fought with sticks and stones." It's the same thing with the whole new sound system. The synthesizers have opened up such a world of sound that it's almost impossible to have a sound interesting enough. But, nevertheless, I would say that the field is open to original ideas. How you get there is a big mystery to me. I just don't know.

EL: Is a formal education in composition and orchestration critical?

EB: I would advise, as I have advised all of my protégés, to learn everything that you can learn about music. Jazz, folk music, ethnic influences, orchestration, composition, conducting. Learn everything you can learn, absolutely everything. It is true that a few charlatans will wander into the field. Charlatans wander into the field out of so-called popular music basically uneducated. The uneducated ones may achieve temporary success, but they'll never last. They can't, the field is too competitive. Now I've had several protégés that have done very well. My daughter Emily is going to be a composer. But all of them have had formal training. It is not a field for amateurs. It is much too sophisticated—especially these days. There's very little support. If you're young and you get lucky enough to do a film, there are no music departments or music directors. Basically, you find yourself running a music department. You have to know how to hire an orchestra, and you should know how to orchestrate. You definitely have to know how to conduct, and, in addition to all that, you have to know it all mechanically. You should know synthesizers, you should know about computers, you should know about music editing. It's a lot to know. Those who are going to survive in the field are those people with the best equipment.

EL: Any other advice for a young person entering the field?

EB: Get all the training you can get. Be prepared. If you are already a composer, there are other courses offered at universities these days. There are excellent courses offered at UCLA, for instance, that will help you become conversant with film language. If you have any chance to attach yourself to a working composer as an apprentice, do so. All of my protégés studied with me first. Either I knew them personally, or when they appeared their training was so impressive that I said to myself, "This person can make it." But in each case, in every single case, their equipment was very impressive.

Maurice Jarre

. . . .

Maurice Jarre began his career in France composing and conducting symphony music. Originally composing for a French theater company, he began film scoring in the sixties and has since scored over fifty films, including *The Life and Times of Judge Roy Bean, Taps, The Year of Living Dangerously, Witness, Gorillas in the Mist,* and *Enemies, a Love Story.* His scores for *Lawrence of Arabia, Dr. Zhivago,* and *A Passage to India* each earned him an Academy Award, and he received a 1990 Academy Award nomination for his score for *Ghost.* He also received the Legion of Honor from France and is a French Commander of Arts and Letters.

EL: Can you briefly summarize your formal education and your music education and how it prepared you to work in film?

MJ: I started to study music quite late—when I was sixteen. Before I was sixteen years old I had no idea of the difference between a C and a D. One day my mother said, "Why don't you go with your sister to attend piano lessons?" So I went with my sister and I was mesmerized by this music. I started to really love music from that point. After that I started to listen to concerts and records. Then I decided I would like to become a conductor. Of course, when you are sixteen years old and you don't know anything about music that's impossible. My parents were joking and saying, "You want to be a conductor and you don't even know your notes!" So I started to make a lot of musician friends. When my father realized that I was serious, he said, "If you get your degree in engineering, I'll give you permission to study music." It was a kind of blackmail. I just had to become an engineer first and at the same time study counterpoint, harmony, and so forth.

EL: Were you studying piano specifically?

MJ: I was just starting to study piano. I knew there was no way to do anything with the piano because it was too late. You have to be trained from the age of two or three years old. So I started to study technique. Finally, I met Charles Munch, a wonderful man who was the conductor of the Boston Symphony and French Orchestra. Charles told me that if you want to become a conductor and you're starting late, you should start to study an instrument that is rather easy. A violin is out of the question because it takes so long to accomplish; it takes about ten or fifteen years before you will be able to play in an orchestra. The goal was to be an instrumentalist in an orchestra in order to understand the conductor's role. So I went to the music conservatory in Paris and studied theory and started to study percussion. After three years I graduated and started to substitute in different orchestras in Paris, and I started to make money. During this time I had my degree in engineering. But it was not possible to continue with what my father wanted me to do.

I started to work as a percussionist in different orchestras in Paris. At the same time I studied orchestration and more sophisticated elements in music. During this time I met the director of a young theater company, Jean Louis Barrault. He was looking for two young musicians to play the music background for his theater. Every performance was accompanied by music. He chose me and another young man named Pierre Boulez who became a good friend and very famous composer. He was a wonderful pianist. We both played many different instruments. I played all the percussion instruments. We had about twenty different instruments backstage in the theater: timpani, xylophone, vibraphone, glockenspiel. Every possible percussion instrument—we had an ondes martenot, and, of course, a piano. When we needed violins or trumpets, we used a record player. It was about 1949. We didn't have a decent tape recorder. So we doubled the sound of percussion, piano, or ondes martenot with what the violins or trumpet were playing on the record. The audience thought there was a huge orchestra backstage. There we were—just Pierre and myself trying to jump from one instrument to the other. It was one of the best experiences in my life. It was fun. We stayed together for four years. Of course, we became good friends. Later he went into his own field and I went into my own field. After that I became the music director of the French National Theatre. At that point I started to compose for the theater—music for about sixty or seventy plays from Chekhov to O'Neill, from Brecht to Molière, and, of course, Shakespeare. It was wonderful training for composing and also for conducting. We had an orchestra every performance, about twenty-five people. I was conducting every performance, conducting practically every night. It was really very good training for a lot of things. First of all I met a lot of interesting people—writers and playwrights like Cocteau, Camus, Sartre, and so on. Sometimes I had very, very few days or even a few hours to write some things for a performance. One time, for a particular Molière play, the director had told me he didn't need music. At 10:00 A.M. the day of the premiere he said, "Maurice, I'm sorry. I need about ten minutes for tonight, you have to save me—you have to write!" I had time just to write. By eight o'clock we had the music rehearsed and we played. That's the reason it was wonderful training. As you know, when you work on a film sometimes the deadlines and the pressures are really hard. That kind of training when you are young can be a big asset when you are a little older and have to do a film score in two weeks.

EL: How did you get started in film?

MJ: A young French New Wave director asked me if I was interested in writing the music for a short film—not a feature. During this time in movie theaters in France every performance had a cartoon, the news and a short before the feature. It was a great opportunity for young directors, young producers, writers, and composers to try their tools. That was my first assignment. Later the same director asked me to do a feature. After that I started to work with different directors. Then I did the music for a film called *Sundays and Cybele* which won an Oscar for Best Foreign Language Film. Sam Spiegel saw the film and liked the music; he came to Paris to meet me.

Sam Spiegel liked the way I had done the score and he asked me to do the music for *Lawrence of Arabia*. It was funny; I went from three instruments to one hundred and twenty for the score of *Lawrence*. Sam asked me to be a part of the team of composers for the film. He said, "I want three composers. I want Khatchaturian (the Russian composer) to do the Arabic music, and I want Benjamin Britten to do the British military music." I asked, "If you have Arabic music and British music, what am I going to do?" "Well," he said, "you're going to do the dramatic music, and you will coordinate the rest." I thought, "What a great honor to work with these two great musicians and composers!" I was very impressed. After a few weeks I was in London starting to work like mad. Sam said, "Maurice, I have some bad news. Khatchaturian cannot leave Russia." (During this time there was no way for him to go abroad.) "Benjamin Britten wants one year to do a third of the score because he has some other work to write." I said, "Oh, bad news!" (Of course, I really thought it was great!) He said, "Maurice, I have to go to New York for one week. When I return we will see what we are going to do." When he came back from New York he said, "Maurice, I have great news. I made a deal with an American composer to write ninety percent of the score and you will write ten percent." I said, "Who is the composer?" He said, "Richard Rodgers." Richard Rodgers? This is strange. Sam said, "He read the script and he thinks he can do the themes. He will send you the themes, you don't need to go to New York and he doesn't need to come to London. He will send you the themes, you will do the orchestration and arrangements and you can still write ten percent of your own music." I couldn't believe that. By that time it was the end of September, beginning of October. The premiere of *Lawrence* was already set for early December, I think. Also, the original length for the film was about three hours and forty-five minutes. I thought, "How can I do all this work in so little time?"

Finally the themes arrived, and I met David Lean for the first time. I saw the film. I saw forty hours of film. Forty hours! Practically one week! It was so beautiful and so great. When we met there was a pianist who played the musical themes. David Lean appeared and listened to Rodgers' themes. He didn't like them at all. He said, "Sam, this is really ridiculous. It's not at all right." (At that time I didn't know that Richard Rodgers didn't even want to see the film. He said he would work from the script. Sam Spiegel didn't want to pay for the trip to London to see the film.) So it was really very, very strange.

After the British pianist played the themes David was going to leave. Sam turned to me and said, "Maurice, don't you have anything to show us?" I said, "Sure, Sam. I have some things I could show you. It's rough—ideas and things." So I start to play—I played a theme which eventually became the *Lawrence* theme. I remember David came over and put his hand on my shoulder and said to Sam, "That's exactly what I want. That's exactly what I would like to have in the picture. Sam, why are you going to do all these trips around the world? This young chap is the one who should really write the music." From that point I had about six weeks to write the entire score of *Lawrence of Arabia*. When I got the Academy Award nomination, Sam didn't want to pay for the trip to the U.S. because he said I had no chance to win. I found out later that he said the same thing to the art designer and to the editor who were also nominated. He didn't want to pay for these trips to Hollywood. Really funny.

After that William Wyler wanted me to do the music for *The Collector* but he wanted me to work in Hollywood. I was thrilled because after London, Hollywood was a dream. I wanted to know how they worked. About twenty years later I became an American citizen.

EL: Can you describe the kinds of conversations that you might have when you sit with a director for the first time? What kind of a vocabulary do you use with a director who is not musically sophisticated?

MJ: It depends on the director. It also depends on if you have worked with the director before, or if it's a new director and you know nothing about him. When you have worked together, or you know the director, it's much easier. Even if he's not musical at all you start to build a kind of understanding and a common vocabulary together. If I've never worked with a director before, my approach is to let the director talk as much as possible about his film, about his concept, about his view on the music and to record what he says. The director who knows nothing—who does not know anything about music—is sometimes the easiest director to work with. First of all, he is open. Second, he trusts you a little bit more. You can really start to play things for him. If he is a good director, he has good intuition and sensitivity. It's not so difficult. The problems come up when a director has a little bit of musical training and thinks of himself as a music professional. That is really very difficult because their egos are in the way. I've had experience with this type of director. One director told me he wanted to have the main theme played by the oboe. Great, OK. So in the orchestration the main theme was played mainly by the oboe. We arrived at the recording session and played the first piece. He said, "Maurice, I thought you told me you liked the idea of the oboe?" I said, "Yes, the oboe *is* playing the theme." He turned to the orchestra and said "No, no, no!" and he pointed to the clarinet. "That's what I mean." So I put the theme in the clarinet and he was very happy. That's an easy problem. When you start to talk about concept and musical and technical things it can be a little bit more difficult. Some directors know music very well. They know opera, symphonic works, songs, pop music and electronic music. At that point it's not difficult at all because you have a common vocabulary. When I did the music for *The Damned* with Visconti, he said, "Maurice, I would like this sequence to have the feeling of the second movement, third symphony by Mahler." You know what one is talking about. The same thing with Peter Weir. Peter has an even bigger spectrum. He can discuss electronic music to opera. In the four films I did with him there was no problem because I knew exactly what he wanted.

EL: Do you have a philosophy about film composition that you bring to almost every piece?

MJ: I love music and I love film. You have to understand that when you do the music for a film it's not going to be a symphony or a sonata. It's going to be a collaborative work. You have to understand that you are going to be a fifth of the team that will make the film. You should really submit 100 percent of your talent and humility to the director. It's his film, it's his concept; even if you don't agree sometimes you still have to go with him. You can argue and explain your point of view and intuition, but if he does not agree you have to finally do what he wants. I think one of the basic problems with composers is they think they're going to write their masterpiece symphony in the film. It's not that. It's a totally different discipline. You have to be concise. You have to make your point in a matter of seconds or minutes. You have to try to create a third dimension and have the humility not to be obtrusive and serve the film. Sometimes you must explain what the viewer doesn't immediately understand by just looking at the film. It's fascinating work. It's very interesting and combines inspiration with discipline. This discipline is much harder than any other kind of work like writing a piano sonata, or a concerto, or a symphony, or a ballet or opera.

EL: What kind of research, if any, do you do? Literary or musical?

MJ: Again, I come back to my training in the theater. When I did *Lawrence of Arabia*, I knew a little bit about Lawrence because he was such a great figure in the contemporary world, but really not in detail. So I started to read all the literature, different biographies of him, trying to understand the complexity of Lawrence.

When I studied music and conducting at the Paris Conservatory of Music all young conductors were asked to acknowledge their musical culture. You had to write a thesis on five different ethnic musical cultures. I had chosen Arabic music, Russian music, Indian music, the music of South Asia and the music of the southern United States.

EL: That's quite a variety of musical style and heritage.

MJ: I had no idea that twenty years later I would use practically all my study and research for *Lawrence of Arabia*. This training also came in handy when I did *Resurrection* (American country music), *Shogun* (Japanese), *Tai-Pan* (Chinese), *The Year of Living Dangerously* (Indonesian music), and, of course, *Doctor Zhivago*.

EL: Life sometimes works out beautifully, doesn't it?

MJ: You have no idea; sometimes it's really strange. When I was a student I thought, "What is the point of a conductor studying Arabic or Indian music?" For instance, in Indian music they don't treat music like we do; they have a special notation which I studied. When I did *The Man Who Would Be King* for John Huston I wanted to have real Indian musicians playing true Indian instruments. When I wrote the parts for them I wrote in the special Indian notation. We were using the London Symphony Orchestra, and there were these six musicians dressed in white, on their knees, playing Indian instruments with incense burning. When the other musicians came in and looked at these six guys, they instantly said, "Oh my God, we'll be here for one month. They'll never be able to play with us." We did the first piece without any mistakes from the Indian musicians and recorded all the music in three days. At the end of the third day the full orchestra gave a standing ovation to these six guys. It was a very, very touching moment. John Huston was delighted because it gave a very, very special feeling to the soundtrack.

EL: Do you still conduct and orchestrate your own scores?

MJ: Yes. Also, about six years ago, I realized that there is a large audience for concerts of film music. I have done concerts in Japan, China, Spain, France, Chile, and Canada. I show a few film clips and explain to the audience how the music is recorded in the studio. I play the theme on the piano, then with the full orchestra. I show the film without the music and then I play the music with the film. This gives the audience the feeling they are attending a recording session in a big studio in Hollywood.

EL: What a great learning opportunity.

MJ: Music for film can enhance the film or even help the picture. David Lean said, "You know Maurice, don't forget that sometimes you have to be the doctor of the film. You can make a bad cut or a bad scene better."

EL: What other advice would you give to young people as they prepare to be film composers?

MJ: They should, of course, have as strong a musical background as possible. We are in a new age. They must have a knowledge of electronic music, not just to save money. Also, try to experience some things other than music. Read. Know what's going on in the world. Have the brain not only focused on one single thing, but watch the sea. Listen to the noise of nature. Have something more in the brain than just technique. I have the feeling we are going toward excessive technique and much less to the general feeling or sensitivity with all the noise we hear—the pollution of noise. People cannot listen to a piece of music unless it's one hundred decibels. It's a sickness. They are going to lose their hearing—not only their hearing but the sensitivity of the ear. Sometimes it is great just to listen to silence—like nature. We go too much for the technical point of view and we lose our contact with nature and natural sounds. When you are going to compose you don't compose only with rules. Rules amount to nothing. Look at paintings, read, understand general culture . . . and the rest is pure luck!

Herbie Hancock

■■■■■■■■■■■■■■

Herbie Hancock was born and raised in Chicago, Illinois, where he began
playing the piano at age seven. At the age of eleven he peformed with
the Chicago Symphony Orchestra. He earned a B.A. degree from Grinnell
College and has studied at Roosevelt University, the Manhattan School
of Music, and the New School for Social Research. He has worked with
numerous musicians, including Miles Davis, Chick Corea, and Oscar Pe-
terson, and in 1966 he composed his first feature soundtrack for the
film *Blow Up*. He has since scored several films, including *A Soldier's
Story*, *'Round Midnight* (for which he was music director), *Jo Jo Dancer,
Your Life is Calling*, and *Harlem Nights*. He has also composed the music
for the television specials "Hey, Hey, Hey, It's Fat Albert," and "The
George McKenna Story." Mr. Hancock has gained international recogni-
tion for his outstanding work, winning two Grammy Awards for Best R&B
Instrumental Performance, a Grammy Award for Best Jazz Instrumental
Composition, and an Academy Award for Best Original Score for *'Round
Midnight*. He most recently composed the score for *Livin' Large*. In 1989
he formed Hancock and Joe Productions.

EL: Can you briefly describe your formal music education and how it
did or didn't prepare you for film work?

HH: I started playing piano when I was seven. I took classical piano
lessons and continued lessons until I was twenty-one years old. I went
to college when I was sixteen but I was an engineering major first—I
was trying to be practical. I continued piano lessons in college, and at
the end of my second year I changed my major to music because it was
ridiculous for me to think that I was going to do something else. I
already knew that I was going to be a musician by hook or by crook.

I studied orchestration and took harmony, theory, and sight-singing and then found out that I already knew harmony and theory and sight-singing because I had learned it playing jazz, which I had started playing at age thirteen or fourteen. I learned theory and harmony from other musicians, from playing and from figuring things out and from talking to musicians. Basically, I learned it from the street. I took the courses in college and looked at the textbooks and said, "I already know this stuff! This is what it is!" I even had some disagreements with the instructor.

EL: Your goal at that point was to be a professional musician—as a performer or as a composer?

HH: As a performer.

EL: When did you start getting involved in film work?

HH: In 1966, Michelangelo Antonioni asked me to do the music for *Blow Up*; I'd never heard of him. I'm sure that when he told the people from the film company that he wanted me to do the music they said, "Herbie who?" At the time I was a sideman with Miles Davis' group and I had my own recording contract with Blue Note records. I also had been composing.

EL: How would you characterize the difference in intent between straight composition and composition for film?

HH: Composing music involves just that one medium. The music has to be complete within itself because it's the only medium involved. It has to tell a complete story by itself. In writing for film, the boss is different. When you're writing music for a record you're the boss, and when you're writing music for a film, the director's the boss, at least in spirit. It's the director's dream that you're trying to realize, and what seems to work for me is to have the feeling that in helping the director realize his dream, I realize my own. Also, the music is there to support what you see on the screen.

EL: When you sit down with a director and talk about what it is he or she wants, what kind of references do you use? Musicians have their

own vocabulary but I would imagine not all directors have a musical vocabulary. Do they play other music for you? How do you discuss what they want?

HH: There's not that much of a difference in the language. We use the visual representations of textures in music. It's not foreign to use words like "palette," "pastel," and then there are other terms that are generic to the art form; the term "dynamics"—there are different kinds of dynamics. There's a lot of overlapping that happens. Even with emotional kinds of words, like "irritation" or "longing," you can still use those same kinds of words because they have a dramatic context.

EL: When you do a film, when do you like to join the production team?

HH: I like to come on as soon as there's a script. Whether I read it right away or not is up to me and my schedule, but the sooner I can get a hold of something the better. That way it can kind of mull around in my being for a while. Many times the film is shot and all of a sudden somebody says, "Oh my God, we don't have any music yet!" and the music becomes a last-minute thing. I actually haven't noticed that so much lately because in most of the modern films, the music has become one of the major selling points. It's become a very important medium for the commercial success of the film. It gets a lot more attention than it used to.

EL: When you're watching the rough cut, at what point do you start playing with stuff and at what point do you know that what you've done is set, that it's really right? Do you ever feel you could live with the film for three months longer and do an entirely different score?

HH: I suppose that varies with the individual, but with me, there's a point where it almost feels like I've fused with film. I've studied it so long and so hard and so intently that I know every line, and I've milked the film for everything that I can in terms of understanding the film. I view the film many times, either in previews or on a movieola, where it's flickering by and we stop to examine certain parts of it. I also talk with the director while we're looking at it, over dinner, in all kinds of situations at every hour of the day. At a certain point (and I'm always glad when I get to this point) it feels like some kind of fusion with the film has occurred and the music really just starts to flow out. I'll see a scene, and something just comes out. If I mess with it for a while, play around with it, change harmony here or there, or decide to catch a certain hit point or not catch one, just fooling around with it a little bit, I get to a point where it seems to settle by itself. It just seems to work. In other words, the scene comes on, I play the music to it, and it just feels right; I get a gut feeling about it. There are often constraints and I hate it when I have to let a scene go if I don't have quite that

gut feeling, but one has to be practical. Unless it makes a major difference, you have to stop nit-picking after a certain point.

EL: How much of your orchestrations do you do? Do you turn it over to
somebody else?

HH: Just recently I decided to turn it over to somebody else. In the
beginning I was learning as I was doing them. I wanted to cover as
many bases as I could myself just to develop the skills to do it and to
do it better and better each time. At a certain point I felt confident
enough that I knew how to orchestrate well enough to do a film. It's
such a demanding job to do all of those functions by yourself that I
feel my energies are better spent creating the music; there's a lot of
drudgery involved in physically writing the stuff. I'm not saying that
the orchestrator is only doing busy work, he's not, it's just that it's time
consuming. Conception consumes it's own time, but physically having
to write it out is the part that I don't like to do at all. This is why I'm
so happy about the new technology.

EL: Would you talk a little bit about that? We know about the way
computers can change the way screenwriters write; has it changed the
way musicians write?

HH: It's changed the way I write. I don't mean that what comes out of
me is creatively different than before, but the physical act of having to
take a pencil and write it on the page slows down the creative process
so much; I don't have to be bothered with that anymore because of the
Macintosh computer.

EL: Can you briefly describe the computer setup that you work with?

HH: I've got a Macintosh II and a 150-megabyte hard drive inside, a
total of 280 megabytes in external hard drive, and four 1.2-gigabyte
drives. Actually, two of the 1.2-gigabyte drives are being used with an
IBM computer because one of my instruments works with the IBM. You
need a lot of memory because it is a sampling instrument. I have a
color monitor because I'm spoiled. I like working in color; I get bored
with black-and-white. I have an interface to my instruments called a
MIDI Tap by a company called Lone Wolf. They have a fiber optics

system that can work independently of the Mac or can be connected to the Mac through its serial port. I have some new software so that I can access the MIDI Tap from the Mac because the Mac is so much more graphic. The MIDI Tap has a very small two-line screen, but with the Mac's large display I can see all the connections simultaneously with the MIDI Tap. I'm able to set up my whole keyboard rig and all the programs, I can even set up the rig and have a particular program for each instrument.

The set-ups are called landscapes. So I give them a name and set up and store several of these different landscapes. Every time I switch landscapes, my setup updates according to the new landscape and I just store it. Also, I primarily use a program called Vision from Opcode for the Macintosh as a sequencer program. Basically the sequencer program is one that allows the computer to remember the keys that were played by the user, to record those key depressions rhythmically, and to play the instrument by sending out that same information electronically back to the keyboard. The instrument thinks that someone is pressing the keys down because it's receiving the same kind of information that it receives from the keyboard.

Basically the keys of the electronic instruments are switches. They look like keys but physically, inside, they're just pressing switches down. The switches cause some kind of electronic event to happen. The computer causes these same events. So the instrument responds because it doesn't know the difference. Essentially what it does is play the keyboard back to me. Before we had to put things directly on tape. Today a sequencer program can function like a tape recorder, you're limited only by memory. In the beginning, the sequencer programs used to allow you to have a few notes. Now it's amazing—I've never exhausted the memory of my computer, and with a sequencer and the new software that's available, I haven't even come close to it.

EL: So all this stuff has sped up the process?

HH: With tape recorders you can work with separate tracks so that you can play a simple part of the composition. Then if you want to record another part, you go back, play back the first track, and record on the second track. The sequencer can do the same thing. You can play certain things on a track, and then go back and play that track back and record on a second track. In the past, on tape recorders, you were limited to twenty-four track tape recorders. Now they have new digital machines that are thirty-two track and forty-eight track, and if you go beyond that you have to actually take two machines and link them together. With the sequencer, since the only limitation is memory and there's lots of memory available now, you can go way beyond forty-eight tracks. If I make a mistake on a track, instead of going back and erasing that track, I just record another track. If it's completely useless I just delete it, but if there's anything on there that I might need, I just save it and go on to another track. I might do six or seven passes on one part because I might like a little bit here and little bit there of different passes. Then I'll decide, for example, the seventh one is the one I want to use. I may keep the other ones in case I might want to move a couple of notes here that are from one part and merge or replace that same section on the final part that I've done. Of those seven tracks, the final one is the only one I'll use, so that becomes a single track for me. The rest are just as though I put them in parentheses. I can go on and have an unlimited amount of tracks. I've actually never used more than fifty or sixty tracks.

EL: It sounds like what you're doing is superior to using old technology, that the process is easier and more flexible.

HH: Oh, yes. The thing I'm most accustomed to is playing keyboards as a performer. Many times it's much easier and quicker for me to compose right at the keyboard. On the other hand, I've found that one develops a style of playing and certain physical habits on the keys from having played for a number of years; they can also be a kind of a hang-up. Your fingers might fall in certain places at certain times out of habit. Whereas, if you conceive away from the keyboard, your mind is much freer. So, many times I may still use pencil and paper to jot down ideas or even carry a small microcasette tape recorder to sing ideas into and then do the work of development at the keyboard. It's a system that works very well. Because of the technology we're at the point where we don't even have to simulate or synthesize instruments much anymore with keyboards because a lot of the newer instruments are sampling instruments. The samples have the same or even greater fidelity than a CD. A lot of the samples of orchestral instruments are really the real sound of the instruments and the samples are as good as what we hear on record. You can't say that they are synthesized sounds anymore. The term synthesizer has become a generic term. We still use that word, but they really aren't synthesizers any more than a CD is synthesized.

A lot of orchestrations can be done at the keyboards. Depending on the musical content, there doesn't have to be any difference between having samples and having live musicians play. The restrictions are that some live player did make that sample and that live player might not necessarily have been a good player. Also, you have to consider the way one manipulates an instrument to get the different textures or effects that are possible on an instrument. With a violin, for example, you can play the string very close to the bridge or you can play it very close to the wood where the frets are and get two different sounds. You can pluck the string, you can play with vibrato or without it. There are all kinds of other effects you can get by even striking the strings with the wooden part of the bow. There are a lot of different techniques involved with violin playing or string playing that you can do at will if you're physically playing the violin.

On synthesizers, each one of those different sounds is a different sample. Touch sensitivity of the keyboards, even though it's much more highly developed than when they first began, is still in its infancy on those instruments. It gets pretty involved when you try to play some of the nuances that are possible with live players on the keyboard. It's not so easy to switch through those different effects. On the other hand, it's possible to do things because of the technology that would be impossible on an acoustic instrument.

For example, you can sample a certain note at a certain pitch of the instrument and play that note far below the physical range of the acoustic instrument, or far above the range. It may not sound like that acoustic instrument anymore but it can be an unusual sound. Often, you need to be able to write out parts. There are programs developed to take notes that were played and electronically convert them to notes that you can see on a screen and even print them out using a printer.

There are different fonts and various diacritical marks available in music—trills, mordents, flats and sharps, all the different rests, all the different kinds of tonguing for brass instruments, different types of bowing techniques, slurs, ties, and even beamed notes. What comes out looks like what you buy in a store from a publisher, and it can all be done at home. You don't have to write the music out anymore, you can let the computer do it. Many of the copyists are using the computer for final copies.

EL: Do you think it's important that you don't live in a vacuum as a composer, but that, if performance is feasible, you get out and play a lot and hear a lot?

HH: Definitely get out there and hear a lot. Playing a lot helps. I am a performer, so it's really second nature for me to go out and participate. You don't have to be a performer to do film scores, although I think it helps. You don't have to do it to the extent that I do it—it's really the major part of my career. It certainly helps to know a certain amount about keyboards. The piano is basically a small orchestra, it's a rhythmic instrument, and a harmonic instrument. It's much easier to write using the piano as a foundation than any other instrument, I think.

EL: Any other advice you'd give to a young person?

HH: Orchestration is a very important thing to study. Formal training alone is not enough. You have to go out and physically listen; seize every opportunity to apply what you've learned, and test it out even if it means getting together with musicians and forming some kind of chamber group that you can write for, or finding a situation where there's a band that gets together occasionally that you can write and arrange for. Try different things, even with the technology. The technology is a tool for serving us, but if we haven't developed our ears to be able to hear what's possible, then the technology has no real function; it has no place to go.

FOURTEEN

■ ■ ■ ■ ■ ■ ■ ■ ■ ■ ■ ■ ■ ■ ■

★ Special Effects

As technology has advanced and audiences have become more sophisticated, there has been a number of what have been referred to as "special effects movies." Although many of these films have been fantasy or science fiction films, the use of special effects has spread across all film genres and is used in both small- and large-budget films. Special effects are conceived in pre-production and executed in production and post-production. The creation of special effects is heavily reliant on an assemblage of a variety of specialists in the areas of model making, matte painting, animation, miniatures, robotics, and computer design.

Special effects personnel are usually hired through a contract with the effects company/house for whom they work. A script is offered, the company places a bid, and an agreement is reached.

Robert Greenberg

■■■■■■■■■■■■■■■■■

Robert Greenberg was born in 1948 in Chicago, Illinois. After graduating from Arizona State University with a degree in Mass Communications, he studied business management at DePaul University. Before starting R/Greenberg Associates with his brother Richard in 1977, he served as general manager in charge of manufacturing and overall sales for Royal Crown Cola of Canada. R/Greenberg Associates created the Oscar-nominated special visual effects in *Predator,* the Tri-Star Pegasus logo, the Pillsbury Doughboy, and the opening title sequences for such films as *Dirty Dancing, Home Alone,* and *The Bonfire of the Vanities.* Most recently, R/Greenberg Associates created the visual effects for Jonathan Demme's *Silence of the Lambs.*

EL: Can you characterize what it is that you do?

RG: Simply put, we are involved in merging three separate fields of imaging technology: the film industry, the video industry, and the computer industry. We merge these fields together to enable us to create images for any release format. On the print end, we create images for newspapers, magazines and billboards, which requires working at very high resolution. On the broadcast and feature end, we work in design, live action, motion-control filming and robotics, model making, computer graphics, graphic and cel animation, optical printing, editing, special visual effects, and digital video production.

We work on everything from the openings and special visual effects for feature films to the directing, producing, editing, and completing of over 100 commercial projects a year. We also work on feature film trailer graphics, T.V. network identity packages, logo designs for everything from features to print advertising, and even special effects for theme park rides. We're just opening a new division for interactive multimedia, so we really cover all the bases. We do handle, on an editorial level, mixing and sound, and often subcontract the musicians and voiceovers for different projects.

In commercial and feature production, we work for clients all around the world. We have a production partnership with a well-established company in Tokyo and representation in several European countries. We're not the largest in any specific area of production, but we are one of just a small handful of extremely diversified and integrated production companies. We mix together all the disciplines by interfacing our production departments in a way that allows creatives in each area to interact easily with one another. The foundation of the company and the basis of each project is design. Many of the designers and directors at the company come out of a formal design background, which heavily influences the look of our productions.

EL: What was your training?

RG: I actually got into this business through an odd set of circumstances. I started as a general manager and vice president at Royal Crown Cola. I was pretty good at sales. I worked my way up through the sales offices and through production until I became general manager and built the company's Canadian facility.

My brother Richard came out of a graphic design background, and I started a business with him in 1977 with no formal knowledge of filmmaking and without any client contacts. I learned the process pretty quickly from him. My interest was really in the two areas that we're best known for, diversification and integration. Now we have ten live-action directors, a staff of ninety, and a large base of freelancers.

From the architecture of the studio to the working philosophy, the company is based loosely on the Bauhaus concept. The Bauhaus put together a diverse group of artists and craftspeople under one roof in order to create new dimensions in art and technology. Their extraordinary accomplishments resulted from the free exchange of ideas between people from all disciplines. That is the idea here as well.

EL: So who are all the people that you put together to work on a feature?

Garret Kalleberg

RG: The "architects" are the designers, directors, producers, editors, video engineers, visual effects supervisors, set and lighting designers, cinematographers, and still photographers—all the people who are responsible for the overall "construction" and look of the final image. The "textile designers" or craftspeople are the grips, gaffers, hair and makeup designers, model makers, lab technicians, etc. These are the people who bring to life a particular aspect of the project through their highly specialized crafts.

People on staff here come from backgrounds in opticals, special visual effects, still photography, video engineering, mechanical engineering, computer science, robotics, graphic design, illustration, and all sorts of arts and crafts. The idea is to develop an environment where you extend people's creative boundaries so that they have room to discover abilities they never even knew they had.

EL: How is your company structured?

RG: The company is set up with divisions that are simultaneously autonomous and interconnected. Film laboratory work, film-to-tape transferring, and super computing are examples of the few capabilities we do not have in-house because they require a lot of work for the minimal creative benefits. So these are things we still go outside for, but we have in-house virtually all the creative tools available today.

EL: Describe a couple of projects that you have done that you think really maximize that creative capacity that your team has.

RG: Well, really they all do. A pair of projects that come to mind are the feature films *Predator* and *Predator 2* for which we created the special visual effects. We had to design a creature who is invisible yet somehow remains visible to the audience; the notion is "visible invisibility." We invented the production system and the required equipment, a CompuQuad special effects optical printer, for which we received a Science & Engineering Academy Award. We've used the printer on a number of complex feature films.

The *Predator* productions are very good examples of how the creative and technical process here works. First, we had production people here who understood thermography from a previous project. That's how we created the predator's vision. During the live action filming the alien was really someone in a red suit, and because the jungle that he was from was always green, we were able to pull separations from the color difference and then create what is called a Fresnel or faceted-lens effect. The background actually is showing through the form that is created by the red-suited running figure. We enlarged the background and composited it in out of sync, creating this very unusual, moving prismatic effect that gives you the form of the creature. I think that creating the predator utilized a lot of the creative capabilities that we have.

On *Zelig* we developed a system for steadying archival footage because we wanted to put Woody Allen into archival backgrounds. The problem was that the early camera systems were not what is called "pin registered." Pin registration involves making camera images perfectly steady so that you can shoot somebody separately and put them into the scene, in addition to a lot of other image manipulation. We designed a special way of doing that for this film. The visual effects are key to the dramatic content, and yet they were all created completely behind the scenes. We worked with Gordon Willis and Woody Allen on shooting new footage to match the archival images, and we developed a way of "aging" the new film elements to match. We had a ball actually taking the negative and putting ashes on it, running it through the synchronizer too fast and all sorts of stuff like that. We do a lot of what we call "optical surgery."

EL: When a director or producer comes to you, they're investing their vision in you. How do you come to see the same thing in your minds? Do you present them with storyboards? What's the common language?

RG: Oftentimes you can find examples in the real world. It was very easy on *Zelig*, for example. The film's producers would show us a scene with Babe Ruth and then say they just want Woody Allen in there. The object is to make it really look great and believable. In a film like *Predator*, where the script calls for something totally unreal (and there are many options involved in creating that creature), storyboarding is the beginning stage. We draw something, usually going through a succession of ideas in this manner. The next stage is testing, which generally, for whatever reason, people usually don't do enough of. For example, in *Wolfen*, they hadn't figured out how to create the special effects until all the principal photography was shot, so consequently they were limited to doing something that could actually work with existing cinematography. That's just one example, but there are hundreds of films where they just develop the technology after the fact. So storyboarding and testing are critical.

EL: I'm amazed by the invention involved here. You obviously have to be out there on the edge creatively, but you're in business. How do you budget all this stuff when there are so many unknowns?

RG: A lot of it comes from experience. A lot of it comes from being able to pull together people you work with and to trust their decision-making, problem-solving, and creative abilities. You sit down and work through an approach and come up with budgets. I also came out of a business and corporate background, which I think is particularly important because when you come down to it, studios, ad agencies, and all of our clients are more bottom-line conscious than ever. I think in the producing profession, they are going to be even more so in the future. Part of the creativity and the problem-solving really boils down to figuring out how to force a never-been-done-before one-of-a-kind project into becoming a reality. More often than not, it's too little too soon—the budgets are almost never enough and the schedules are too tight. We've had to invent an unusual method of producing, and we are on time and on budget, no matter what the obstacles. We have computers that record our job history so that we can look at our job costs at any given point in time. We have a history, which has made us aware of the importance of being extremely diversified as well as buttoned up.

EL: Is budgeting your biggest problem?

RG: Our biggest problem is not the work or the budgets, it's primarily the unpredictable nature of the business. You don't always know where your next project is coming from.

We're really dealing with what I call "one-offs"—products we create only once. You usually can't amortize the cost of developing a new technique for one production over a large number of projects, and that's why producing visual effects and "combination" projects is so expensive. Essentially, even though we don't like the term "manufacturing," for lack of a better way to explain our work, we are in the business of manufacturing very special images. Because our industry has such incredible peaks and valleys, we must depend heavily on our experience and reputation to continue to bring the work in. Diversification is also what really keeps us going, so theme parks and interactive multimedia are the logical next step for us.

EL: Is that what's most frustrating about the profession?

RG: What's most frustrating is that you are either too busy or too slow, and there never seems to be the ideal mix of projects and schedules. Not only are you never sure of where the next job is coming from, but you are being asked to do the impossible on ridiculously short schedules, inventing the technology to get the job done as you go along. In contrast to government construction projects that are inevitably delayed and over budget, we do not have the luxury of being able to change completion dates or spend more than originally planned. That is stressful.

You must also be flexible enough to work with people in different industries who all work in different ways. The feature film, commercial, theme park and corporate video production fields are all so different, yet without diversification we would have been out of business a long time ago. We really need to be able to rock and roll in different ways.

EL: How would you advise someone to train for this kind of work? I understand there are a lot of different kinds of people working here.

RG: People must be computer literate. Whether you're a writer or an artist or a photographer, everybody is embracing computers, particularly computers that are "user friendly." If you invest in a personal computer and a video camera, you can simulate almost anything that we're doing here. There are a number of really terrific programs at colleges, such as the School of Visual Arts, MIT Media Lab, the Cooper Union, NYU, and Columbia on the East Coast, and UCLA, USC, Art Center, Cal Arts, and the AFI on the West Coast. There are programs that involve a lot of computer simulation at NYIT, Stanford, RPI, MIT, Cornell, Ohio State, and Harvard. These programs do give you some special training and hands-on experience.

I'm also a firm believer in young newcomers trying to get jobs as production assistants. Many of our people here, probably 25 percent, started as messengers. Apprenticeships are great. Try to get on a feature crew as a production assistant or work for a commercial multimedia company like ours.

Developing business skills is important. It helps to be a self-starter and to be able to manage your workload and delegate responsibility. Management skills are not just great for business but also for creative roles, such as directing and producing—really for all the disciplines. There are courses people can take to acquire these skills, but I think the best preparation is on-the-job training.

Michael Backes

••••••••••••••

Michael Backes has worked with computer technology since 1984. He was one of the pioneers in the application of the personal computer to the challenges of film production. From screenwriting and production scheduling to sophisticated 3D computer animation and real-time scene simulation, Mr. Backes has attempted to push the limits of personal computing. As a consultant to director James Cameron during the making of *The Abyss,* Mr. Backes supervised the first MacIntosh computer system to be used for many of the behind-the-scenes tasks on a major motion picture. As a consultant, Mr. Backes counts among his clients: Apple Computer's Advanced Technology Group, three major film studios, and The American Film Institute. He has also lectured on computers and the film business at UCLA, ACM Siggraph, and to many user groups.

EL: How would you characterize your work with computers and film, and what is happening in that field?

MB: Currently I'm working with directors, writers, art departments, and, occasionally, special effects companies on using small computers in the production of films. The inroads for small computers into films came primarily through the special effects pictures because they usually employed the individuals who were either the most technologically literate or enthusiastic. It's a relatively new phenomenon, it's happened primarily since 1984. The introduction of the IBM PC and the Apple Macintosh got people to think about using computers in film. In 1984 and 1985, Lorimar did a film called *The Last Starfighter* that used a great big Cray computer to do special effects, and there was a lot of computer envy out there. Everybody wanted to jump into the application of computer technology in filmmaking, but at that time a Cray cost was twelve million dollars and the small computers just didn't have the horsepower. A lot of people started using the personal computers just as word processors. With the introduction of the Macintosh and the availability for the first time of a computer that could do graphics very easily, people started to say, "Gosh, why can't we use small computers to do graphics, storyboards, or a little animation to show us how a motion picture scene plays?" At the same time, on the financial side, people were starting to say, "We can take these spreadsheet programs and use them for budgeting and scheduling our pictures, and it will make the frequent process of revision a lot easier." You can ask a lot "What if?" questions like "What if the studio gives me less money?" which is the usual question you have to ask. It's a three-pronged thing: graphics, word processing, and numerical manipulation that got the computer in Hollywood's door.

EL: Can you name the areas of film where computers are being used?

MB: Basically, every job title in the industry could be affected to some degree by computer technology, though some less than others. There are no computer programs for grips yet, but there are probably computer programs on managing the grip truck. You've got screenwriting programs for writers, computer editing suites for both film and video for nonlinear editing, storyboarding programs for production departments, painting programs, 3D and 2D animation programs, and computer-based video assist systems on the set while you're filming. It's pretty wide-ranging. Obviously there's tons of software for scheduling and budgeting pictures. Now there is software for writers that allows you to break down a story idea. There's a new program called Plots Unlimited that has literally thousands and thousands of little pieces of plots. Pretty soon we'll have an artificial intelligence to help you plot stories.

EL: How did you get involved in this?

MB: Via computer—I was pretty much self-taught. I had taken computer classes in college but I hated them. Then I bought an Apple Macintosh and got hooked—on computer games. When I got bored with the games I said, "What real work can I do on this?" I met Ron Cobb who is a production designer and futurist. He worked on the Macintosh and had worked on *The Last Starfighter* as a principal designer. It just took off from there. When we got color and real horsepower in the computer we started to think, "Wow, we can do things like 3D graphics." By the time *The Abyss* rolled around, we were just starting to get the software that was really useful. By then I was totally hooked.

EL: Describe your work on *The Abyss*.

MB: Ron Cobb was working on it doing some design. James Cameron, the director, had owned a Macintosh for a while and was interested in using a Mac on a movie. He wrote the screenplay on a Macintosh, and Charlie Skouras, the production manager, did the budget and managed the schedule on the computer. Van Ling and I worked to develop a system to storyboard and do some 3D graphics animations of some of the bigger props as well as the day-to-day graphics management. It was the first major Hollywood movie to use the Macintosh for all that stuff and probably the first to use a personal computer to manage the pre-production graphics.

EL: How much did your experience as a screenwriter and as a former film company executive play into your understanding of how to link computers with film?

MB: My experience helped me understand how the movie industry works, as much as anybody with my experience can understand it. I was an executive for three years at a small studio, I've been a screenwriter for about four years, and between those two experiences I understand how the game is played. The biggest lesson to be learned here is that if it saves you time it will be used, if it just saves you money, it probably won't be used.

EL: Why is that?

MB: Because filmmaking is all about time—you never have enough time to do anything because every extra day is interest lost on somebody else's money. Film is that interesting marriage of art and commerce: I figure you might as well be aware of both. But the commerce definitely has a capital C. Computers will only be used if they save people time. The other key question that has to be addressed by people making software for filmmakers is that filmmakers usually don't have time to learn how to use software. You have to use a metaphor in your software that the filmmaker already understands. If you want to design a motion picture camera simulator, your controls on the screen better work like the camera so the people who want to use your software are comfortable. So the most successful software for filmmaking consistently works like regular things in the film world.

EL: How do you keep on top of the abundance of software in film?

MB: Much of the software I use was not specifically designed for film but is applicable to filmmaking. The idea is that a pencil is applicable to filmmaking in the sense that you can write a script or sketch a storyboard with it. There are other software tools out there that are very applicable. I just read like crazy—I read all of the trades, in this case Macintosh-specific trade magazines, looking for software that might be applicable. I'd say 40 percent of the time I contact the company before they even realize that there's a market for their software in the film business. I say, "Hey, did you know your software could be used in the movie business?" The best example of that is when I was working on *The Abyss*, there was a guy in North Carolina named David Smith who'd written a game called "Colony" where as you move the mouse on your computer you fly in real-time 3D through an environment. When I saw it I said, "set," when he saw it, he said, "game." I called him and said, "I want to send you some blueprints and I want you to take these blueprints and put them into your game so I can walk around my set in real time. Like most people, people in the computer business are fascinated by movies.

EL: Is this an open or closed field for somebody who wants to break in?

MB: I think it's incredibly open because I can't do it all. I'm asked to do things like the AFI/Apple Computer Center for Film and Videomakers. There are definitely positions out there on productions. What I like to do now is go in and set up a system at a company and have somebody else run it. That frees me up to get into more cutting-edge software that I'm going to try to bring to the film community. I think there's a lot of opportunity. I think there's opportunity for programmers and incredible opportunity for artists. There aren't that many opportunities out there for artists besides designing Hallmark cards and doing traditional graphic design. This is an area that is really quite interesting—the idea of using computers to do design work for film. It's a fascinating area and it's brand new, there's a lot of opportunity.

EL: How important is film school or film apprenticeships for somebody who's going to get into this?

MB: I think the more you learn about film, the better off you are. Film is an important art. You're not going to learn how to do the stuff I do in film school but you'll learn about film in film school and that's extremely important. As far as apprenticeship goes, you have to find somebody to whom you can apprentice yourself to learn this—it's difficult. A conventional film education is certainly helpful and highly recommended but you have to wed it to a technological education. My background was incredibly eclectic. I majored in Biology and English in college, and I wasn't into computers at all. I came out to L.A. and started working for a producer and just got hooked on the film business. If I was going to do it with intent, if I was a student in college and was asking, "How do I get into computers in the movie business?" the first thing I'd do is study computers and technology, get it down, and study a practical language like Object C, or something that is actually usable in software development as opposed to something like COBOL. A lot of this stuff is graphics driven. Then study cinematography and filmmaking, watch as many movies as you can, and try to figure out how a computer could help—because when a computer can't help it'll just hurt. Often you'll see people get excited about technology. But technology is not some magic wand that you wave over your life and it makes it easier. You bleed a lot on the cutting edge—if you want to get out and use the latest and greatest, you're going to have a lot of blood on your keyboard.

EL: What is your greatest frustration?

MB: Frustration with software that usually hasn't been completely tested; the great stuff is always the brand new stuff, and the new stuff is always the stuff that doesn't have all the kinks worked out of it so you get system crashes, etc. In a millisecond you can lose a week's work; it can be frustrating. At the same time, it's kind of like being a sculptor who has the big block of marble, and when you're done, it's a beautiful sculpture. When you see the results on film for the first time, and you go "Wow!," and then you show it to other people and they say "Wow!," and they incorporate it into their movie, and get "Wows!" from the audience—that what's it's all about.

EL: By the year 2000 will computers have radically changed Hollywood? Or will the change be modest?

MB: It will probably be a smaller change than what's really needed. The film business has been the slowest to change technologically. Our sound systems haven't changed that much in seventy years. I think it will be a while, but, yes, there will be an enormous change just because the whole world is moving towards computers. It's simply inevitable that computers will change the world. There will be some things on the computer horizon that we haven't even thought of yet. Media and computers haven't gotten married yet, but they're definitely engaged.

EL: Any other advice for a young person who really wants to get into this field?

MB: The bottom line is that it's a great field for generalists. If you have wide-ranging interests, technology and the film business wed two great things: technology and art. It's really an exciting field. You have to write your own ticket. If you have the imagination and the ability, it's a great area of the film industry to get into because you can wear a lot of hats, meet a lot of interesting people, and you can get into snooty private clubs.

Scott Ross

Scott Ross began his work in film and music at Hofstra University, graduating with honors in Film/TV in 1974. After settling in San Francisco the following year, he gained business experience as sales manager of a large chain of retail audio stories and went on to found his own production company, providing technical operations for HBO, Showtime, and independent television productions. In 1982 he became the director of production for One Pass, a video post house, and moved quickly through the ranks to become President of One Pass in 1985. During those years he engineered the design and construction of a $2.5 million mobile production unit and directed national commercials, music videos, and an Emmy award-winning jazz special. Lucasfilm, Ltd., recruited Mr. Ross in 1988 to serve as Industrial Light and Magic's director of operations, and by the end of the year he was appointed ILM's General Manager. Currently, he is group vice-president for the LucasArts Entertainment Company.

EL: Would you briefly summarize your formal education and how it may have prepared you for what you're doing today?

SR: Between 1969 and 1973 I attended Hofstra University in Hempstead, Long Island, majoring in film and television. Then I went on to the New School for Social Research, from 1973 to 1974, majoring in film and television.

EL: When you were studying as an undergrad and then later at the New School, what was your specific interest in film?

SR: In my junior year, I went out on tour with the Miles Davis band as a sound engineer and I was a concert chairman at my University.

As many of us were in the late sixties, I was very much involved with music and I decided I wanted to be a musician. I started studying music but I was so behind musically, formally, that I couldn't cut it academically on a musical level. I turned at the time to what was another interest of mine, nowhere near as keen an interest as in music— and that was film. It was the closest thing to a creative environment in which I could be involved where I had the necessary skills to qualify for a degree. I was not thinking of pursuing it as a career when I got out of school.

EL: So once you graduated and finished your formal education, how did you set out to pursue a career in film?

SR: Through my musical contacts back in New York, I was working as a mixer on the road with rock and roll bands and with jazz bands. When I came to California, I started pursuing a musical career, but I was starving to death; things weren't working, and I decided to give it up. I decided that since I had an undergraduate degree and part of a graduate degree in film and television, I would pursue that. I saw an ad that Hewlett-Packard was looking for a media director for their corporate television programming. I interviewed for the job and was told that they couldn't hire me because I couldn't muster the security clearance to get the job. That evening I went out with my then-girlfriend, my now-wife, and we ran into an old college friend from back East. We told her my story, and she said that she had a friend in the television industry and could I write out my background and send a resumé. I pulled a napkin off the table in the restaurant and wrote on it that I had worked with Miles Davis and with other rock and roll bands. I gave it to her and a month later received a phone call from this fellow who was providing technical crews for all of the broadcasts of sporting events in the Bay Area. Would I and could I possibly pull cable for $4.50 an hour tomorrow for the San Jose Earthquakes? Of course, I was living on alfalfa sprouts and starving, so I said, "You bet, what time should I be there?" That's how it started. Over a period of years, I learned a lot about television and became a camera person, an audio person, and a technical director, and really got involved in sports and entertainment specials. Then I was hired by a company called One Pass in the Bay Area

© Lucasfilm Ltd.

to head up their operations. After four or five years, I became president of that group and served for about two and a half years. Then I came over to Los Angeles.

EL: How would you characterize what you do and what ILM as a whole does?

SR: Let's start with ILM as a whole. ILM provides visual effects for three different markets right now: the feature film market, the commercial market (broadcast commercials), and theme parks. A definition of visual effects would be the manipulation of filmed images in such a way as to make the unreal real.

EL: Within that, what specifically is your role?

SR: I have been quoted before and I'll say it again, my card should say Scott Ross, Janitor, because I work for 350 of the most talented people I've ever met in my life. While I have the title of vice president/general manager and my responsibilities are to lead this company, if truth must be known, I try to create an environment and opportunities for these 350 brilliant people.

EL: As the man who runs this operation, what do you look for in the young people who are coming into ILM? What characteristics, educational backgrounds, enthusiasms turn you on in terms of choosing new people entering your company or your field?

SR: Well, there are specialized areas. In our company we have many, and let me just name several: computer graphics, optical, editorial, animation, model, creature, camera, production, matte painting, art department, and it goes on. We're generally looking for people who are specific to those areas. We look for two different kinds of people: 1) very experienced who have either worked with us in the past or have worked with our competitors and are well known, famous leaders in the industry and 2) new people. Where do they come from? Well, if it's an art department person we're looking for, an art director, we want somebody with the ability to draw. Usually they're coming out of universities. They generally have a keen interest and sense of the history of visual effects and understand the medium. We ask them to send us their portfolio, and if the work is incredible, we hunt them down. We will go after them. The first criterion is that the work has to be absolutely incredible, and that's in every category. If you're a model maker, you have to build models as no one has ever built models. If you're a producer, or a production coordinator, you have to be organized and understand the process as no one else has understood it. That's the basic criterion.

EL: How does one who balances the management of 350 creative individuals and keeps a company running at the same time foster and nurture individuality, spontaneity, creativity?

SR: How does one do it? Blind luck and stupidity. It is the most difficult thing that I've ever done; it becomes more difficult every day, and it's what keeps me on fire. I remember when I was in high school one of my high school history teachers had a quote that he used a lot (it was 1967 at the time), and he said "Where anarchy reigns, chaos begins." In a creative environment, the creative people generally try to push towards anarchy. The role of the "suit," (I guess I'm the "suit" in this business) is to be able to pull it back as much as possible towards structure. Just as you think you have the proper amount of structure, you need to push a little towards anarchy. It really has to be somewhere in the middle, but for fun, I think you need to push it a little bit more towards the anarchistic.

EL: When you deal with a filmmaker in your feature film work, commercial work and even the theme park work, what is the vocabulary, the common ground, in a field of so many specialists? Is there an intermediary?

SR: When a project comes in, we generally put a three-person team together; a producer, an art director and an effects supervisor. Our effects supervisor is similar to the feature film's director. They're the lead, key creative persons who control the project from beginning to end. That team is put together because film is the most collaborative form of art around. It's also commercial, and we can't forget that. You've heard these well-known terms that I think are tattooed on my forehead, "on time, on budget, win an Academy Award." Those three statements push our company forward. You need to have a team put together that has the creative side, the technical side, and the business side as a triangle and attach it to the project. If you falter in any one, you didn't do your job.

EL: How important is film school for folks coming in?

SR: That's difficult, you hit on a good one there. Many of our computer people are computer scientists coming out of Cal Berkeley and such technical schools. The problem is that the language is very different; they don't understand our language, and we don't understand their language. We've been successful because we've had a computer graphics department attached to this company for almost eight years, so a lot of walls have been broken down, but there are still problems of language and syntax. Regarding film school, if you're a specialist and we're looking for an artist, it probably is helpful that a person went to some form of design school and also has a passion for films and possibly took some undergraduate courses in film as well. Most important, and this is the thing I would stress the most, you must really want to succeed in our business, and you really need great interpersonal skills. That's why I think college is so important.

EL: What's the most frustrating thing about your profession?

SR: Business in itself is frustrating because you never have enough money and you never have enough time. I think in the creative process as well, you never have enough money or time. On the other hand, it's bittersweet because that's part of the excitement.

EL: Can you describe, in feature work, at what point a filmmaker comes to you, even for the initial meeting, and at what point you get heavily involved? Can you generalize the length of a commitment to a feature?

SR: Well, it really runs the gamut. For example, there are projects that we've been involved with before a director's even been assigned to it. The studio has a great script that seems to have a great deal of visual effects. So they'll shoot us off a copy of the script and ask, "What do you think? What's your ballpark on it? How would you approach it?" That's the earliest we could get involved. Oftentimes we judge without the insight of a director, and he or she might have a very different take on what it is. Some directors hand it over and say, "OK, I want you to develop these creatures, this look, and these visual effects. Here are the sequences. Come back with storyboards and ideas and concepts, not only on how you would do it, but what it would look like." Some directors are very, very straightforward and say, "Here are the storyboards, this is what I want you to do; I need the boy to fly from here to here, I need the girl to do this and turn into a monster; and here's what the monster looks like. Can you do it?" So the involvement can run the gamut; it's not cut and dried.

EL: Is your field open or closed for a young person?

SR: It's both. Our industry is considered by those who are outside of it as being glamorous. Those of us who are inside recognize that it's the furthest thing from glamour that you'll ever see. Since it's considered a "glamour" industry, there are many people who want to be involved in it. The entry level, getting through the door, is very difficult because many are lined up outside the door. My experience has been that once you're in, if you're as good, as dedicated, as creative, and as crazy as you think you are, you can rise to the top very, very quickly.

EL: Is there a way you can characterize the kinds of films that are most attractive to ILM?

SR: The most important thing in a film is that it moves somebody. It doesn't need to be (and probably shouldn't be) the effects that do the moving; it needs to have a great script. We look for films that are uplifting; while they're commercial and generally not art, they're films that show the better part of the human spirit, films you would take your kids to and feel good about the message they got.

EL: Your company is a real leading-edge company. Do you see yourselves as setting trends, or trying to detect trends? Is innovation a big part of what motivates everybody there?

SR: If you were to ask, "Has our company been involved in new techniques?" I would point to the work and say, "Absolutely." Not to tip my hat too much but the most exciting, innovative, visually innovative piece of film, I think, in 1989 was the 35 or 45 seconds of the water-pseudo-pod in *The Abyss*. As a visual impact, I think it was probably the most visually exciting piece of film that was produced that year, and it was a new technology. We are one of the few companies that actually have significant R and D budgets and a staff dedicated to innovations in the field of visual effects.

EL: You're still a young man, but during your career have you already seen significant changes in the filmmaking industry? How do these affect you, and can you identify others that would be helpful to a young person thinking about this field?

SR: There are positives and negatives. One of the positive things is the world is becoming a global village (to use a tired phrase), and because of that films are now international films. Blockbuster movies have to be blockbuster international films because the costs of films are so extraordinarily high that you need an international box office. The good part about that is that it's making the world smaller. I believe there are several ways to make an international film: one way is through music, because that's an international language, and another is visual imagery, because that's another international language. Because the international film is becoming much more prevalent, it uses much more special imagery, and we're excited about being involved in that. A negative is that one of the reasons for pushing that international flavor is that films are becoming so expensive above the line. The stuff below the line is getting squashed, so the technicians making the film are being pushed further and further away from the creative process as a cost-containment process. The folks above the line continue to make more and more and more money. So it drives the price of the film up.

EL: Any general advice you'd give to a young person entering the field of film in general?

SR: To encapsulate my philosophy . . . If there was only one thing I learned at film school it was that when you get the opportunity, you should work harder and smarter than anyone else.

FIFTEEN

⬛ The Critic

Film criticism appears in daily newspapers, weekly and monthly news magazines, and trade journals, and on commercial, cable, and public television. There has also been a gold rush of movie review books to accompany the home video market. Criticism has become a popular form of creative nonfiction writing, which now rivals fiction as a viable commercial avenue for writers. The film critic has achieved great power; both print and media critics have taken on celebrity status and can influence the public's tendency to attend or not attend certain films. Responsible criticism relies on describing, analyzing and evaluating the art form. These skills must rest on solid writing skills, a bedrock of knowledge of film history, familiarity with the filmmaking process, strong analytic abilities, and a love of the art form.

There is no union or guild for this field. The salary of a film critic usually depends on the medium in which he or she is featured and how established the person is within the field.

Leonard Maltin

■■■■■■■■■■■■■■■

Although he has earned a reputation as one of the country's leading film historians, Leonard Maltin is best known as the film correspondent and historian on the popular syndicated television program "Entertainment Tonight" and its weekend edition "Entertainment This Week." He is the author of *Of Mice and Magic: A History of Animated Cartoons, The Great Movie Comedians, The Disney Films,* and *The Art of the Cinematographer,* and his annual paperback, *Leonard Maltin's TV Movies and Video Guide,* is considered a standard work. He has published articles in numerous magazines, is a contributing editor of *Video Review* magazine, and his daily feature, "Leonard Maltin on Video," is heard on more than one hundred radio stations. For nine years he was a member of the faculty of the New School for Social Research, and he continues to lecture at colleges and institutions around the country. He served as Guest Curator for the Bicentennial Salute to American Film Comedy at the Museum of Modern Art and has acted as a consultant for a variety of other film projects. Most recently, he has written, hosted and co-produced a number of original home video programs, including "Cartoons for Big Kids" and "Bugs and Daffy: The Wartime Cartoons."

EL: Can you briefly summarize your formal education and how it did or didn't prepare you for your profession?

LM: I have a bachelor of arts degree from New York University. When I was choosing a college, I had a lot of self-debate; I was already being published and had been running my own film magazines since the age of 15. I was already quite focused and enjoying modest success; I was heading in the direction I wanted to go. Of course I was too much of a straight arrow not to go. I'm glad I went, not so much for the education but for the life experience, for the social meaning of going through that experience. The best thing that happened for me was that I worked on the school paper. NYU had quite a professional daily newspaper, and I quickly became the movie reviewer and then later the entertainment editor. I wouldn't have traded that for the world, it was a wonderful experience. It was so wonderful it caused me to cut many classes. That's the best background imaginable for doing what I wanted to do.

EL: While you were at NYU, were you formally studying film?

LM: No, I was not. At the time I was there (I enrolled in 1968), they didn't have a Cinema Studies department, and the film division was geared much more toward filmmaking, which was not my real interest. I decided not to major in film and instead majored in journalism. I was able to audit a number of film courses and really had the best of both worlds. The orientation of that department was toward working professionally—many of the courses were taught by working journalists and they encouraged you to be working too. That was the approach at NYU; I was able to turn in carbon copies of some articles I'd written for publication as assignments and they didn't disparage that, they were delighted. That wouldn't be true at many other schools and I was grateful for that. Also, getting to take film courses was great. I took a wonderful course on documentaries that was very useful as well as many others.

EL: When you left NYU, what was your next professional step?

LM: It was a very confusing time for me when I left NYU. I had been freelancing all through college, and I had published three books while in college. When I got out I thought I would just keep doing the same thing, but there were problems. If I was going to work on my own, I would no longer have any social contact and that was difficult to face and deal with—it's the lot of any writer. I considered getting a teaching job somewhere so that I could teach film and have a foundation of income and security from which I could then work on other projects and continue to write books. I had learned even at that moment in my life that you can't make a living writing, certainly not film books. This presented a problem because you can't get a teaching job with just an

undergraduate degree, and yet I had come to really hate school. I didn't hate NYU, I just hated school. I didn't want to sit in the classroom one more minute. I really didn't know what to do. Then a friend said to me, "Why don't you teach at the New School?" and I said, "Would they have me?" and he said, "Yeah, that's the great thing about the New School, if you've got a good idea for a course and you can get people to take it, they'll have you." I went to meet the dean of that division and suggested I teach a course on animation, and they said "OK, we'll try it" and enough people signed up that I did teach that course. I ended up staying there for nine years. That was a wonderful experience, and it gave me exactly what I wanted—more than I thought I would get out of it actually. I had contact with people who were interested in the subject (nobody was taking that course as a requirement). Having to articulate your ideas on a subject forces you to think them through, and having a class as a sounding board and as a stimulant is doubly helpful. During the years I was teaching that course I started formulating a book on the history of animation that I finally did publish. It was a really good experience that I enjoyed very much. It was a great social experience too, because my class became the hangout for all the cartoon buffs in New York City, and many of them still miss it to this day.

EL: You obviously value interaction with other people. Do you see criticism as an isolated profession or as a social one? What's your philosophy on interacting with audiences or viewing with audiences?

LM: It depends on the job at hand. When I was reviewing for this show ("Entertainment Tonight") for instance, I didn't want to meet with filmmakers for a very simple reason. If I met a filmmaker and liked him or her, I'd feel very bad about giving a bad review. It sounds simplistic but it's a very real problem. Some people can do that; some people have the ability to separate their professional self from their social self. I have a hard time doing that. I'm not saying it's impossible, but it's difficult. I don't have that many friends among filmmakers; I know some, and I know some better than others. The first time I had to go on the air and give a bad review to a film made by a friend of mine was very difficult. It was also very difficult for him to accept. We had a real rift, and we patched it up eventually. It was Joe Dante, and the film was *Gremlins*, which I didn't like. What's funny about it is that Joe had made that film for his friends. It was rife with in-jokes, and he had done it as a goof. His friends didn't like it and the public ate it up. Last year Joe's producer Mike Fennell called me and asked if I would do a cameo in *Gremlins II* playing myself giving a bad review to *Gremlins I* and then being attacked by the gremlins. I thought it was rather poetic, so I said, "Sure." I wrote jazz reviews for a long time (another great love of mine), and in the jazz community there is such a blur as to be almost nonexistent—the line between jazz writers and jazz critics and jazz players and jazz fans—they all hang out together. It's very hard to separate yourself as a critic. There are other facets to that question too. When I review a movie for this show my reviews are always very simple, very brief. They are always mere impressions of the movie. I think they are valid in the context and I think they serve a purpose, but they are what they are. That's a lot different from writing a Pauline Kael–length essay in the *New Yorker*. Those are two different things. It may well be that for someone writing an essay of that depth and that seriousness, meeting the filmmaker could be beneficial to fleshing out your own understanding of what the intentions, goals, and problems were. I don't think meeting the filmmaker would have any great benefit to somebody who does very short newspaper or television reviews. I think it could be more of a hindrance.

EL: What do you see as the purpose of criticism in the nineties?

LM: The problem is that what is called film criticism today is not what anyone would classically define as criticism. Again, it doesn't invalidate it, but I think we've lost the semantic difference between a piece of criticism and a simple review. Most members of the general public read a newspaper review or watch a television review for one reason only: to find out if the film is any good and if they should go to see it. That's all they want out of that review, that's all they're expecting, that's all they're asking. Critics serve as a consumer guide, period. That's valid and it serves a genuine purpose, and a lot of people are grateful to have that service, but it's not criticism. Criticism in the classical sense is a serious, thoughtful essay on the film that enlightens, illuminates, debates, and discusses the merits of the work. Often in doing so, I'll have to give away the ending, something I don't think is ever permissible in a simple review. Serious criticism will take some time to chew on its subject. Most people aren't looking for that. That's why I don't read that many critics. I'm only interested in reading a review if it's going to give me something I don't already know or I don't already have. I'm looking for graceful writing, knowledge, and intelligence, and I'm looking for someone to stimulate my thoughts on the subject, and there aren't too many people that do. I think many critics will tell you the same thing. Why should they read another critic? What are they going to gain from it unless that critic gives them food for thought?

EL: You've written so much, and you are truly a historian. Is that immersion in film history critical in order to review contemporary films?

LM: I think if you were the managing editor of a newspaper, you'd no more dream of sending someone to cover a football game who'd never covered a game before than you would assign the sports reporter to cover the gardening show at the coliseum. It just would never happen, it isn't done. Where movies are concerned, however, the prevailing attitude is that everybody knows about movies, therefore everyone can write about them. It's true, we've all seen movies all our lives, and it's true that everyone seems to have an opinion about movies, so that in theory anyone can write about them and perhaps write intelligently about them. Without some background, without some knowledge and without some love for the subject, I don't think you're worth a damn as a critic. In print it still happens all the time; it's happened at the *New Yorker* several times in the past couple of years while Pauline Kael has taken a leave of absence. They've assigned some writer, a general writer on the staff, to cover the film beat for a while; the *New York Times* did it most noticeably when they hired Renata Adler. It happens all the time in television—the apocryphal and yet valid story of the editor working late at night and opening his mail and finding two tickets to the ballet for that night; he looks around the office and sees a guy sweeping and says, "Hey you! Take these tickets and go out and see the ballet and write a review!" That still happens all the time, because nobody really takes movies seriously in that context. I think to be a worthwhile critic you must have knowledge, and you must have love, and if you're missing either one of those, you're not any good.

EL: What's frustrating about your profession?

LM: When you work in television, you're always frustrated by the time limitation. I can't think of anything else that's ever frustrating about it.

EL: When you review a film, do you see it more than once?

LM: I don't have time to see it more than once. Again, if I were writing a serious, lengthy essay, I would feel compelled to see it more than once. To do the kind of brief, summarizing reviews I would do on this show, there is no need.

EL: What kinds of educational paths might you suggest for a young person who was considering entering the field of film reviewers, film critics?

LM: There are two answers to that. I think anyone who is foolish enough to want to pursue this career should get to know their movie history, know it well, and see it not as a chore but as a mission, as a voyage of discovery. The other thing would be to get a well-rounded education, not just a film education. It's not an original thought on my part to say that the problem with the whole film industry today is that it's feeding off itself far too much. You have filmmakers and film executives and even film critics who know nothing but film and have no life experience, no literary experience, and no historical experience. One of the things I like most about watching old movies is that they give me a sense of history. Not only history over the centuries but most especially twentieth-century history, and I revel in that. I'm always discouraged when I talk to young people who have no sense of recent history at all. There's no more painless way of learning it than watching old movies. What was on people's minds in the forties, or the fifties, or the thirties? Watch the movies and they'll tell you. I heard a great quote from Cicero: "Not to know what happened before you were born is to remain forever a child." I believe it. Schools often do a poor job teaching us about contemporary history, or even current events. There's nothing more interesting and there's nothing that's taught more poorly.

EL: How important are journalistic skills or the study of critical standards?

LM: Writing skills are crucially important, not only for a critic but for everybody. Communication is so crucial in our lives and so few people know how to communicate well. This is something you're not going to learn in school. A good school can help teach it to you, a really good school will teach it to you properly, but by and large, I think people have to want to learn how to communicate well. They have to keep their ears open and learn from their mistakes as well as the mistakes of others to communicate more effectively. That includes speaking as well as writing. I think learning by doing is the path that has to be followed here.

EL: Is it an open or closed field as far as job opportunities?

LM: I always tell young people who write to me the same thing: Get published. Get published somewhere, anywhere, a school paper, a local shopper that's distributed for free in your neighborhood, a newsletter from an organization you belong to, just get published. If you can't get published, do what I did, publish yourself and give it out to people. If xerox machines had existed when I was a kid, I could have ruled the world. I didn't let very much stop me anyway, but when I think about what I had to go through when I was a kid just starting!

EL: What was the name of your publication?

LM: I had several. When I was in the fifth grade, a friend and I decided to do something of our own, and we produced the first issue of a quasi-newspaper. It had a circulation of three because we had an original and two carbon copies. The reason I did my little publication when I was in high school was because they wouldn't let me write for the paper; I was a sophomore and they didn't want any part of me on the paper. I said, "To heck with it, we'll do our own." I did, and that's how I wrote and expressed myself. You cannot write in a vacuum, you have to write to be read. The reader is your partner, if you're not reaching that reader, and with luck getting some response from that reader, you can't know how you're doing; you can't improve and get a sense of yourself. That's why I say get published, get published somewhere, anywhere, and then make sure people see it, make xeroxes, send it to people. Send it to friends, send it to people you admire, send it to relatives, leave them off in places, get yourself read, but also get yourself the experience of writing, writing on a regular basis, writing to a deadline, and writing to a space limit. If you're writing for a school paper, they will impose disciplines on you that you won't impose on yourself. Those disciplines are important, too. When they say to you, "We've got to have the review in an hour," you've got to gather your thoughts in one hour and get them written. You can't spend a month pondering what you want to say, you have to say it. If they say, "You only have four inches," you have to do it in four inches of type. These are important things to deal with. But the most important thing is to do it.

EL: Any other advice that you would pass on to a young person?

LM: Only that nothing is impossible—nothing. If you're determined to do something, if it's something you feel you want to do and have to do, then you have to find a way to try make it happen. It's tough for me to give advice because luck has played so much a part in my life, luck and timing. Being in the right place at the right time and having good things happen. You can't invent that. Some people may not have the breaks that I had, but somehow I always believed in myself, and I believed in trying to make things happen, and finding a way. I think if you're good, if you have talent, and if you have determination, then you can create your own rules sometimes and forge a path, even if one is not officially open to you.

Sheila Benson
■ ■ ■ ■ ■ ■ ■ ■ ■ ■ ■ ■ ■ ■

Sheila Benson began her career as a film reviewer for KTIM AM/FM radio in the early seventies. After eight years as the film critic for the Pacific Sun in Mill Valley, California, she moved to Los Angeles. Since 1981 she has been a film critic for the *Los Angeles Times*. Ms. Benson is a member of the National Society of Film Critics and Los Angeles Film Critics Association, and she has served as a jury member for the Montreal World Film Festival, the Berlin International Film Festival, the Manila International Film Festival, and the Hawaii International Film Festival. In 1987 she garnered the Woman's Building Vesta Award for exceptional achievement in journalism. Ms. Benson has published articles in numerous magazines including *TV Guide, Film Comment, Elle*, and the *London Sunday Telegraph*.

EL: At what point in your life did you discover writing and/or criticism?

SB: Not until I was 40, very late in the story. I was living in Marin County, where I thought I would be for the rest of my life, having children and husbands. I had gone to New York, had been married, and my photographer husband wanted to live in Sausalito. There was no reason not to, what else was happening in our lives? We settled there, and marriages and divorces ensued. In the early seventies a friend suddenly got a fifteen-minute daily program on the radio and said to some of her friends, "You are going to talk about food, about gardens and about movies." I said, "I am not." And she said, "Then you may never talk about them again; you may never talk about them in the car on the way home and steam up all the windows."

EL: Were you passionate about films?

SB: Apparently so. I had done a little bit of freelance writing about which I know little. I then started to do movie reviews for fifteen minutes a week on the radio at 8:30 in the morning for free. When I started I was so green I paid my own way into the theaters, sat down, and when the credits came, I began to write them down. I thought, "Vincent Canby must have to sit through these things three times to get the stuff right." I learned subsequently about press kits and that they were frequently wrong. They'd say, "So-and-so, an Academy Award nominee," and I'd say, "No he wasn't, he was co-nominated with So-and-so, I know that." I did an awful lot of reading and research for those fifteen minutes because I had no faith that I could talk that long. (That has since changed.) I thought I'd dry up. After a year and a half of free work, I wanted some kind of monetary return. There was an opening on the little weekly paper up in Mill Valley called the *Pacific Sun*. I started writing regularly for them, and it was there that the *Los Angeles Times* found me.

EL: How many years elapsed between the time you really started writing and when the *Times* found you?

SB: Well, I think I started writing in '72, and they found me around '78 and used me as a stringer for a while. Then Charles Champlin asked if I'd like to come down and "play second string" to him during August when everybody is off on vacation. I said, "Look, I've got a life; I've got three children here; I can't do this; give me your home number, I'll call you tomorrow." I had taken a vow four years earlier that if I were going to do this, I was absolutely going to do it. That meant I had to see every film that was released, because that is your vocabulary. I went over to The Pacific Film Archives as often as I could to catch up on all the great stuff and to fill big holes in my background. That was an enormous help. To afford this I worked in every store in downtown Mill Valley; at one time I had four jobs. Then I began working for magazines. The first was *Mother Jones* and there was one called *New Times*, and one that was called *New West*, which became *California*.

EL: Do you think that your view as a critic changed when you moved down here and were suddenly in the middle of the business?

SB: Not my view as a critic, but I know that I wrote differently. While living up north I remember writing, in regard to *The Other Side of Midnight*, a very bad movie, that I felt that one actress had been rather badly advised to do as many nude scenes as she had because "never had anyone exposed so little so much to so many." Now I would not write that at the *Los Angeles Times*. Writing it in Mill Valley was like writing for my pocket; the actress would never see it. That's something very personal; if she was badly advised, she was badly advised. At the *Pacific Sun* I was convinced that the individuals in question would never read or see it. Here I know that everybody reads the *Times*. It took me probably a year to get my full voice back. I don't think I'm cruel or unkind, although there are actresses out there who would disagree with me about' that.

EL: Does being a critic impede your ability to develop friendships with filmmakers?

SB: Yes, what I would love more than anything is to know people, particularly on the craft level, because that's where my family operated, and I loved that. I would love to sit with my feet up with an editor and have the editor tell me what *he* sees when he sees a movie. I would love that. Sooner or later, I hurt somebody's feelings and they get pissed as hell at me, so I don't necessarily know that many people in the business. There is that problem.

EL: Has the role of the critic or reviewer changed? What is the role of criticism today?

SB: It's about three or four different things. There's always the matter of standing between the audience and what is now a $7.50 ticket. There's also the serious thought about the history of film, the craft and the art of what is being done and said. Handling that is not always easy in a newspaper; it's very different at *The New Yorker* where one can pick one or two films a week every two weeks to write about.

EL: Working on a daily, how much research are you able to do?

SB: A lot. San Francisco was a great training ground for me because the movie was seen on Tuesday and the review would come out on Friday.

EL: What's your schedule now? Can you describe the assignments?

SB: Generally (and this is changing now) you have three weeks with a big movie. If a movie comes from a book, I let the movie tell me the story first. Then if I don't know who that character lurking over there is, it's because the film is not clear. I think you have to be able to say, for example, that *Garp* is not *all* of that book, but it is absolutely the heart, and it doesn't matter that some characters are gone. One has to be able at least to mention it. You can also get too corseted by comparing book to movie. I see the movie first, though sometimes I do a lot of reading if it's a period film, or I'll browse through a costume book.

Up north, I would begin writing at 11:00 at night and write until 6:00 a.m. at a table in the dining room. Things come up almost subliminally if you have that concentration and that quiet. I never wrote on a typewriter. A typewriter implied doing something important, and I knew better, and I knew the noise would scare me to death. I always wrote in pencil on a yellow legal pad . The great change in my life has been the computer because it offers the greatest flow and the greatest access to almost subconscious references.

I know people at the *Times* who write everything down quickly, then go back and fix it. I am not that; I am a massager. I get a first paragraph and then I do it again and again until I like it. Then I go on to the next one. Sometimes I outline, sometimes I don't. It's like money in the bank if you have a lead and an ending. Once you know where you want to begin and what you'll say at the end, it's wonderful.

EL: Do you ever read other reviewers?

SB: I try not to read them before I review, but we all do afterwards. Of course, probably 85 percent to 95 percent of the reviewers writing now began at the knee of Pauline Kael, and we all smelled and sounded like Pauline. I don't think I do now, but for a long time there was always the matter of comparison with her take on a movie, of feeling, "Oh, I missed that." She set the standard to a degree. So did Dwight MacDonald, then later on James Agee. If you were lucky, you learned about Manny Farber. Pauline was the one we all cut our teeth on, the one who made it OK to like movies passionately and not just objectively.

EL: Was there anything else that made her the standard?

SB: She made movies accessible and very clear. She's got that great background in philosophy, and she's able to break a film down intelligently, which she loves to do. I think that she can take a position and hold it against all comers, and yet I can disagree with that position passionately. I think that criticism is presenting only the best case one can for one's arguments. There is no right or wrong way to look at a movie. There is no single correct review. There is one person's very best arguments told in plain and forceful language. That's why I love the National Society of Film Critics books, which used to have three reviews of the same film. There *is* no book on criticism, incidentally; if students are going to study anything, I recommend multiple reviews of the same film.

EL: Is there an advantage to being on a daily and being well-known?

SB: Oh, it's very useful. Once in a while people will second-guess you and *think* that you're going to hate something. People who found that I loved *Blue Velvet* were very surprised. As preparation for being a critic there is no substitute for living a while; there just is not. I will defend somebody who has been through marriages, divorces, losses, births, and *everything* against the smartest 26-year old just out of film school. These experiences deepen your understanding, and I say that in spite of the fact that the motion picture business is currently run by very young people. They are not necessarily making the best movies.

EL: What are the overriding pressures or frustrations?

SB: Space, right now. At the moment we are in a dire space crunch. All newspapers have had huge losses since the first of the year. When there are 60 percent fewer jobs to be advertised, your want ads fall off. When three huge department stores merge, you have one ad instead. When retailers can't sell, they advertise less.

EL: Do you find that it is a solitary profession? Or on your paper do you have a team? How much contact do you have with other reviewers?

SB: I do go to movies with people who I think will like them. If I have *loved* something and somebody else has not liked it, I don't wish to listen to how much they didn't. It's not going to change what I write or feel, but it's no fun to go to movies by yourself.

EL: Do you see the movie with the public?

SB: Yes, sure, every way, across the spectrum.

EL: Does it make any difference if you see it as the only person in the theater or when it is filled with hundreds of people?

SB: No, it does not. That old saw about having to have a packed house to laugh at comedy is nonsense. This is not going to be regarded as a terrific example but I saw Elaine May's *Ishtar* with seven people. There are parts of *Ishtar* where I thought I was going to die laughing. Don't tell *me* you can't laugh by yourself, particularly if you are not self-conscious about making a fool of yourself in a small group.

EL: Is this an open or closed field for young people to pursue?

SB: The existence of fewer and fewer newspapers is proof to us that people are not reading. I worry about it a lot. I don't want to say this is a closed field; I never want to discourage anyone. I worry about the fact that all the newspaper conferences and surveys indicate that people are reading less and probably picking up the "thumbs up and thumbs down" approach more.

EL: The kind of ninety-second spot on the news or in a magazine that says, "This is about this, I thought it was great; go see it," has that hurt criticism like yours?

SB: I don't think it has hurt written criticism particularly, because one can't say what needs to be said in sound bite time. I think that's even true in the half-hour program, where four films can be discussed. Tell me, if they didn't have film clips, how many people would watch? Do you know that we make our film clips ourselves? In the last analysis I still think there's a place for the written analysis.

EL: What would you recommend as appropriate educational paths in the nineties for a young person?

SB: English, history, all the literature courses in the world, art history, the liberal arts. A smart person with a background in philosophy and in history and some ability to express one's self is going to be much more interesting than somebody who has spent his or her life in the dark, in front of a screen; that is a hermetic life. There is such a thing as a movie nerd. It doesn't make the person any less loving about the subject; it's just that all their references are to other films. I think that's limiting.

EL: Do you picture your audience at all when you write?

SB: No, I really don't. I hope it's a *friend* out there. On the luckiest level it's half of a conversation and the ping back from the other side is the other half. I got a letter from a director once that made me cry and I've kept it. This was at a very down point in my life and it made me think, "OK, this is why I do it." He said a lot of people had enjoyed his film but I seemed to have really gotten it, to have been privy to conversations that had taken place during the making of the movie. It was really wonderful. Of course it can be a pretty pissed-off ping, too. I had one director's entire family call me: his mother, his brother and three months later *he* wrote me a four-page letter. That was one angry director. That's also fair, because not everybody is going to love you; this business is not a popularity contest.

EL: So you have to become thick-skinned?

SB: No, you can't ever become thick-skinned. You have to know it's not a popularity contest, then speak out, make the best case for every-thing, and let the chips fall where they may.

EL: Do you think that critics have become increasingly imbued with power?

SB: No, on the contrary, we can throw our bodies in front of *Rocky V*, and all we will get for our trouble is the footprints of the audience on our backs as they rush in to see it. Frequently people in your life will come up to you and say "Boy, were you right, was that *awful.*" You feel a little useless when you've gone to some pains to suggest some-thing, but I know the feeling—good or bad, you just want to see it yourself.

EL: What other advice would you give to young people about the profession?

SB: Go to every art show you can; listen to classical music; and hear Bruce Springsteen (if you can get in). Be open to everything, be an absolute sponge, soak up everything, even things that seem irrelevant. It's amazing the stuff you eventually use; suddenly something clicks in, it may be something you heard recently, or saw or read years ago. You had no idea you would use it and there it is. A very interesting recent movie, *The Natural History of Parking Lots* (not, incidentally, a documentary), had a composition in one outdoor scene that was reminiscent of a Thomas Eakins painting. Later I met the director who told me, "He's one of my favorite American artists." That's why I include such material because if it hits something in you, maybe it does with other people.

Richard Schickel

■■■■■■■■■■■■■■■■

Richard Schickel is a film critic and author who currently reviews movies for *Time* magazine. He has published several books, including *Schickel on Film*, a collection of his longer essays, *Hollywood at Home: A Family Album, 1950–65*, in collaboration with photographer Sid Avery, *D.W. Griffith: An American Life*, and *The Disney Version*. He has worked on several television productions, including the TNT programs "Gary Cooper: American Life, American Legend" and "Myrna Loy: So Nice to Come Home To." Mr. Schickel's current book is a critical-biographical study of Marlon Brando, and his upcoming television show examines the career of Barbara Stanwyck. He has held a Guggenheim Fellowship and is a winner of the British Film Institute Book Prize.

JF: Do you think young filmmakers have a sense of film history, a curiosity about this medium?

RS: I think the picture is very, very mixed. We've had a generation of filmmakers—Coppola, Lucas, Spielberg, Scorsese, etc., who are romantically infatuated with movies from the past. They've seen everything; they quote from older films very gracefully. Their knowledge is serious. I feel that after that generation, the slightly newer group has not been using the past as well in films. One sees an attempt to rebuild the spirit of film noir, but it seems to me they're not doing it very well. You have to know those older films in your bones in order to use those references gracefully, casually, and authoritatively. As for the next generation, the kids coming out of film school seem to have even skimpier knowledge. You would think that when they see the current masters borrowing things, it would stimulate their interest and push them to investigate the use of older movies. That doesn't seem to be happening. What one sees in short films by young directors and film students is usually a lot of technical proficiency. They really do know how to set up a scene and shoot it nicely. But narratively they're not as strong as they should be. Setting aside all those other considerations, if I have one general observation about current movies, it is that their narrative strength is much diminished from those made even as recently as the late sixties.

JF: When and why did this happen?

RS: All the clichés are applicable; the excesses of information that we have to process and deal with is distracting. I think television, certainly MTV, has diminished everyone's attention span, including that of film-makers. We have to make a distinction between the manner of a film, which may be very allusive and fast-moving, (which is not bothersome as long as it's well thought out) and a narrative substance which may be thoughtlessly developed. I really think people are not as conscious of the logic of storytelling as they once were, whether it's because of the many distractions in our lives, whether it's because we're not exposed in popular literature to solid storytelling, whether it's the fashion for narrative fragmentation that is so chic these days in modern literature, I can't say. But this is a serious problem in terms of movies.

JF: Can you comment on criticism as a career?

RS: To this day it remains clear to me that to be a full-time movie reviewer who writes about nothing but new movies as they appear is not a fit job for a human being. Set aside the pay scale for movie reviewing, which really is not very good (except on television), the real issue is that you are a prisoner of the system at that particular moment in time. In other words, your subjects are constantly imposed upon you by what happens to be released. You are caught forever in your contemporaneousness; you can never step back from it; you can very rarely bring to bear any substantial historical or aesthetic perspective on this particular little object that's in your view this week. I never felt that was enough for me, and I didn't think it was healthy to be so involved in the business. Both with *Life* and *Time* you're really confined to a very short space, with never a moment to step out and expand from it. This is true of most people; the only reviewer who ever has had true essay space has been Pauline Kael. But if that's a frustration there is also a need based on a sense that there really is something more to life then this week's movie. One has a need for more mental exercise and the simple ego need to write more expansively, and hopefully, more substantively. Books fulfill some of that need for me. About the time I signed up with *Life* I started my first serious book. Then, near the end of the sixties, the PBS station in New York asked me to write some narration for some documentaries about film. Those were my first television assignments. I found that I liked that, too, for different reasons— it brought me into the process of filmmaking. I think the main thing I enjoyed was just the sheer fun of it. It was more fun to make something—even though it was a television documentary—than it was to review something. It was so much more stimulating.

JF: How has filmmaking helped you as a critic?

RS: The more I got into the process, the more it changed my critical view of movies. What I began to realize is that most movie reviewers, including very good ones, haven't the faintest idea how a movie gets done, what processes and choices are made, or of the slapdash improvising that is responsible for the best and the worst. It is a much less conscious process than most critics imagine it being. Also, I have a feeling that because most critics have a natural literary bias, they're actually impervious to the real language of films. It's one of the reasons why Stanley Kubrick's movies (I regard him as one of the two or three greatest living filmmakers) are always so poorly received critically. Stanley is talking in a language that is utterly foreign to reviewers. *Barry Lyndon* is a prime example. It may not be the movie of his I like the best, but it's the movie that most clearly exemplifies my point. It's as simple as that Henry Jamesian dictum, "Landscape is character." A movie is a great medium for landscape, and the landscape that Kubrick projects in *Barry Lyndon* is telling the story of Barry Lyndon. It's in the light of the gaming rooms, in the fold of a costume or a drapery, it's in the walls and ceilings of the location he has chosen. All of that is dictating the character and the destiny of his really incredibly inarticulate protagonist. The more you look at movies, the more you become conscious of the unspoken language of film. All movies that one deeply cares about are movies that in some way or another have caught in the mind imagistically, rather than narratively, oddly enough. It seems to me you need that narrative for the immediate gratification of the audience and the immediate securing of their interest, but memory tends to deconstruct movies, and so one loses touch with the narrative flow. You just barely remember who did what to whom in a movie you saw some time ago. What's left are images in your mind that are there forever and sometimes those images are linked to dialogue, back in the days when they wrote good dialogue.

That's another area of concern at the moment; one actually *hears* very few good movies anymore—dialogue that sounds real but in fact is more pointed, more vivid than real, is an art that seems to be lost at the moment and is something that is wrong with movies at this particular time. Other than Woody Allen's work, I'm awfully hard pressed to think of movies in recent years that have particularly caught my ear, even though lots of them have caught my eye. Dialogue in movies is almost as much an image-maker as the camera is, because good dialogue stirs images in your mind. That aspect of image-making is at a vast discount now, another function of general cultural illiteracy. Persons who used to write movies as a rule came out of either theater or fiction, and they had a certain standard in this regard that the film student coming out of a course in screenwriting is not likely to have. Even actors who came from the stage had an ear for good dialogue and would insist upon this. It is perhaps not as true now. People are unaware of the language of film, almost all movie reviewing is just a form of moral criticism.

JF: Do you find it difficult to review a movie in a brief article? How do you feel about the recent popularity of television reviewers and their limited time to describe a movie?

RS: All critics are dealing in brevity. Richard Corliss and Roger Ebert got into a quarrel in *Film Comment* on the subject. Ebert claimed that in some of his reviews he was able to devote more words to the subject than Richard did in his review in *Time* magazine. It's not really a question of how many words as such; it really is a question of a point of view. The basic duty of a movie critic or any critic is to characterize that movie fairly. In a funny way, in the process of fairly and accurately characterizing it, he will have done 9/10 of the job of passing judgment, because that characterization will imply the narrative drift of the movie, the moral point of view of the movie, something about the performances in the movie, and raise some questions of directorial choice, of how a scene was realized, how it was shot, that kind of thing. If you simply and accurately characterize what is going on on that screen, you've gone a long way toward fulfilling the critic's real obligation. The reader then has a good sense of what he might see, a good sense of what the critic has seen, and probably an understanding of what the filmmaker intended to do, whether he succeeded or not. If you look at Edmund Wilson's articles, you would be astonished at how infrequently he actually passes judgment in a review. Very often his work reads like simple plot summary. His art is in how he has summarized the plot, what he has stressed, and why. The almost inferential criticism is the most interesting.

The television critics present a number of problems for the rest of us. In recent years editors all over have begun pressing reviewers for less nuanced writing, much flatter judgments. It lowers the terms of the discussion of movies, which has never been exactly exalted in any case. Brutal negation panders to the lowest element in the audience, the crowd that loves to laugh over other people's mistakes and misfortunes, while the unmediated rave panders to the industry, which wants to make reviewers adjuncts to the marketing process.

This is a real problem. In all the years I've been doing reviewing it's only in the last decade and most powerfully in the past five or six years that I've started receiving phone calls from publicists, the day after seeing a movie, requesting my opinion of it. This was really pretty rare in the sixties and seventies. There used to be a certain deference, a willingness to wait a week or two until the review came out. Now you'll get a call the day after the screening. You get a sense someone feels the movie's in trouble—the anxiety in their voices and the number of calls rises. This is something I really don't like. I'm always frank; there is no point in lying to the guy on the other end of the phone. It's almost like my little television review of what I may or may not write in the next couple of weeks about the movie. I don't know what that bodes for a movie, but the callers sure do care, and they don't make any distinction as to whether I'm a good critic or a bad one. They're just looking for enough blurbs to fill up their ads.

JF: Today we don't see film without some context; the media gives us so much information about the director, the producer, the actors . . .

RS: Indeed, more than we need to know, and yet the things that seem to me of real interest they still don't know much about. Every week the newspapers publish this week's top ten grossing movies. Everybody knows about someone's marriages, addictions, troubles of all sorts. What the public still doesn't know much about is the true mystery of movies—how a sequence of shots is put together to achieve the desired effect, how an actor actually digs into a part and brings something to it, what post-production involves, or how decisions made in post-production affect what's seen on the screen. All those things fascinate me and I still don't know much about them. I never make a TV documentary without learning something new of a technical nature.

JF: Let's continue talking about the language of film.

RS: You would think that the new generation of critics coming out of film schools would bring to the critical process greater sophistication and more technical information. If they do, are they going to lose the other thing that also is important about movies, that is, the ability to locate them in the culture of the moment, place them in some kind of historical perspective, see an individual movie as the product of a number of careers that have come together at this point? All those things are also very interesting.

As a matter of fact, that's where I think as a writer I'm living more intensely these days, not in week-to-week reviewing. For example, when Olivier died, *Film Comment* asked me to do a long career piece about him, and I had a wonderful time writing that. I was able to step back and look at a career that I admired, trying to analyze why it had turned in certain directions at certain times, and just appreciating those moments he had provided that I will treasure forever. To me that's enormous fun. Right now I'm writing a book about Marlon Brando, and in my eyes it isn't a biography of him. Brando was a terribly significant figure to my generation, so this is really about my generation responding to a particular actor. I'm trying to see how certain things that happened in terms of American history in general and movie history in particular affected his career, affected his ability to do what he wanted to do. I think I'm more passionate in that writing than I am in writing this week's review for the magazine—which doesn't mean that I scant on that review. I just get more satisfaction out of the other.

In the sixties, as the literary world made the earth-shaking discovery that movies were an art, it was great to be young and a critic in New York. You felt you were part of something that was hot, and people wanted your opinion on all sorts of matters, but some of that has disappeared now. In other words, movies themselves have lost some of their urgency for that crowd because, in general, they have stopped addressing them regularly. I wasn't nearly as good a critic then as I am now because I didn't know as much as I know now. By this time, I've seen thousands more movies than I had when I was blithely opinionating on this subject in my early thirties, and I'm a better man for it. I'm bringing a lot more to the role of critic than I used to.

JF: Would you say that that's probably true for the filmmaker also?

RS: Sure, the more he does, the more he knows. Obviously, if you're doing major motion pictures, each new time you're going to find things out. In Elia Kazan's autobiography he says, "It doesn't get easier when you get older; it gets harder." The reason it gets harder is because you know more, and the more you know, the more you'll try, in my case, to cram into your little space in *Time* Magazine, or book or television show. I used to knock off reviews in two or three hours in which my moral opinion of the movie was firmly set forth. Now it generally takes me all day to write one of those eighty liners, and the reason is I know more, the space hasn't expanded but my knowledge has. I think it's your obligation as you get older to work harder and engage harder with your subject, whatever your subject is. Otherwise, there's no point in putting in the years that you've spent to learn your trade, your craft, or your art.

JF: Has the audience changed?

RS: Every economic decision is essentially based upon catering to a very young audience with only one variant allowed. The fall releases of the "serious pictures" are intended for critics, prizes, and Oscars. This is also a shame. One of the things I've tried to do as a reviewer and as a critic is to speak to the common reader, and, by extension, the common viewer. The notion is that movies are not, any more than literature or music should be, the exclusive property of a narrow group. One can find language with which to make and to talk about movies that has a general appeal to literate people. The general public may not be the world's experts in movies, but they are not uninterested in movies, just as they are not uninterested in all the other aspects of their culture. That's the audience I'm trying to talk to when I review movies, and it's the one the moviemaker should be trying to reach as well. That audience will include a very large number of bright young kids, but it will also include a lot of bright old people in their eighties who have plenty of time to go to the movies. In other words, the best thing about the movies of the thirties and forties was their audience. Those movies functioned at different levels for different parts of the audience, and no audience was necessarily excluded from any of those genres.

JF: What else has changed?

RS: Another thing that's disastrous for filmmaking is this notion that the first weekend is everything. There's a much greater attempt to outguess the critics. In other words, certain movies will not be shown to us because they're afraid bad reviews might lower their opening/weekend grosses. That wasn't true before. At least one studio in this town does not let a national reviewer see its movies in time to review them prior to release, no matter what the movie is, or whether you can help or hurt it. The funny thing is you could as well help it as hurt it. I don't like being maneuvered around by these people.

JF: Are there any trends in criticism that bother you?

RS: I don't like being treated as if I'm an adjunct of Marketing. But I don't want to pretend that everything wrong with reviewing is the studio's fault. I'm awfully conscious of my own failures, liking or disliking some movies more than I should have on first glance, and sometimes flat-out missing the point of the movies. I'm disturbed by magazines bringing the general audience the wrong sort of knowledgeability, which is gossip knowledgeability. The problem is that the right knowledgeability about movies is almost irreducible in prose. If you were actually to sit and analyze a single brilliant sequence, you would not only far exceed *Time* magazine's space, you would exceed any known space in any known magazine. Finally, we all have practical problems, things that prevent us from achieving whatever ideal form we're striving for. I think practical criticism should consist of an accurate characterization of the movie, some attempt to place it in a context, whether historical or current social context, and some attempt as well to locate it in the large career of its principal makers. I don't think it's part of our job to predict or care what kind of an audience it immediately gathers. I don't think it's our business to pass gross personal moral judgments on movies. That's irrelevant. Criticism should not impute motives to the makers of the film. I think we should stay away from the whole question of marketing. I don't write profiles of people, I don't like that kind of celebrity journalism particularly. Nor do I read very many of my fellow reviewers. Inevitably I see the *New York Times* review or the *L.A. Times* review and that's about it. Nor do I try, any longer, to see every movie that comes out because we can't review every movie. But when I look at reviews I want to find out the same thing any reader wants to find out. If I have a spare afternoon, is this a story that might interest me? Does it sound from this review as if there's something interesting going on in the filmmaking that I could learn? To the degree that humble journalism can do it, that's what we should do, and probably all the rest of the stuff I've talking about as an ideal is better done somewhere else, more than likely a book or some kind of article for a specialized magazine of some kind.

SIXTEEN

⊞ The Publicist

Publicists represent individuals, projects, production companies, studios, and/or networks. They may work for a small or large agency, a studio or network, or choose to freelance. They are the liaison between their clients and the press. It is their responsibility to properly and positively present their clients to the public via print and electronic media. Publicists design indiviual media plans to suit each client. Elements of that media plan may involve interviews, press releases, and attendance at key events.

According to the Publicists Guild (818-905-1541), scale for a Senior Publicist for a studio is $1,228.34/week, while minimum for a Senior Publicist at an agency is $1,083.12. A publicist may join the guild as long as he/she is employed by a studio, agency, or television station that has a contract with the guild.

Mickey Freeman and Joe Sutton

Mickey Freeman

As a reporter for *Daily Variety* for five years, Mickey Freeman wrote a weekly entertainment column. He then served stints as head of publicity for a television and radio station, account executive with a public relations company, and director of public relations for an electronics company before starting his own firm, Mickey Freeman and Associates. The company later became known as Freeman & Sutton when Mr. Freeman became partners with Joe Sutton.

Joe Sutton

Joe Sutton began his career as a publicist with Rogers & Cowan in 1960. He joined Mickey Freeman & Associates in 1961 and became a partner the following year. In 1969 Mr. Sutton left Freeman & Sutton to become a personal manager. Three years later he joined MCA as executive vice president of their music division and later started his own company. In 1981 he and Mickey Freeman re-formed Freeman & Sutton.

EL: How would you characterize the role of a public relations person in the film and television industry? What's your function?

MF: In simple terms, our basic function is to get the client before the public and to give our client credibility. The more good press they get, the more they're out there; the greater their value. You have to make the client a valuable commodity. In the simplest terms that's what we do.

JS: I think it's placement whether it's a corporation, production, an institute, or an individual—a matter of putting them in front of their industry and the public in the way they want to be presented. You present them; you place them; you guide them; and you construct the format for their presentation.

EL: When someone comes to you, how do you begin to develop a plan for this process?

JS: Take the American Film Institute. You identify what it is and identify its parts. You take those parts, and you cohesively present them so that the entity is known as one. All the parts create the image or the identity of the institute in the community and the nation. When you take a personality, you take their vehicle, whether it's a motion picture, a television series, or a movie of the week, and you present what he or she is as a dramatic actor. You take the reality of that person and present it honestly, but in the best light you can. You're always trying to present the positive. Once the industry becomes aware of them the public almost automatically becomes aware.

EL: Has having a public profile always been important, or is it more so now?

JS: It's more important now than it has ever been. It used to be press, now it's presentation. It has nothing to do with being a press agent. You have to present, you get campaigns, you get people associated with charities; you're aware of their personal lives. It's a package that is so complex. Your presentation involves why and how and where. Sometimes it's what you don't say rather than what you say. There are people who do charity work that don't want anyone to know about it; there are other people who do charity work that helps the charity when their involvement is known. It's a very complex business. Many times it's what you don't do that's important and not what you do. It used to be a reaction, but now it's a thought process.

MF: In the early days, the trades especially, called us "flacks" because all it was was "flack"; that's what the press agent sold. Most of them were guys who came out of nowhere. They became "flacks," and they sent out gags and gimmicks and the press would use that. Today you can't sell that to the press. There's too much sophistication. It's become a business, and it has to be planned and worked at.

EL: What is at the core of your business?

JS: It's all about relationships. The press is always there—it doesn't come and go. I don't mean this to slight talent because we couldn't live without the talent, but the talent comes and goes and evolves. The press remains the same and even when a member of the press changes, he'd have a list for the guy taking his place—saying this guy's honest; this guy you've got to watch out for; this guy will not tell you the truth. When you know you can talk to somebody who has faith in you, you're valuable in a public relations presentation. You can't make up anything about anybody. Everybody's looked at through a microscope today—there's no baloney. If someone says, "The P.R. man is full of baloney"—baloney! The P.R. man has to have more integrity than anybody in this business.

MF: You have to know your people. Joe and I have always been straight with the press. There are some offices that put down the press and protect their clients, but we protect our clients by being honest with the press, being straightforward.

Joe can call Army Archerd anytime and say, "Look, this is what happened. Please don't use it right now." Army knows that when it can be used, Joe's going to call him and say, "It's yours." We feel that is very important. That's the way we run our business.

EL: Do you think that the press at large is more focused on this field today, or do you think that the country has had an increased interest in film and television?

MF: I think it's probably both. I think through the years the public has become very sophisticated. When you see as much entertainment coverage as people see—the TV is on all day long—they know what goes on. They know what's funny, what's not, what's working, what's not—they become very sophisticated. The press itself is extremely sophisticated.

JS: With the amount of tabloid press, either television or editorial or radio, you have to tell your client, corporation, or individual that if you play, you're going to pay. If you play straight, you're going to play easy;

if you play crooked, you're going to get killed. You cannot cover for a married woman or man who goes out to a nightclub with someone else. It's going to be on the front page of every tabloid in the business, on television, "Entertainment Tonight," *TV Guide*. *TV Guide* used to be a straight, nice little publication; today you can read more in *TV Guide* than you can in the *National Enquirer*. They're addressing that inquisitive individual who wants to know the gossip. But gossip can be good; it doesn't have to be bad. You really have to warn your people; "If you want to do it, do it in good taste."

EL: Is the writing creative or journalistic?

MF, JS: Both.

EL: What other skill does a P.R. person have to have?

JS: An understanding of every client. Every client is different; every production company is different; every movie is different, every television show is different; there's no formula. Every time someone walks in the room, the formula changes, not the methods, but the formula, the creation, what we are looking for. The first thing we do is find out what we're dealing with and then where we want to go with the client and for ourselves. When you have a long-range goal you can get there because the road is defined. We're here and we want to get there. It's just as easy as going from L.A. to New York, but if you don't know where the hell you're going when you get on the plane, you fly around in a lot of circles and you can land right back in L.A. So when you have a goal and understand what your resources are, then you can achieve it.

MF: You have to have a good bedside manner; you have to be able to deal with people. You deal with a lot of different people, a lot of different egos, a lot of different problems, and the psychology involved in that is overwhelming sometimes. You can be talking to one person one minute, three minutes later you've got another client, then another and they're all very different people. You have to be able to change gears quickly. Joe and I run a business and we always know what's going on with every client—we're there for every client. A lot of the bigger offices will put somebody in charge, and the guys at the head won't even know what's going on.

EL: How many clients do you handle?

JS: We don't talk about that. Take us away from here, and individually we should be able to handle ten people without any problem. When you have fifteen support people working, we could handle fifteen clients or we could handle 150 clients without any problem. It depends on how much they pay you. Obviously you want to get more money so that you can be more selective and handle fewer people. We're a medium-sized company with a lot of power. There are a lot of big companies with no power and a lot of little companies with a lot of power. It depends on your relationships with the press and with your clients.

EL: How do you attract clients?

JS: Other companies may do intricate, involved presentations—we don't. This is what we are, and this is how we present ourselves. This is our job.

EL: When you hire the young people who come in and work for you, what are you looking for? Do you look for collegiate background? Do you look for experience?

JS: You look for background and you look for personality. There's a unique personality needed to be a publicist. You have to be understanding. You have to know that you're not going to make as much money as an agent or a lawyer. You're going to make good money.

EL: Starting salary under $20,000?

JS: Yes, $12–15,000, and we're doing them a favor to give them a job.

MF: We have people starting at the front desk and we move them right up. We move a lot of people up. Joe and I feel that they really need that break, and it's worked very well for us. There are some wonderful people here. We get along well and we try to keep it that way. We feel it's very important. You have to come in here every day and be together. If we don't get along, you've got friction and it takes the fun out of it.

EL: What kind of majors have the young college people come in with?

JS: Business, Journalism, History, Communications, and Arts.

MF: We even have an attorney; he never wanted to practice law.

EL: How stressful is this profession?

JS: Very, if you're not the personality type. If you are the personality type, it's like coming to play every day. It's like playing football, or baseball, or golf for me. I come in here and have a good time. It's a wonderful way to make a living. You don't have to have a sledgehammer, there are no rocks and no rules.

MF: The tougher part happens on those days where you can't make something work, and somebody comes down on you. You keep trying to do the best you can and it doesn't quite fit together. We all have that. Overall, I think because of our approach we're able to work out most problems. We've been very lucky; we don't have a lot of turnover with clients, and that really makes us feel good. Getting clients is not the hardest part—it's keeping clients. We do that. We've had very little turnover in the past nine years. Joe and I have been in business together for at least nine years and before that we were together nine or ten years.

EL: How has the media explosion ("Entertainment Tonight," etc.) made your job easier or more difficult?

JS: It hasn't made it easier, but it has made it more important.

MF: The media explosion has made it easier because there are more outlets.

EL: How do you maintain relationships with this continuing boom of people?

MF: You get to know everybody because they keep moving around. Things bounce back and forth. There have been times in our business when all of the sudden talk shows went out of favor, and everybody said, "We don't want personalities." We've been through all of that. The number of newspapers is way down; we used to have seven newspapers in this city we could go to. Now we have the *Daily News* and the *Los Angeles Times* and then we have to go to Orange County. So that's very different. But there are so many television and cable shows that are out there now. Television news has also become a source for public relations.

JS: It's a very interesting business, and it's a tremendous business of the future for young people. If you look at the president of the United States, he's all public relations, 100 percent. How he treats the media, how he's presented to the media, how he dresses, what he does, everything is public relations.

EL: I'm interested in the ethics of what you do. Do unethical P.R. people stay in the business?

MF: Yes, I think so, they may run out sooner or later. We know companies that are unethical and still get clients. Some people are very good at getting clients but they don't keep them. They just keep running them through because they're not doing the job for them. That does exist in this town. That's not to say there aren't a lot of very good offices, and there are people who work hard at what they do. As in any business, doctors, lawyers, etc., you get all types.

EL: How sophisticated are your clients when they come to you? Do they come in and know what they want, or do they just put themselves in your hands?

MF: Most of them don't know what they want or need, but it depends. You do get people who have been in this business for twenty years who know the business. But you get a lot of young people who have had very little experience and they don't really understand it. We work with them; we explain it to them.

JS: It's as though we work with a primer with them and each primer is different. It's never the same because everybody's different. That's why I said there are no rules; every client is different. There are guidelines, but every client is unique.

MF: You've got to protect them. If there's an interview set up, somebody's got to be with that client because you never know exactly what they're getting into. Most of them know, but every once in a while I've had clients who start to come down on somebody in the cast of a particular show, and I say, "Don't do that because you're going to get murdered." They learn and we try to teach.

EL: What are the advantages and disadvantages of being a professional and also running your own business?

JS: You don't work for anybody. You're your own boss. Big or small, you're master of your own fate. The disadvantages are that you have to run a business, and running a business is tough. Forget about being a great public relations person, you have to be a great businessman. Just look around this office. There are twenty people here. If you multiply it by the people dependent upon those people, there are maybe a hundred people living off this company. So if you're not a good businessman, those hundred people are going to suffer. The responsibility is mind-boggling. It's a two-edged blade; you have to be a great P.R. man, but that doesn't ensure anything. If you're not a good businessman, your doors are closed. It's very difficult.

MF: There are people who are self-starters and those people can run the business. You really have to get out and be self-motivated because that keeps everybody in the organization motivated. These people work like hell.

EL: What are average days? How many hours are you and your staff putting in a day and how many days a week?

JS: I couldn't even count the hours because do you count dinner with clients or dinner with the press? It's working, so it could be twelve to fifteen hours a day everyday. It could be five days a week; it could be six days a week. However, our people are usually friends, even though they're clients, or they're associates. Our day starts at 8:00, 8:30 a.m., everybody's here and we work until 6:00 p.m. Because we're a West Coast company, all East coast outlets are closed at 3:00 or 4:00; the papers and electronics here go to bed at 7:30. Their day is over at

3:00; they're putting their shows together. Our day is over at 4:00 as far as getting anything into print, on television, or on the radio. All you needed when I was a kid was a telephone, a piece of paper and pencil, and you were in business. Wherever Mickey and I were in those days, we needed a phone and that was it. Today you have to be equipped. You have to have state-of-the-art computers, fax machines, lists; you have to have state-of-the-art everything. It's so competitive; it's so far-reaching; it's so sophisticated that if you don't have the tools to service people, you can't get the news out. If you have one piece of news, "Mary had a baby" and you wanted to get it out, you have to get it to five hundred desks around the country. Those are just the key desks. You have to be able to reach a source to get the information to those people immediately.

MF: We don't even use the mail, I think the only time we use the mail is to pay our bills. Everything else is fax'ed or Fed Ex'ed or whatever. If we send stuff to the *Los Angeles Times*, we fax it and then call to see if they got it, because there's so much fax out there now that a lot of the papers never get it, so you have to recheck.

JS: What's really great today is that there's nothing that cannot be marketed. We're not really public relations people; we're in marketing. You can present a lawyer and market him; you can have lawyers calling a lawyer if you do it correctly. If he becomes the expert in a certain field of litigation and all he does is create newsletters to legal journals, you've marketed that attorney, or dentist, lawyer, charity, school, event, anything. That's what's interesting about our business. You can graduate from college today and come in on a professional level. When you're a public relations person and you work in this industry, you are a professional. You can work anyplace. We have people go out of this office who can work any place, any city, who, what, where, why, when, call information, call. It's so basic and it's a very easy business if you know when and whom and why to call. You have to know what a story is; you have to know what and for whom a story is good.

EL: How much of what you do is instinctual?

JS: A lot! But it's also too involved and too important to base it simply on instinct. It's got to be planned, to be programmed, to be thought out, and then it's got to be presented.

EL: Are there moments when you do rely on your gut instincts?

JS: All the time.

MF: Yes, we've been doing it for so long we just know where it can go immediately. It's not just instinctual, and we try to see among the people who come to work here who has a feeling for the business. There are some people who know a story and know what they can get in print. Some people don't quite ever grasp that. We try to find the person who can.

JS: I think this is a gambling business, but you have to know that when you gamble, you're not going to lose. You can gamble and you may not win, but you have to make sure that you don't lose. If you lose, it can be catastrophic.

EL: And irreparable sometimes?

MF: Could be, yes. We can have a press conference for somebody and nobody shows up. That's a losing situation.

EL: We've talked about the fact that the young people you hire come in with a variety of backgrounds. How deep a knowledge of film and television do the people you hire have to have?

JS: You don't have to have much, but you have to be able to learn. You have to learn who the players are. The most important thing as far as I'm concerned, after integrity and honesty, is creativity. You just can't sit behind a desk; you must be creative; you must understand what a story is, you must understand how to present it, you must create the mood. It's a playbook and you must create the plays. If you don't, it just sits there, stagnant.

MF: You have to understand too, that not everybody can do everything. Certain people do certain things better than others. Some people are just better talking and being with clients. Some people write, some people really don't. Some people are better in public than others. There are people who want to sit in the back room and write and don't want to bother with anybody. There are all those types of people, and they all have their place. It's great to find somebody that's well-rounded. To find somebody that can write, is creative, handles people well and is not afraid to get out there with the press, that's expecting a lot!

EL: You build a team then.

JS: It's not a team, it's a family. You can wake up in the morning and come home at night and everybody has done different things, but there's food on the table. Everybody contributed a little; the house is clean; the table is set, the food's on the table; the beds are made; there are nine million things that go in. That's what happens here. There's a family of people that create the end result by presenting our clients to the public and to their own industry.

EL: How much do you court the press outside of a specific client or event?

JS: If a new editor comes into the *Hollywood Reporter* or the *Los Angeles Times*, for instance, Mickey and I will make a point to call, take him to lunch. It's just an introductory lunch so that when he gets our call, there's a face, there's a voice, there's an identity, and there's some kind of relationship established. They look for that because they want to know with whom they're dealing, the clients you have, what do you do. You always introduce yourself to the press, always, but it's not courting. You court the press by the intelligence of your presentation to them regarding your clients.

EL: So then your relationship with them is fairly specific as it relates to an event, a client, etc.

MF: Members of the press will come in, and all work differently, so what Joe and I will want to know is, "How do you work? What can we do to help you? I don't want to call you at 3:00 if that's a lousy time for you." Those are the things we need to know.

JS: Soon it becomes very personal: "How are you doing? How are your kids? Who won the game? What's going on?" That's the nature of relationships. It's amazing what people will do when they know they can trust you. They'll use the stories they have to use, but it's the stories they don't have to use that make you a good public relations office. That's the secret because everybody has to use, "There was an earthquake." When there's an inch to grant, they'll give it to you rather than to some other guy, and an inch or a second can be very important.

EL: Is it a hard or an easy profession to break into?

MF: It's rather difficult. There are a lot of people out there who want to be in it. There are those who want in when they're 35 or 40 and that's almost impossible because there's nowhere to start where there's any money. You can't say to a guy that's got two kids and a wife, "Well, we can put you on the front desk for a year at $1200, $1500 a month," that's impossible. Young kids come in and we train them.

EL: So that's a good time to come in, right after college?

MF: A great time.

EL: What advice would you give to young people coming out of college who want to enter this field?

JS: Learn how to write. We send people that work here to night school.

MF: If you want to come in you really have to be willing to work. Kids coming out of law school can get $60–70,000 a year. You're not going to be able to work in this business at that level. You have to be able to come in and say, "I want to work and learn." Because no matter what you've taken in college you have to learn the business on a day-to-day basis. If they're willing to do that I think you can earn a nice living. After two years it isn't bad. I got into this business because I didn't want people giving me orders; I have a lot of trouble with people telling me what to do. I decided I'd better be my own boss or else I'd be in trouble my whole life. Obviously we all take orders from somebody; that's part of life, but it's much less when you have your own business.

EL: Any other advice?

JS: Just be open, be imaginative, get all the education you can, and never stop writing. I think the most important thing in this business is to listen to what people are saying, listen to the client, listen to the press. Keep your mouth shut and listen. Listen, listen, listen.

Michael Levine

Born in Manhattan, Michael Levine briefly attended Rutgers University before starting Michael Levine Entertainment, a concert promotion agency based in New Jersey. In 1977 he moved to Los Angeles to establish *TV News Magazine,* which he owned and published for six years. For a short period in 1979, he also worked at the nation's largest public relations firm, Rogers & Cowan. In June of 1983, Mr. Levine initiated the Michael Levine Public Relations Company, which is now known as the Levine/Schneider Public Relations Company. During the past eight years the company has opened offices in New York, London, and Las Vegas. Mr. Levine is the author of several reference books, including *The Address Book—How to Reach Anyone Who's Anyone* and *The Environmental Address Book,* and also serves on numerous advisory boards, including the Academy of Television Arts and Sciences and the Neil Bogart Laboratories for Cancer Research.

EL: Could you briefly characterize your role as a public relations specialist?

ML: In a metaphoric sense, a publicist is similar to a gift wrapper in a department store. We attempt to attach an attractive appearance to a personality or project and create a demand for it.

EL: How do you set about creating a demand for something?

ML: Someone wise once said, "What we need is an ever-changing plan for an ever-changing world," and it's certainly true in the entertainment industry. Our company represents entertainment personalities. The first thing we do is write a media plan, a campaign strategy if you will. Of course, it's important to remember that the best public relations campaign is the campaign that doesn't look like one at all. We develop a fairly specific plan that is tailored to meet the mutually agreed objectives of our client. We write a plan and then go out and try to implement it through our contacts in the media, radio, television, and print. It's important to understand that public relations is misrepresented to the extent that it's usually viewed as only press releases, and it's far more than that. It can be the firmness of a handshake, or it can be the attendance of an appropriate event. There are many more colors on the palette than would first appear.

EL: How do you attract clients?

ML: In the beginning, it's very difficult; it was for me and would be for anyone. I describe getting my first few clients like trying to push a wet mattress up a spiral staircase—it didn't seem to want to go. It becomes significantly easier as you go along. This is a problem not only faced by aspiring press agents but by almost every area of the entertainment industry. The entertainment industry responds to supply and demand just like any other industry. There is massive supply, namely the many people who want to be in the industry, and there is very little demand. There are very few jobs and a lot of applicants. The beginning of a career, whether it's as a talent agent, manager, publicist, or filmmaker, is very difficult. There is almost a weeding out, a boot camp–type initiation that one has to go through. This is why the William Morris Agency mailroom and other mailrooms have proven so important.

EL: Is there a parallel to the mailroom in the public relations?

ML: There is a somewhat new parallel that really did not exist until about ten years ago. It's called internships, and they can be life-changing. Our company maintains one of the most dynamic and largest internship programs in the entertainment industry. Most good firms have fine internship programs. Ours calls for a three-month/nonpaid commitment, fifteen flexible hours a week, for college students. It is the best way of getting visceral, palpable "hands-on" knowledge. Albert Einstein said, "Real knowledge is experience," and I certainly agree. I would encourage it not only for anyone interested in public relations, but anyone

interested in any area. In any business you'd be very well-advised to augment your textbook knowledge with real experience.

EL: If a young person had been an intern at your firm, where would they start?

ML: In an entry-level position.

EL: How long might they expect to stay there?

ML: The process has historically taken about two years. It depends how talented and determined the person is. Are they really ambitious, or do they have a burning, maniacal rage? There's a big difference. Are they interested or obsessed? We know people who are very ambitious, but who don't have a burning maniacal rage and so they can't accelerate the process. For the first five years I worked two shifts. I would work from 9:00 A.M. to 6:00 P.M., go home and take a shower and work from 7:00 P.M. to midnight. People would ask me how many years I had been a publicist and I would say "ten" because of those two shifts. Generally, if you start in our company in an entry level position and you can last two years, you're pretty much on your way.

EL: Since most young people attend a four-year college, what areas of specialization would you recommend if they wanted to attend liberal arts college and then enter your field?

ML: Most of the interns we have are journalism and communications majors.

EL: How important are writing skills?

ML: They're not unimportant (and I know I am in disagreement with some traditional P.R. representatives), but writing skills are not the "be all" and "end all." You can be an exceedingly competent publicist without ever winning a Pulitzer Prize. It is important to be able to communicate, that's the business we're in, and writing is one form of communication. But inspired, innovative, colorful writing is more important than technical skills. All things being equal, better to write than not. It is not the only mode of communication. Verbal communication is critical.

EL: How did you get started in the business?

ML: When I was growing up, all my life I had two interests; one was the entertainment industry and the other was politics. For example, when I was in elementary school and I would look at the map of the United States, while most children's eyes would go to either the place they were born or the place they were living, my eye (I was born and raised in New York City) always would go to California. When my friends were ten years old and reading car and wrestling magazines, I was always reading *Variety* and the *Hollywood Reporter*. I was fairly vocationally obsessed with the entertainment industry.

EL: What are the advantages to having your own firm?

ML: That choice and those advantages are very personal. There are people who are meant to have their own company and there are people who are not. Most people are not, not because they're inferior in any way, they're just not. There are massive advantages and massive disadvantages. But for the people who are, there's almost not a choice.

EL: Can you briefly describe what the advantages and disadvantages are?

ML: The disadvantages are the unending pressure and decisions that go beyond the representation of a client: a sick employee, a decision as to whether or not it is appropriate to move our company to all recycled paper even though it's 30 percent more expensive. It's unrelenting pressure, like being held under water. For some people that is both an advantage and a disadvantage. For people who truly love the craft of public relations, you have to divest yourself of some of that to do other work. When a person on your staff comes to you with a personal problem, you have to attempt to become a psychologist and support that person even though you have your own obligations as a publicist. The advantages are when things go right, you get the credit. You do have a feeling of accomplishment. It is not for most people, and about three days a week I wonder if it's for me. I've handed in my resignation to myself about twice a week for the past five years.

EL: But does the pressure also keep it exciting?

ML: I can't emphasize enough that there are certain personality types who are born to do this and most are not. 99 percent of the world live in buildings. 1 percent of the world build buildings. That's the way it is, and that's not bad news.

EL: How do you approach your relationship with the press? Is it heavily dependent on personal relationships?

ML: It is personal. The post-Watergate world is a lot more candid then it was thirty or forty years ago. It's built a lot more on honesty and reliability. In the thirties and the forties, there was very stunt-oriented P.R. stuff that doesn't work anymore.

EL: Because you represent personalities, do you ever find yourself working against publicity in an effort to guard someone's privacy?

ML: There are times when more publicity is appropriate, and there are times when less publicity is appropriate. It has all the feeling of riding a bicycle down a hill—when to apply the brake and when to feel the acceleration of a bike going at its own rate. If you go too fast you're going to spill out, if you don't go fast enough, you're going to fall.

EL: When your clients come to you, do they know what kind of a profile they want, or do you have to formulate it for them?

ML: It is a rare client that has any sense about public relations. A very interesting thing—people define the world in their own terms. They tend to project out on the world what is their world. It's my responsibility to have the more sober view.

EL: What is most exciting and what is most frustrating about your profession?

ML: The most frustrating thing is that it's infinite. At the end of a twelve-, thirteen-, fourteen-hour day, there is never a completion. You can always make one more call. If you worked in Detroit and you were building cars and you knew that a very good day would be the completion of five automobiles, at the end of the day you have the happiness of knowing that you completed more than you anticipated. In our business, there is always one more call to make, there is never that sense of completion. The most exhilarating thing? Feeling that you have done something interesting and memorable and inspired. For example, about two years, I designed an idea to have Charlton Heston host "Saturday Night Live" and that was a somewhat untraditional idea and it worked beautifully. The media said it was the work of quite a shrewd public relations expert.

EL: Is public relations an open or closed field to a young person?

ML: It is both open and closed. It is like the entertainment industry in that way. It is crying out in its soul for new, fresh, interesting, innovative people. However, there is a very large, well-fortified, prickly imaginary wall that lies between the inside and outside of Hollywood or the inside and outside of the public relations business. How one is going to negotiate their way over that imaginary wall is the challenge. So it's both open and closed. I know that there are many in the creative world that find deep sadness in the fact that there is such a wall. Although it was a difficult wall for me to climb (and I don't look with envy on anyone who has to climb it today), I think in the final analysis it provides a much needed friction that will be extremely useful and beneficial to moving forward through the desert as a career continues: I am glad it's there in some ways. I don't think there's a person in the history of military service that liked boot camp. On the other hand, I don't think there's ever been anyone in the history of military service who has gotten themselves in a difficult situation and wasn't happy they went through it.